Because it was Beautiful

My Life & Loves

by Alexander Eliot

BECAUSE IT WAS BEAUTIFUL

Copyright ©2016 by Winslow Eliot. All rights reserved, including the right to reproduce this book, or portions thereof, in any form. No part of this text may be reproduced, transmitted, downloaded, decompiled, reverse engineered, or stored in or introduced into any information storage and retrieval system, in any form or by any means, whether electronic or mechanical without the express written permission of the author. The scanning, uploading, and distribution of this book via the Internet or via any other means without the permission of the publisher is illegal and punishable by law. Please purchase only authorized electronic editions, and do not participate in or encourage electronic piracy of copyrighted materials.

Cover painting and illustrations by Alexander Eliot

Designed by: Jefferson Eliot
http://www.jasperlark.com

Photo of Alexander Eliot by Robert Lax

Visit the author website:
http://www.alexandereliot.com
Website by: Tom Stier
http://www.tomstier.com

ISBN: 978-0-9857184-3-5 (paperback)
ISBN: 978-0-9857184-4-2 (ebook)
ISBN: 978-1-939980-90-8 (kindle)
ISBN: 978-1-939980-91-5 (audio)

Published by: Writespa
http://www.writespa.com

Dedication:

For the Woman Clothed with the Sun

Contents:

1: Way Back When
   Childhood & Youth   7

2: Women Then
   Man's Better Half   91

3: Artists Yes
   In Praise of Excellence   149

4: Mythosphere
   Sweet Mysteries of Life   207

5: The Blessing Way
   My Joys and Desires   289

6: Coming of Age
   As Above, so Below   391

Book One: Way Back When

Childhood & Youth

Ancestral Voices

Growing Pains

Preppie

Down in Black Mountain

Indian Summer

1. Ancestral Voices

The impressions received by little children mainly relate to breathing, heartbeat, and body-motions. One is drawn to wonder, prone to ponder, in precarious rhythm.

The first paradox confronting a human newcomer is that one has two separate parents. Soon it becomes clear that Mom and Pop are not as they seem. Instead, they're probably a King and Queen in Once Upon a Time, and wild animals when darkness falls.

If the stork story isn't right, how did we ever get here? To borrow cosmological terminology for a biological event, one's self started out much tinier than a dust mote drifting loose in a parental "Big Bang."

It takes two to make a child. Or a quarrel. Or a rhyme, for that matter.

I was sitting on our kitchen stoop, at Northampton, Massachusetts, surrounded by soft sunshine, and playing at nothing particular. God would stop by now and then, in a familiar sort of way, to hand me toys. At this point I can't picture them, except that they gleamed. Kitchen utensils perhaps, or geometrical objects?

God was a child, just my sort, but perhaps a bit older. He, or She, seemed to enjoy playing with me.

I lived through eighty-one percent of the twentieth century. My career as an art journalist, novelist, foreign correspondent on the cultural beat, eager lover, and comparative mythologist, was lucky indeed.

But there's no use in receiving unless one can give back, so I've decided to convey the true story of what happened, and introduce the following fellow-seekers, all of whom conversed with me, and most of whom became friends—

CAST OF CHARACTERS

My boyhood counselor, an Indian chief
Alfred Stieglitz, and Georgia O'Keeffe
Henry Koerner, comrade Robert Lax
Diane Arbus at her empathetic max
Beloved Anne Dick of Beacon Hill
Peregrine Eliot, the Cornish Earl
Kaaren Kitchell, Richard Beban
Masao Abe, Charles Laughton
Salvador Dali, Dong Kingman
Greg Chadwick, Frank Mason
Buddhist Robert Thurman
Dalai Lama, Rex Harrison
Humanist Konrad Kellen
Ted Williams, Ben Shahn
Kind Bernard Berenson
Edward Hopper with Jo
Brash Taitetsu Unno
Count Ottavio Zazio
Rocky (K.O.) Marciano
Diego Rivera, of Mexico
Dark-browed Frida Kahlo
Henri Matisse, Pablo Picasso
Compassionate Phil Cousineau
Benny Goodman, King of Swing
Ryong Song, Willem de Kooning
Frederick Sontag, of whom I sing
Suggestive sculptor William King
My own deep-hearted partner, Jane
Who saw me through time and again.

I used to wake up, having wet my bed, and creep into Pop's bed for dryness, warmth, comfort, and stories. He was terribly afflicted with stammering, but never on those early mornings. When a father makes up a story for his child, then the story, plus the child, and the father himself, all become one thing in a way.

My favorite tale concerned a bird family. Falling from its nest, the fledgling encounters a hungry cat. In the nick of time, his parents come swooping to scare the cat away and rescue him.

Did a tear trickle down Pop's cheek when he told that one? "No," he'd say. "Just my eyes watering."

A generation ago, on the day before Pop passed out of his body, I was alone with him, sitting sunk in awe and sorrow on a chair pulled close up to his bed. Opening his eyes, Pop saw me there, and raised himself on the pillows—

"Are you here ALSO, Boy?"

I could see, and would always remember, that Pop was looking, shining, speaking, not out of loss and pain but from a beautiful abundance unknown to me.

But the blind side of my brain mistook Pop's radiance for miraculously returning health. I called for others to come and look, whereupon he scrunched up in a spasm of agony followed by coma once more, and death soon after.

I assumed that I'd never see him again. But people do come back, in dreams at least. At the beginning of January 1999, my father chose to visit me that way.

"Sit down, Boy," Pop began, "and listen carefully. I've always hesitated to interfere in your life, as you must be aware."

"True. I should have thanked you long before this."

"I'm doing so now, because your work must change."

"What work? I'm in retirement."

"Denial, you mean. Remember how you coined the word mythosphere a quarter-century ago? It's appeared in all your books since then, and even gained some academic currency."

"Yes, a few professors have picked up on my ideas, but who the hell cares?"

"Nobody cares! I'm telling you the time has come to address your own struggle directly."

"Impossible, Pop. Writing is an indirect pursuit."

"Listen to me."

"I'm listening..."

"Don't be afraid of poetry!"

The extreme intensity of Pop's command astonished and unnerved me. Surfacing to wakefulness, I went over our conversation in my mind. Only then did I recall that my father himself no longer lived. Not in the breathing, reading, physically extended sense.

THE QUICK & THE DEAD

I said to Pop: "You
gave me quite a start!"
He seemed to smile
inside my heart—

*"Was I so sudden?
That's all right.
We dead, you see
are fast as light."*

In his young manhood, Pop had composed fiercely romantic verse. While courting Mother, for example, he sent her a postcard with these rude lines, which rather upset her generally unflappable father—

*Old men are dead.
'Tis time to bury them
In some soft spot.
Swift may they rot.*

Pop was among the first Americans to undergo Freudian psychoanalysis. He hoped it might cure his stammer, but the treatment went nowhere until at last the great god Pan appeared to him in a dream.

It seemed that Pop had chosen to perch upon a low stone wall, enjoying a fine October day. Pan came along, greeted him with avuncular good cheer, and sat down to chat for a timeless while. Then, standing up again, Pan told him with affectionate regret that they would have to part!

After giving Pop a hug, the god leaped over the wall, and trotted off into the yellow woods.

Delighted at this development, Pop's doctor declared him cured, despite the fact that his stammer was as crippling as ever. As the analyst explained the case to my future father—

"You've unconsciously decided to opt for the real world!"

Anyone who presumes to speak for a definable "real world" knows nothing of independent mental effort. So if Pop were wiser he'd have fluffed off his serenely nutty and more or less unconscious analyst.

Instead, he deliberately turned his back on Pan's domain, renouncing verse along with his promising career as a "little theatre" director, and accepting a Smith College professorship instead.

I composed my first poems in prep school. I also practiced boxing there. Our coach, who was a retired prizefighter, taught me never to lead with my chin—

"Show them lateral movement!"

In the arts, as in sports, business, warfare and politics, lack of confidence is by far the most insidious weakness. For me, there was a second factor as well. In youth I felt overawed by Howard Nemerov and Robert ("Cal") Lowell, two sharply budding poets whom I knew as friends.

"Poetry *is* competitive!" Cal used to say. Pronouncing it "pouetry" in his highbrow way. And Nemerov sneeringly tore apart the only verse I dared lay before him. That's the reason I always kept my own poems private, except on postcards to friends.

These days, I couldn't punch out a wet wall of Kleenex. Nor do shame and blame concern me any longer. So Pop spoke truth, and this old postcard scribbler ought to let rip at long last.

"*Ut pictura, poesis (As in painting, so in poetry).*"

That's what the ancient Roman poet Horace declared, and I agree. Gesture features in painting, poetry, and design, all three, so I sometimes incorporate the gesture aspect by imparting distinctive profiles to my verses.

Horace also advised a colleague to: "Mix a little silliness into your scheming."

FROM THE COMMITTEE-ROOM

This poor mortal's cobbled prose
by wobble-bobbling measure goes
and passes understanding at a walk.
We dub the dumbbell "Alexander Awk."

Much better stuff he might rehearse
if he'd just practice rhyming verse
and jettison his jet-stream woes.
It's not impossible, God knows.

My mother, Ethel Cook Eliot, once composed a book called *The House on the Edge of Things,* dedicated to her own mother. Then, in 1975, at age fifty-six, I wrote one called *Zen Edge,* dedicated to "The Woman with the Koto."

There's continuity between my ongoing effort to explore the "Edge of Things" and Mom's volume.

The protagonist in Mom's book was a boy named Kenelm, who follows a flying autumn leaf deep into the forest. That leaf becomes a

crimson-caped "Stranger Woman," who turns back of her own accord at last, and teaches Kenelm how to make songs that show—
"Where the beautiful roads go."

My favorite childhood treasure was a toy birch-bark canoe, crafted, as I'd been told, by an Algonquin Indian. Doesn't black-flecked white birch bark look as if it contains an indecipherable text?

In her upper reaches literature flows like a Shenandoah whose shelving rocks and glittering pools contain mantic epics. Lower down she's a Danube dappled with scrolls, folios, and vellum volumes. Finally we drift out upon a mile-wide Mississippi ripple of sun-spangles interleaved with cloud-shadows.

Still she flows on, as in Vachel Lindsay's poem—

Then I saw the Congo creeping through the black
Cutting through the forest with a golden track

It's fun to glimpse authors who pass between the trees fringing literature's universal stream. Some have lovers by the hand. Others are stalked by enemies or locked in struggle. They're seldom alone, yet many seem lonely.

Lewis Carroll's *Alice in Wonderland,* and *Alice Through the Looking Glass,* compellingly illustrated by Tenniel, drove me to press my nose against the mirror on our staircase landing, in vain attempts to peer sideways past the edge of its frame.

The Story of Dr. Doolittle, written and illustrated by Hugh Lofting, put me in communion with the surprisingly moral animal world, including a wistfully philosophical "Pushmepullyou."

Robert Louis Stevenson's *Treasure Island,* with N.C. Wyeth's sincere, deeply glowing illustrations, took me on early adventure. The author made Long John Silver so vivid, while purposely keeping his soul secret, that I never could decide whether to detest or admire the pirate cook.

But the book to which I kept returning in boyhood was *Palgrave's Golden Treasury* of poems. Although I couldn't often make sense of it, the verbal music got to me.

NOCTURNE

Now I'm growing old, I keep
meeting someone in my sleep.
A warm contralto, sweet and kind
she sings to soothe my crinkled mind.

When daylight comes, I can't recall
her consequential choruses at all
but she'll swing back into sight
like the Milky Way, tonight.

My godfather Padraic Colum used to recast world mythology in swift story form, for children. I assumed that I must be the hero of his Irish volume called *The Boy Who Knew What the Birds Said."*

I remember him as a deep-voiced, gloomy fellow sitting astride our fire bench at teatime on a winter afternoon, gazing into the flames while speaking in low, buzzing tones to Mom. What about?

My younger sister Patience Anne recently informed me on the phone that our mother had told her, as one woman to another, of being propositioned by Colum!

Mom was piously inclined, respectful of Mary Colum, devoted to Pop, and something of a shrinking violet. Hence, madly bally Paddy found himself forever banished from her sight! I've sometimes wondered what happened to my godfather. Now I know why I never saw him again...

Wild animals have been around millions of years longer than our kind. Who knows whether or not they forged ahead on the theoretical front?

Consider, for example—

DR. ARACHNE'S THEORY

When a cool glob of spider spittle
happened to land smack upon
a piping-hot, pot-bellied
cosmological teakettle
did actual time occur
and energy/matter
scatter not a little?
That's a hidden riddle
for insect science to settle.
We get glimmerings of light
at many a shimmering web site.

Socrates and Plato asserted that the world which we perceive consists of ephemeral, shifting and tossing "shadows" cast by a larger, loftily swinging "reality." This has always been a difficult position to embrace with confidence. One tends either to ignore it or to make a pearl of it, as oysters do with intrusive grain of sand.

My *Socrates, the Person and the Portent* (1968) wrestled with the Platonic concept of "forms," yet failed to grasp the fact that these are not remote absolutes after all. They flow freely through us and around us!

Or do they? Might I be guilty of what S. T. Coleridge called his own "Lycophronic tenebricosity"?

This morning I'll mount the stairs of London's Burlington House (in imagination of course) and revisit a favorite work, painted by an amiable Frenchman under five feet tall, who flourished a luscious paintbrush.

Jean-Honore Fragonard composed "The Swing" way back in 1767. The painting in my mind's eye shows an unkempt chateau garden. There lies young Baron St Julien, supine, leering up at his mistress. Perched upon a high swing, she swoops aloft, caressed by summer breezes.

She wears a straw hat with ribbons, a bow-tie neckpiece, pink silks, satins, and white lace. Within this elaborate costume, doubtless, her lithe physique exudes a subtle sheath of sweat. She's no "sex object" but a vivacious, sensual "subject," and free-swinging spirit in her own right.

In the flesh, that is, redolent with rosemary, anise, and fennel, which perfume the French Midi around Grasse.

The Baron's plump-cheeked, hard-puffing private priest has been delegated to push and pull her swing-seat from the rear.

"Push HARDER, Father!"

While singing out that shrill command, she lifts her knees, exposing the petticoat and offering the Baron a slantwise look at what we ourselves can't see. I refer to her most intimately possessive aspect, with its dewy dollop of pubic hair. Gazing fondly down upon her laid-back nobleman, she kicks up one foot, carelessly loosing a satin slipper in the process.

HOMILY

> Immemorial mountains tremble.
> Temples shudder. Down they tumble.
> Comrades crumple. Suddenly they die.
> But all the same it's dumb to grumble
> when a beauty flips her slipper high
> aslant the sultry September sky.

I recently cleaned out a steamer trunk. Near the bottom was one of Mother's diaries, dated 1928. That was my ninth year of life, and Grandfather Cook's last. My final meeting with Mom's dad occurred during the night that followed his unforgettably dreadful funeral, where—

VISITATION

I totally REFUSED to "View the Body."
Even REFUSED to "kneel and pray."
Thus causing general dismay
until Mother said, Okay.

 That night, he came down
through the ceiling, really sky.
Getting into my bed with a sigh,
Grandpa gave me his OWN good-bye.

Mother's newly discovered diary informs me that when I woke up the next morning I told her about my visit from Grandfather Cook's "ghost." Mom had cross-examined me on the matter, and carefully recorded our entire dialogue. Here it is, unedited—

"How did you know it was Grandfather?"
"I saw him."
"Did he have a body?"
"Yes."
"Could you feel the body?"
"Yes."
"How could you see who it was in the dark?"
"I don't know, I just could."
"What did Grandfather look like?"
"Like himself, only much younger!"
"What?"
"Yes, and as he lay down on his back beside me, he sighed like this." (Axy sighed softly.)
"Was it an unhappy sigh?"
"It might have been a tired sigh, or a relieved sigh. Not sad."
"Were you glad Grandfather came like that?"
(Surprised) *"Did you think I wouldn't be glad?"*

"Did you remember he was dead?"
"Of course."
"Were you awake?"
"Wide awake."
"How long did Grandfather stay?"
"I don't know, 'cause I went right to sleep with my arm around him."
"How I wish he would come now, and I could see him."
"Oh, Mother! People like he is now only come for a reason."
"There would be a reason. To comfort my loneliness."

Axy laughed, MERRILY, and, said: "He doesn't have to come to comfort you. He can do it without coming now. Don't you understand THAT, Mother?!"

Mom's 1928 diary shows that she was a lot more strict in her thinking than I ever realized. Further on, she wrote—

"Last night I made a promise to God, to my beloved dead Father, and to the Little Flower, to try and purify my heart sincerely if Father will show himself to me in such a way that I cannot doubt his survival."

Just now I found, tucked into mother's diary, a yellowed sheet of notepaper which reads as follows—

"April 23rd, 1927. To my beloved wife, Carrie Louella Cook, on the fiftieth anniversary of our wedding day.

> *Fairer than on your earlier wedding day,*
> *Sweeter, more loving, wiser every way.*
> *As the young sapling changes to the tree,*
> *Majestic in its beauty, strong and free,*
> *To shelter in its branches the wild birds,*
> *So thou a refuge art, to those you love.*
> *And, loving much through many years of life,*
> *I hail thee model matron, mother, wife.*

Among my early American ancestors was a well-heeled transatlantic importer, based in Boston, named Samuel Eliot. He lived through the "Boston Tea Party" and subsequent American Revolution. When it was over, he returned to business as usual with our former oppressor, naturally enough.

As our taciturn Republican President Calvin Coolidge one asserted—

"The business of America, is business."

Eliot's biography includes the following passage:

"On the 14th of April, 1770, Samuel Eliot took leave of his kind friends in London, with much content, if rhymes addressed to his wife may be believed. "I give a short specimen:

> "To Albion's shores I bid a long adieu,
> And fly in eager haste to love and you;
> Soon do I hope to clasp in warm embrace
> The Fair, posses'd of every charm and grace.
>
> "Happy the man posses'd of such a wife
> The joy, the comfort, and the balm of life!"

A hundred years from now, will my own verses appear hopelessly dated, like Grandpa Cook's and the merchant prince Samuel Eliot's?

Could be! Henry Wadsworth Longfellow, for example, was America's most hugely popular Nineteenth Century poet, yet he goes unread today, silent as a clam...

Carrie Louella Houghton, who'd married Cornelius Cook, derived from a long line of Yankee farming folk. I recall the old lady bustling about her kitchen and responding to my childishly insistent queries with—

"The PROOF is in the PUDDING!"

Grandpa Cook's own heritage was Scots-Irish Protestant, from Ireland's County Down. I remember him as a straight-backed, twinkle-eyed, lean old gentleman, with a billowy snow-white mustache of the "soup-strainer" sort.

I thought of him as a sea-captain, but in fact he'd been a small-time, vaguely troubled Doctor of Divinity.

When Mother was little, her father served as Congregational minister to a hardscrabble New England farm community called North Gage.

Reverend Cook's own mother lodged with the family, and told the kids a host of fairy stories. She assured them that invisible creatures are just as real as can be.

Little Ethel learned the lesson so well that once, when she happened to notice a rain goblin sliding down the banister of the Rectory's back porch steps, over and over again, she called the others to come look, and made them see it also!

TREMBLING OF THE VEIL

When Mom was little Ethel Cook
unjustly expelled from school
climbing up a rock-strewn slope
behind the Cook family rectory
she happened upon a gentian
who gazed into her tearful eyes
with recognition and surprise.

After some years of virtuous, poverty-stricken service, Reverend Cook finally confronted the unconscious fanaticism of his congregation, among whose many idiotic cast-iron dogmas was this–

"Whoever fails to be baptized in the right religious sect is irreversibly cursed, plunging to Hell forever!"

Eventually, a North Gage infant died un-baptized. What could Cook possibly offer by way of consolation for the bereaved parents? And what should he tell his congregation?

Standing straight up in his pulpit on the following Sunday, Dr. Cook resoundingly damned the Doctrine of Infant Damnation.

Shocked to its hard core, the North Gage congregation almost unanimously canned Cook as a traitorous blasphemer! That was his reward for manifesting the independent quality that still keeps our country free.

Armies can't do it, nor hi-tech security measures either, but "ordinary" people can and do.

Dismissed but unbowed, freed in fact, Cornelius Cook now resolved to devote full attention to the needs of his five scruffy children and long-suffering bride. Moving to nearby Pittsfield, Massachusetts, he enthusiastically embraced Mary Baker Eddy's newly created, unthreatening American religion called "Christian Science."

Meanwhile he entered the life insurance business, which made excellent sense to him, and also contributed occasional gently humorous verses to the Pittsfield Eagle.

AMERICAN STORY

Born again, free and whole
as the captain of his soul
Cook toured Main Street
cordially on his two feet.

Reading more of Mother's diary, I was struck by the following entry for May thirteenth—

"When I was home in Pittsfield last week I was actually afraid he might come up the stairs and into my room. AFRAID. How very strange for me to be afraid. Whenever I was afraid in the night at home it was Father to whom I called, on the pretense of wanting a

glass of water. And now, how strange that his best-loved child should lie afraid in the dark.

"That the one who had come to her in the dark with love and assurance would come and frighten her. This is too bitter. I must never be afraid again in the dark of anything supernatural. I must meet my Father in the dark and welcome him as a child."

Pop served Smith College as a one-man Drama Department, teaching Theatre Workshop, Play Writing, Modern Drama, Shakespeare, Ancient Athenian Drama, and finally Asiatic Drama. As for Mother, she was deeply absorbed in writing her wonderful books.

But Grandpa Cook seemed to enjoy holding my hand on walks and even joining in my games. He was the first adult to actually converse with me.

"It's a good idea," he said one day, "to think something silly!"

"Why?" I asked. "Grown-ups tell me NOT to be silly. Are they out of their minds, or what?" "

"It's not impossible. I hesitate to speculate on that point."

"Hey, are you serious?"

"Sometimes I get that way, but not for long. Seriosity ought to be avoided, don't you know."

"Seriosity?"

"Sure. Far be it from me to say what you should or shouldn't do."

"Oh, I'm used to it. Everybody—"

"Yep, everyone on earth feels justified in ordering other people around.

"Why, Grandpa?"

"Maybe it's because folks can't help their own selves. Anyhow, try thinking silly. You can start with some absurd 'What if?'"

FOR GRANDPA COOK

WHAT IF the Flemish town of Bruges,
were up-tilted to precipitate
a metropolitan avalanche
that nothing could staunch?
The consequences would be huge.
Baroque domes crumble and implode.
Round-bellied burghers in brown derbies
hurriedly abandon the doomed urban abode
whose Belgian chocolate, fine lace and lip-rouge
business interests they so splendidly bestrode.
Rumbling downslides tumble marble halls.
Collapsing masonry takes a terrible toll.
Canals become clangorous waterfalls
and cargo barges somersault to spill
blackly clattering cataracts of coal.
A mere boy brings the mess about.
by spreading his toy blocks out
on his family's brass tea-tray
and deliberately upsetting
everything in fancy-free
extremely SILLY play.

When I was little, our family spent most summers at my Eliot grandparents' vacation home at Asticou, on Mount Desert island, Maine. Their shingled mansion, with its verandah overlooking the Atlantic, stood a short stroll uphill from Great-grandpa Charles W. Eliot's shore-front estate.

C.W.E. was in retirement following a forty-year run as President of Harvard.

Mother once told me she had loathed those summers. The extended Eliot family's complacently self-righteous neo-puritan vigor exasperated her.

There was one bright spot, however. During dinner at Asticou with C.W.E. present, one of Pop's teen-age sisters maliciously announced—

"Ethel smokes cigarettes in her room!"

Shocked silence ensued, until C.W.E. responded—

"Thank you, child. You have taught me something new. Never would I have suspected that a perfect lady can INDEED smoke!"

After dinner at Asticou, I used to play "Authors" with Grandma and whomever else cared to join in. The game hinged upon the identities of one's cards, each of which was engraved with a particular author's portrait.

My favorite card represented the early 19th century author Edgar Allan Poe. In my daydreams he was actually "Houdini," a darkly brooding escape-artist of the day.

But there was no escape for Poe. A verse-maker of the first order, Gothic tale-teller, detective story inventor, acutely abusive literary critic, and masked rider of the purple page, Poe composed at a remote and lonely gallop.

He profoundly inspired Baudelaire, who translated his verses. Thanks to Baudelaire's influence, Poe became the grandfather of modern French poetry.

And thanks to Arthur Conan Doyle he also inspired the great British detective story tradition, capped by Agatha Christie.

His final work was an astonishing prose-poem titled *"Eureka,"* for "I Get It," which outraced actual science by a century.

Despite his amazing gifts, the man himself endured opprobrium, suffered poverty, and drank himself to death at only forty, fallen face-down into a Baltimore ditch.

What was he thinking? We'll never know.

THE DEATH OF A POET

Blow
hurricane

Drown
my brain

Break
dear heart

Crack
right apart

 Until great-grandpa came along, American colleges had been finishing schools for rich boys. They learned a little Latin, less Greek, a soupcon of Science and a fistful of history, plus nighttime drunkenness and whoring.
 By hard thought, organizing ability and willpower, Charles W. Eliot changed the face of American schooling. He turned his university into a secular beacon of "elective education,"—choosing one's own studies and receiving proper post-graduate training in the professions.
 But positive initiatives sometimes produce negative consequences, and today's strictly business emphasis on "professionalism" has resulted in forgetfulness of the larger human adventure.
 This in turn has brought about a severe dumbing-down of our educated elite, so-called.
 No elitist, Eliot regarded self-education as an ideal goal. Any intelligent person can achieve cultivation over time, he urged, by reading the classics for fifteen minutes daily.
 America's leading publisher, John Collier, accordingly challenged Eliot to compile a list of his own favorites.

What resulted from that was a hugely popular publishing phenomenon, advertised both as *"The Harvard Classics"* and as *"Dr. Eliot's Five-Foot Shelf."*

Great grandpa abjured all alcoholic beverages except champagne, which he regarded as purely festive. He once confessed—

"I made a poor speech last night, prolix and diffuse. In fact I was INTOXICATED. I had taken a cup of coffee."

C.W.E. never cursed. All that he required in order to express severe disapproval was: *"Goodness gracious!"*

Once, however, when he sat at the helm of his commodious old sailboat called "The Hearty," out at sea, a sudden gale snapped the mast in two, and Eliot was heard to shout—

"THUNDERATION!"

Another time, when Doctor Oliver Wendell Holmes, Senior, blandly inquired why Harvard's Medical School should not be allowed to "jog along well enough as always?," C.W.E. amicably replied—

"Because you have a new President!"

Only later, when he'd left the premises, was it noticed that he had wrenched loose one arm of his chair.

I've always supposed that the great man and I had nothing in common. On the instinctive level, however, genes will tell, and there is an Eliot tendency to veil violent emotions in seven-fold calm.

C.W.E. respected "childhood dreams," but for children only. Subjective activity detracted, in his view, from one's usefulness to society.

"Flee introspection!" he used to say.

That injunction reflected the outward, upward and forward-looking philosophy of life which formed our Founding Fathers and empowered young America.

It was already waning in his time, and introspection has since become the recommended therapeutic norm.

Duty marched foremost in the stern, impassioned tread of C.W.E's moral parade. As for Beauty, she rode well in the rear, blushing and waving, by no means bare, aboard a velvet-upholstered chariot. Humor hardly appeared.

During Great-grandfather's reign a gifted Harvard baseball pitcher lost his scholarship on account of poor grades. Concerned alumni petitioned Dr. Eliot to have the scholarship restored.

"But," the President asked, "is the boy reliable?"

"Oh, he wins all right

"I had been told," C.W.E. declared, "that he makes as if to aim the ball one way, and actually hurls it at a slightly different angle."

"Yes indeed, sir."

"That did not sound in the LEAST reliable to ME!"

"No, sir. "

"Well, I cannot refuse what you gentlemen request."

C.W.E. drew the nation's few first-rate philosophers to serve on his faculty, yet strongly disagreed with some of their ideas. Especially those of gently ironic, discreetly gay Professor George Santayana, who enthroned Beauty, and put Duty in clown costume. Santayana opined—

"In the heat of speculation or of love there may come moments of perfection, but they are very unstable. The reason and the heart remain deeply unsatisfied. But the eye finds in nature, and in some supreme achievements of art, constant and fuller satisfaction. Beauty therefore seems to be the clearest manifestation of perfection, and the best evidence of its possibility."

My father told me that when he was a fifteen-year-old freshman lying ill at the college infirmary, Professor Santayana dropped in, sat down on his bed, gave him the week's homework, and stayed on to chat about Brunhilde.

She was a Norse goddess who enjoyed sliding down lightning-bolt banisters and snatching up Viking warriors slain in battle.

Wafted to a Nordic Heaven for men only, those heroes whiled away the daylight hours by dueling, savagely slashing and thrusting through each other's deathless spirits. Come nightfall, they all got drunk on barley mead, and boisterously whooped it up together.

"Not an ideal way to spend eternity," Santayana concluded with a sigh, "And not unlike the situation prevailing in Harvard Yard!"

Having published his numinous "Three Philosophical Poets," Santayana escaped to Oxford, and finally Rome, where he expired, aged eighty-nine, at a Catholic convent.

DEPARTURE

Tea-time at the convent
whose mist-colored cat
makes an effortless leap
to the invalid's lap.

"Brunhilde confides in
our patient completely!"
sighs Mother Cecilia
while fluttering fleetly.

The brownies are passed
and the Sisters all clap.
Slack-jawed Santayana
awakes from his nap.

Brunhilde's at ease
on the old fellow's knees.
She's purring: *"Run, run.
Escape if you please!"*

Nodding, he dies.
There's a look in his eyes
of relief, interleaved
with extreme surprise.

Santayana's cat-footed memoirs include a final crack at his former employer:

"President Eliot, who was an anti-humanist, once said to me that we should teach the FACTS, not merely convey ideas.

"I might have replied that the only facts in philosophy were historical facts; namely the fact that people had, or had had, certain ideas. But of course I only smiled and took note of HIS IDEA."

The doughty and yet flighty author Gertrude Stein graduated from Harvard's little sister college Radcliff in 1898. Not long afterward she skipped away to Paris, where her elder brother Leo had already set up house.

Private incomes from San Francisco real estate kept the Steins in salon-keeping, art-collecting semi-luxury.

Women complain that most men talk too little. Do women talk too much? That pregnant issue is often talked about, but only Gertrude Stein made talking too much a perversely appealing and revealing literary style. She once offered the following satiric flight—

"Education is thought about and as it is thought about it is being done in the way it is thought about, which is not true of almost anything. Almost anything is not done in the way it is thought about but education is done in the way it is thought about. In New England they have done it, they do it, they will do it and they do it in every way in which education can be thought about. And that is saying a very great deal."

Would C.W.E. have been amused? It's not impossible, but I'm afraid that Great Grandpa would have mistaken Stein's sly funning for a breathlessly verbose and typically feminine effort to convey the facts of the case.

Stein celebrated her successful same-sex union by writing a colossally catty memoir in her beloved's name: *"The Autobiography of Alice B. Toklas."*

SATURDAY IN THE COUNTRY

Superbly pink from ears to toes
Gertrude assumes a nudist pose
and Alice Toklas, gloating, goes
to clean the Virgin Queen of prose
with gushes of their garden hose.

The summer when I was seven and great-grandfather was ninety-two, pneumonia ("the old man's friend") hugged him tight.

He sent for his great-grandchildren: my elder sister Torka, myself, and our little cousin Paul Fremont-Smith. The Patriarch doubtless desired to demonstrate, for our future sakes, that one can die well.

Blanket-wrapped, swathed in a green silk dressing gown, and propped among the pillows of a chaise-langue, he curled his long upper lip as we came in. Adults generally feared that lopsided grin, which seemed to spell contempt, but I felt it was kindly meant.

To hide the purple birthmark on his cheek, which he regarded as a grave disfigurement, Great grandpa kept his face turned from the light.

Trying not to gasp, he asked us to sing "Swing Low, Sweet Chariot."

We did our piping best with that.

"Thank you, my dears," Great-grandpa responded. "Now I desire to speak with your grandfather. Goodbye!"

C.W.E. confided to Grandpa Eliot that he counted on expiring by nightfall in order to "Catch the Bangor Express" back to Boston for the inevitable obsequies at Harvard.

But the best laid plans of conscientious administrators occasionally misfire. Having missed the week-end Express, Great grandpa took the local, still unruffled, on a bed of ice.

C.W.E.'s final words had been to his nurse. She was about to ask how he was resting, when he put a finger to his lips and sighed—

"I hear beautiful music!"

To what kind of music did he refer? What was it that drew Great Grandpa gently toward his outward-rattling final breath?

When he requested "Swing Low, Sweet Chariot" it was doubtless because that "negro spiritual" was the only appropriate number we'd be sure to know.

In childhood I used to sleep upstairs on our backyard screened porch which overlooked tree-bordered Paradise Pond. On early mornings in springtime, richly varied birdsong awakened me. Sometimes I catch myself thinking I hear it still, although that can't happen here.

Might such music have summoned great grandpa?

The day after his demise, I went to my mother and asked—

"What is Death?"

Frowning darkly to herself, she pondered my query. I could tell that she really cared. Finally, Mom suggested—

"Let the forest think through you!"

Well, I tried that, and somehow it worked for me. I still respect the small boy whom I once was, and I'm aware that my "true colors" belong to him as much as they may characterize me now...

Here's a story concerning my Eliot grandparents, which I once heard from a family member—

Having earned his Doctorate from Harvard's Divinity School, Samuel Atkins Eliot passionately wooed and won a seventeen-year-old Cambridge society beauty named Frances ("Fanny") Stone Hopkinson.

Shortly afterward, Grandfather initiated his career by dashing off to distant Colorado, with Fanny in tow. He wished to serve as missionary to the recently conquered Sioux Indian tribes.

Hence my father, Sam Junior, was born in Denver.

The Natives liked Grandpa's unassuming, amiable style, and were much impressed by his blushing bride.

In fact, a Lakota Sioux chieftain once went so far as to offer "many horses" in return for spending a single night with her!

Young Reverend Eliot cheerily responded with—

"You don't have THAT many horses!"

Fanny was profoundly offended, of course. Her husband tried to pass the matter off as a curious example of Sioux courtesy, which angered her yet more.

Feeling betrayed, she took her infant son back home to Cambridge on the next train.

It strikes me now that Pop's stammer could have originated in his mother's furious departure from his father. That doubtless baffled the little boy, causing him to suppose that somehow he himself must be to blame.

Thanks to vain messianic ambition, young Samuel Atkins Eliot had lost his wife and little son, while merely amusing a few inveterately heathen Sioux!

Grandfather posted an urgent letter to Washington's Bureau of Indian Affairs, which had sponsored his missionary effort.

Native Americans did not require conversion to Christianity, he reported, half so much as they needed release from heavy oppression, a modicum of education, and equal opportunity with white settlers...

Daydreaming now, I've climbed aboard the legendary Midwestern "Rock Island Express." Boozing, low-toned banter and brooding imbue its acrid blue smoker.

Leaning back in my seat, I prepare to enjoy the long ride ahead. My own reflection, young and smooth-browed once again, smiles back at me from the darkened train window. What's more, old-time faces dimly grace the oblong glass of windows gliding shadow-like alongside mine, so I'm by no means alone.

NIGHT JOURNEY

Our brand-new locomotive's wail,
ballooning ahead, creates an eerie while,
where creaking prairie schooners used to sail
in high-wheeled, bedraggled dragon-file,
over virgin grasslands of the USA to be.
Each wagonload, a Paleface family
who brave the danger-laden trail
with tomahawking Omahans
eagle-feathered Wichitans
and other hostile Indians
to pacify, or blow the heck away.

Just think how many of our states, and cities, too, have Indian names. We were Native Indian, Spanish, French, Anglo and African first.

Scandinavians, Germans, Dutch, Irish, Italians, Jews, Chinese, Japanese, Moslems and Hindu folks came along to top us off.

"Our house" really is everyone's house now, and it's about time, too.

Charles W. Eliot undertook to patch up the quarrel between his despairing son Sam and furiously flustered Fanny. Following protracted consultations with her Yankee tycoon father, who became a strong ally, he finally telegraphed Sam to hurry home, because all would be forgiven.

So that was done. Warmly reconciled, Fanny produced six more children: Charles, Elizabeth, Frances, Ted, Roz, and Tom.

Grandpa meanwhile rose to serve for a quarter century (1902-1927) as President of the American Unitarian Association, and longer still as Minister to Boston's Arlington Street Church.

Brilliant Tom—my youngest Eliot uncle—ran for Congress against Boston's charismatic, notoriously corrupt James Michael Curley.

By beating heavy odds to win, Tom Eliot attracted President Franklin D. Roosevelt's attention, and wrote our first Social Security legislation.

That's what keeps this improvident old codger afloat today. When certain politicians rant that Social Security should be abolished, you can be sure that they themselves are in the money, whether by hook or downright crook.

To nail down the Irish Catholic vote, F.D.R. appointed J. M. Curley his new Postmaster General.

In order to demonstrate that he harbored no hard feelings against the Eliot family, Curley soon issued a postage stamp commemorating Charles W. Eliot. During a reception held at my grandparents' Revere Street Cambridge house, which I attended at seventeen, Curley offered the following blarney-stone account:

"America's premier educator once deigned to attend a Harvard-Yale football game accompanied by Edward Everett Hale. As they were crossing the bridge to reach Soldiers Field, a student approached the President, and inquired where he might be going. 'I'm on my way,' Dr. Eliot assured the youth, 'to YELL with HALE!'"

Afterward, I asked Grandpa if that were true, and received the following blandly resonant response—

"Why, no. Your great-grandfather had nothing against Hale, but neither did he condemn Yale. He strongly disapproved of football, and never attended games. No sane student would have dared to accost Harvard's President. Finally, my father would not have permitted the merest shadow of profanity to escape his lips."

One's inner nature participates in the inner nature of Nature herself, by which I mean consciousness as a whole. Hence I don't feel squeezed into some rigid time-frame.

I still respect the small boy whom I once was, and I'm aware that my "true colors" belong to him as much as they characterize me now.

That's the hidden motivation for these seemingly random recollections.

2. Growing Pains

My neighborhood gang had an admirably athletic President: "Dickey-Bird" Cooney. Second, came indrawn, skinny "Bones" Dunphy. Third, sardonically grinning Harry Maynard, from Massasoit Street. Fourth, wall-eyed "Tarzan" Kellog. Fifth, the egg-shaped, genial rich kid "Tub" Janes, who lived in a gloomy big house on Elm.

Sixth and last, but by no means least in my opinion, the small southpaw "Red" Eliot of Paradise Road, appears.

A SCAMP AT HAMP

If I got mad and kicked Tarzan's
smart ass for asserting that
his dimwit Dad could
lick my Dad, then
Dickey-Bird
would order
Bones to chase
me down, and Tub to
sit on me, until I apologized.

Rightly so. Although Mr. Kellog was a hairy ape indeed, and the most prominent local monument to stupidity, I should never have dared to call Tarzan's dad a dimwit. That ran right against our unspoken rule of mutual forbearance.

Tub didn't mind raiding his Dad's handgun collection, so on rainy days we practiced cheating at poker and swiftly shooting each other, in the Janes' attic. Tub was tops at both.

We also boxed, with mitts provided by Tub, in his commodious garage. Harry Maynard excelled at boxing. To everyone's surprise, I wasn't bad either.

Our favorite outdoor games included "King of the Mountain," "Gang War," "Follow the Leader," and "Street Polo" aboard our battered bicycles.

Unlike today's mothers, ours wasted little time worrying over us, but our obscure shenanigans gave them plenty of washing, mending and shampooing to do.

"Two bits" (or one quarter) a week was my boyhood allowance. That purchased Saturday matinee movie tickets, penny-candy, and cap-pistol materials. It also piled up in my piggy bank, to pay for such mail-order disappointments as a "dynamic tension" course from Charles Atlas.

That forgotten figure dared to present himself as "The World's Most Perfectly Developed Man." (I regarded myself as "The Strongest Boy on our Street.")

Atlas advertised in "American Boy" and "Boy's Life" magazines, using a persuasive comic strip approach. The opening panel showed a passing hunk kicking sand in the face of a pretty girl, whom a "ninety-eight-pound weakling" was trying to romance.

Dismayed by his inability to punish the rude fellow, the weakling wisely subscribes to Atlas' course. Returning in superb physical condition to the beach, he punishes the hunk in hand-to-hand combat, and captures the girl's attention at last.

Two beginning cartoonists in Cleveland doubtless read Atlas's ads, which I imagine sparked their creation of America's most popular mythic icon. Back in 1938, Jerome Siegel and Joseph Shuster surrendered all rights to their "Superman" concept to Detective Comics, for $130. Talk about capital punishment! Time-Warner owns them now.

A FINE ROMANCE

Superman was always true
to one beautiful woman, who
ventured with her secret beau
where nobody else dared go.

Although, as loyal boys insist
the couple never even kissed.

Saturday afternoons, we would troop downtown to the narrow Plaza theatre on Pleasant Street, pay one thin dime apiece, and gawk together at the movies. They were "movies" because they moved, and silent because "talkies" had not yet arrived.

The Plaza's pianist sat left of the screen, banging or tinkling out appropriate emotions for each episode.

"Westerns" were my favorites, naturally. I regarded Hoot Gibson as the thoughtful sort whom red-blooded fellows despise. Although no tulip, he was not so stalwart as my personal hero: straight-shooting Tom Mix.

I thought I knew all about them, but how could a freckle-faced, Cap-pistol Kid horsing about in western Massachusetts possibly guess where Hoot and Mix alike were from?

Silver light-reflectors and bug-eyed movie cameras on trolley tracks, glint in the sunshine. Prop-men, script-girls, and grips, scurry worriedly about. The Director gloomily sniffs, frowns, wets a forefinger with his tongue, and holds it high to determine whence the air current comes.

The Assistant Director starts yelling frantically, as about a hundred mounted attackers in war paint and feather headpieces, come galloping up over a nearby rise of ground.

Meanwhile the two stars, in Stetson hats and fringed chamois jackets, sit chatting on horseback —

PALAVER

"Apaches, shmapaches!"
Hoot sputters to Mix.
"They gallop like golems
from over the Styx.

And I'm simply appalled
by the falling-down tricks
of feather-brained extras
who litter our flicks!"

"So shoot 'em, and win"
Mix replies with a grin.
He's a man of few words,
unaccustomed to sin.

Those hard-riding, fast-falling, silent Western film extras were not Native Indians, by the way, but ex-Cossack recruits from Hollywood's White Russian colony.
   Comedies were okay, I supposed, except that the slapstick struck me as hurtful, and even made me duck down in my seat at times. Buster Keaton and Harold Lloyd commanded my full attention, but Charlie Chaplin was too heart-breaking.
   Eyes closed, I can still see Charlie, equipped with his tippy bowler and flexible cane, whipping up hilariously brutal ideas —

INCOGNITO

His shaggy goatish part
in baggy trousers furled
Great Pan cavorts athwart
our oafish twirling world.

Whatever happened to that old gang of mine? Mostly good things, I guess, because the quarter-century following World War Two was the only moment in history when American labor actually prospered.

Dickey-bird Cooney rose to be Foreman at the Northampton Basket factory, and his cheery wife undertook a night job cleaning out buses for the Peter Pan line.

Tub Janes' dad died bankrupt, so Tub labored at the nearby Springfield Valve company.

Tarzan Kellog managed a convenience store.

Bones Dunphy attended Holy Cross College and went on to become a doctor somewhere.

Harry Maynard joined the U.S. Air Force and performed heroically throughout World War Two.

He was one of the first to return to Europe and confront the horror of the whole thing, including his own role. He'd never been wounded, not even a nick, yet suffered internal head injuries anyhow.

"I've slipped and fallen flat," he once confided to me, "in the spilled blood and brains of my crew!"

Having joined Time Inc at my suggestion, Harry prospered as an advertising space salesman. In retirement, he served as President of the Institute for General Semantics.

We two were lifetime buddies, and Harry gave me wise, decisive guidance at two crucial points in my life...

My eleventh summer was passed at "Camp Mohawk," a rustic Berkshire Hills repository for restless and annoying boys. On my first night there, our log cabin counselor informed us kids that he happened to be a Cree Indian Chief!

FOUNDATION COURSE

With saving grace, our native Cree
taught wait and see serenity.
He showed me how to shoot pool
and make believe that I'm no fool
which I keep doing as a rule.
"The Last of the Mohicans" is ME.

"Your red hair and my Indian complexion," the Chief once assured me in private, "make us wiser than most."
"Huh?"
He nodded: "They think the color red stands for sex and rage—"
"Hey, what IS sex, anyhow??"
"Who knows?"
"Don't you?"
"Not yet."
"Oh."
"While shooting pool, for example, we treat this here cue ball as we would a squaw."
"Is that an Indian woman?"
"Right. We can stroke her."
"Okay."
"Yes, and we should kiss her."
"Are you sure? I don't go for that idea."
"I'm sure all right, and you'll find out there's something in it. But don't never, ever, hit her!"
"Why the heck not?"
"Because a cue ball is touchy. You might even say squaw-sensitive. '
"So what?"
"Hit her, and she goes haywire. I mean, plumb tomahawk!"
"That wouldn't bother me none."

"No, but you've missed the shot, my friend, and your turn is OVER."

"Oh. Now I get what you're talking about."

"You do?"

"Yeah. In the first place, don't never hit the cue ball. Instead, you should stroke her."

"Right."

"You can also kiss her cheek when you gotta."

"Fine point, Red."

"Thanks, Chief. You've given me the number one RULE of pocket POOL."

"Good for you!"

Racking up our cues, he added: "A word to the wise never hurts. I myself had to find out the hard way."

"Well, anyhow, you're the CHAMP of our CAMP."

"Thanks, Red. I like the way you talk in rhyme/"

"Do I do that?"

"For sure. You'd galvanize an Indian Pow-wow!"

The next year, having reached the age of twelve, I stood on our front porch In Northampton, swinging at imaginary pitches with my best birthday present: a genuine "Louisville Slugger."

By then I figured I knew quite a bit about life, death, and baseball as well.

My fastball was a slow ball and my out-fielding was way out, but on the other hand my pinch-hitting for the "Northampton Ponies" had been mentioned twice in the Hampshire Gazette, and once in the Springfield Republican!

Across my happy musings strolled a tow-headed, sloppy looking man, ambling down along Paradise Road.

"Babe Ruth!" I thought. "No, it couldn't be."

Turning in at our walk, he said—

"Nice bat."

"Want to try it? Here!"

"No thanks. My name's Frost. I'm a professor, like your Dad, but over at Amherst."

"Oh."

Robert Frost had arrived to discuss a theatrical project with Pop. I can't recall what came of that.

He still remains America's number one rhyme slinger. Consider "The Road not Taken" for example —

> *I shall be telling this with a sigh*
> *Somewhere ages and ages hence:*
> *Two roads diverged in a wood, and I —*
> *I took the one less traveled by,*
> *And that has made all the difference.*

America's reigning poet at the time had one local rival. Namely Wallace Stevens, an imposing gentleman in a gray flannel suit, who doubled as Vice President of the Hartford, Connecticut, Fire Insurance Corporation.

Stevens never raised his voice. Yet it's been said that once, on impulse, he knocked boastful Ernest Hemingway flat! (That's a story which Hem earnestly denied.)

> CLASS ACT
> Reflective his fine shoe-shine.
> Voluminous his girth, well hung.
> Astonishing was many a line
> on Wallace Stevens' silver tongue.

Like most practitioners today, Stevens wrote relatively permissive free verse. He was incredibly adept at slinging subtle stuff in zippy Frisbee style, such as—

> *I do not know which to prefer.*
> *The beauty of inflections*
> *Or the beauty of innuendoes.*
> *The Blackbird whistling,*
> *Or just after.*

I do not know which to prefer, Frost's inflections or Stevens' innuendoes, but I'm aware that the "Blackbird whistling," and the "just after" silence, speak as one. Who can deny that things and events are multi-faceted? So much depends upon the angle from which you observe them.

Pablo Picasso first alerted me to this when, having reached thirteen, I encountered his Cubist paintings in an exhibition at the Smith College Tryon Gallery of Art. Because Picasso's images were new to me, I could easily replay their gray and brown square-brush-caresses on the inside.

Picasso showed me places where Space, Time, and the curiously free play of Thought, rub elbows.

CROSSOVERS

Picasso's sketch of a guitar
entangled with some furniture
evoked a corpse upon a beach
rolling, broken, out of reach.

When I blinked and looked again
the thing became a talisman
of Gypsy music, jokes and wine.
Was I correct the second time?

My third impression overcame
the others like a limpid stream.
The picture's purest pleasure lay
in measured overlapping play.

Recognizing the triple-layered quality of cubism set the direction for much of my life work. It was like waking up one morning in a far-distant country, only to discover that one already understands the language spoken there.

To reach the museum I'd borrowed my father's bicycle. Entranced, I completely forgot to return it on schedule.

This made the ever punctual professor unavoidably late for his class in Athenian Drama. He must have waited anxiously until the last possible moment, and then raced on foot to meet with his waiting students.

After class, Pop showed up at the museum, furious. I heard him roar at the receptionist—

"Where is my SON?"

That was the worst of it. A minute later Pop appeared, and bowled me over with a swift forearm swipe.

His aggression was totally out of character, and anyhow I didn't care. Pop's passing fury only pointed up the timeless thrill of my first purely aesthetic experience...

My awkward age, so-called, proceeded at a typically precipitous pace. This brought waltz and foxtrot lessons which I loathed, and a peculiar impulse to kiss the girls after all, which I suppressed by getting a good grip on myself, — so to speak.

Mother often asked me to kneel and pray for Pop's "conversion."

Sometimes I did so. But finally, following the incident at the Smith College museum, I summoned sufficient courage to ask the obvious question. What might be his own opinion of the Catholic Church?

"I think it's DISGUSTING!"

He'd long made a brave show of tolerating Mother's religion for the sake of family peace, but no more.

I'll never know what led to that spontaneous outburst on his part, but it strikes me now that the early 1930's may have been especially stressful for Pop, and for Mom as well. Apparently, those two wonderful but very different people had briefly mislaid their love for each other.

Soon after Pop's wake-up call, I got a private theology lesson from an Irish-American, deep voiced, black-clad, pot-bellied Monsignor named Patrick Cummings.

He had converted my mother to Catholicism when I was eight or nine years old, Then, on Three King's Day, he'd baptized me (with "Patrick" for a middle name).

So he was only doing his duty as shepherd to the willfully skittering black lamb of a teen-ager in his spiritual care.

Monsignor began with a question: "Do you believe in God?"

I dumbly nodded.

So round, so firm, so resonantly orotund, and tightly packed with implacable logic, was the half-hour sermon that followed. Also, impossible for me to swallow.

Afterward, I sat alone upon the grassy bank that overlooks Smith College's Paradise Pond. I took comfort in the landscape, waterscape and airscape combined, whose numberless crisscrossing rhythms, reflections, cohesions and half-heard music slowly smoothed my agitation away.

Nature's perpetual-motion variety and vast extent envelops all human knowledge in what St. John of the Cross called a "Cloud of Unknowing." We can't ever leap out of that.

As this thought crossed my mind, the whole scene choked solid and stopped dead. I was smothering, crushed in a universal paralysis which I myself had somehow brought about! There's no way to convey the ensuing mental agony.

After what may have been a few minutes but felt like hours, mother Nature shuddered back into her accustomed harmony. I lay sweated out, wrung dry, scared stiff, and shaken to the core.

My brush with horror prompted an immediate change of heart. Then and there, I made a solemn vow to turn around and trade my Judeo-Christian blues for the old gold of pagan mysteries...

Cicero quotes a lost Aristotelian treatise to the effect that if a troglodyte or deep-earth dweller were to emerge upon our planet's surface and pass a single day and night under the sun, moon, and stars, he or she would well understand that such things are the work of deities.

That still sounds right to me. But rationalists in the tradition of Thomas Hobbes disagree. They maintain that our remote ancestors must have found existence—

"Nasty, Brutish, and Short."

Who knows? And are we better off now? One might as well argue that present life is—

"Hasty, Suited, and Bored."

I myself suppose that humanity's prehistoric existence must have been—

Wondrous, Precious, and Dangerous, like the Garden of Eden.

The diversity of religions is good, because it promotes individual spiritual adventure. So, even if there were a deity who wanted us to agree on some single system of faith, we shouldn't.

American tradition favors "freedom of religion," yet freedom and religion make an odd couple. In the Bible, didn't God expressly forbid Adam and Eve to taste the fruit of the Tree of Knowledge?

Eve has two sons: Cain the farmer and Abel the shepherd. The Lord favors Abel, so Cain slays him. And God rebukes Cain—

> *What hast thou done?*
> *The voice of thy brother's blood*
> *calls to me from the ground.*
> *And now art thou cursed.*

I recently dreamt of finding a private journal penned by my father. It was yellowed, stained, and stiff with age. Some of the pages stuck together. But the handwriting was fine as ever, with the clarity of a good typeface.

Pop shaped each letter to contain a maximum of evenly distributed white space, setting it vertically for easy readability. To conserve paper and postage, his script was always the same small size.

Sensing that Pop's text must contain some final advice, I felt eager to read what it said. But I couldn't make out a single word! Why not? I was "nonplussed," as Pop would have put it, like a second-grader called, unprepared, to the blackboard.

At that point I came wide awake.

There I lay, looking up at the darkness of the bedroom ceiling. Minuscule luminescent traces inhabited the obscurity, just as they do one's bloodstream. My heart was pounding.

Why? A bad dream?

Dreams are totally convincing at the time, and baffling afterward. All contain strip-poker aspects, but it's not easy to analyze them down to their underwear.

I guess the American expatriate novelist Henry James dreamt of being birthday-suit-bare, blushing and quaking like an unexplained Colonial fruit Jello, at a Buckingham Palace reception.

Never mind the fact that he could have been the life of what was doubtless a dull party.

Off the diamond, Big League baseball's awesome slugger Ted Williams seemed a bit lonely, proud but insecure. He doubtless dreamt, sometimes, of sinking, swirling, and hopelessly shrinking, like a red cotton athletic sock at the Laundromat...

Each person's cranium encapsulates a modicum of motor-control and commonsense, plus a cumulous cloud of somewhat vaguely registered experience. Incoming data from near and far matters much the most.

Children under seven process this best. Grown-ups do less well, and by the "prime of life" our perspectives have narrowed way down for practical purposes. Can we expand them again?

For me, that is the question.

Much bigger than ordinary satellites, the moon came barreling down out of deep space, impacted our planet and skidded off again, taking along a Pacific-size chunk of Earth's surface.

Minus the huge magnetic pull of the moon, which one discerns directly through the rising and falling of ocean tides, our earthly home would not spin at the ideal speed to support human life.

Earth and Moon interact like mathematics and poetry. Math works with inexorable logic, stripped clean of human feeling, whereas poetry slows down one's thoughts while painting in the emotional aspects of things.

Kenneth Hurlstone Jackson's "A Celtic Miscellany" volume of translations (Routledge & Kegan Paul, 1951) ought to be re-issued. Here's a twelfth century prose poem from Jackson's anthology—

"When Patrick, glorious in grace, was suffering on goodly Cruach—an anxious, toilsome time for the protector of lay men and women—God sent to comfort him a flock of spotless, angelic birds. Over the clear lake without fail they would sing in chorus their gentle proclamation.

"And thus they called auspiciously: 'Patrick, arise and come! Shield of the Gael, in pure glory, illustrious golden spark of fire!'

"Then the whole host struck the lake with their smooth and shadowy wings, so that its chilly surface became like a silver sheen."

The *Life of Brigid* by the Irish monk Cogitosus, dates from the seventh century of our era—

"She was pasturing her sheep on a grassy knoll, when a sudden downpour occurred. She returned home in wet clothes. The sun shining through a gap in the building cast a ray which seemed to her to be a solid wooden beam fixed across the house.

"So she placed her wet cloak upon it, as if it were indeed solid, whereupon the cloak hung securely from the incorporeal sunbeam!"

The saint had seen the sunbeam with her physical eyes, while the eye of her imagination witnessed what others could not. As Brigid spread her sopping wet cloak out upon the sunbeam, her firm, brown, working girl hands confirmed the sun's desire to assist her by means of a great, and at the same time lowly, miracle.

The following Scottish-Gaelic invocation cries out for performance.

The translation is by Jackson and the freewheeling arrangement as verse is mine —

> *Greeting to you*
> *new moon*
>
> *kindly jewel*
> *of guidance.*
>
> *I bend my*
> *knees to you.*
>
> *I offer you*
> *my love.*
>
> *I lift up my*
> *eyes to you*
>
> *I raise my*
> *hands to you*
>
> *New moon*
> *of the seasons!*

Pop derived his personal anti-faith scenario from ancient Manichean and Gnostic doctrine. Decades later, on his deathbed, he left me a note—

"*At my memorial service, NO mention of God.*"

Mom had gone on years before, so I kept Pop's celebration secular as commanded, lubricating it with plenty of wine. His memorial involved about eighty relatives and friends, who formed a broad circle shaded by the sycamore tree in back of his house. Participants took turns standing up to reminisce about Pop. Some offered sly pinches of piety, which may not have amused his ghost.

SEASONS

While I make paper kites of words
April blows highroads for birds.
Come August, cicadas chorus.
Watermelons ripen for us.

Soon, October's gusting cold
turns the foliage red and gold.
Crinkled leaves detach and go
to molder down below.

In wintertime the snow-clad trees
stretch their groping roots at ease.
Now the long, dark starry nights
break open onto timeless heights

I'll conclude this chapter on an upbeat note, with a quatrain from Herman Melville's epilogue to his poem "Clarel"—

But through such strange illusions have they passed
Who in life's pilgrimage have baffled striven,
Even death may prove unreal at the last
And stoics be astounded into heaven.

3. Preppie

At an Ivy League prep school called Loomis Institute my nowhere-to-go sex drive, my coincidentally abstracting intellect, and my appreciation of poetry, all three together, clicked into herky-jerky gear.

The Latin literature course that mildly smiling old Bunny Mills laid upon us boys familiarized me first with implacably practical Julius Caesar and second with flowery Virgil, who never wrote a truer word than these—

> *Sunt geminae Somni portae quarum altera fertur*
> *Cornea qua veris facilis datir exitus umbris*
> *Altera candenti perfecta nitens elephanto*
> *Sed falsa ad caelum mittunt insomnia manes.*
>
> "Two gates of Sleep exist. The first being horn
> through which the spirits of truth easily pass.
> The other is gleaming white ivory, whereby
> gods send false dreams to the upper world."

While at Loomis, I got laid up with flu in the school infirmary. Back then, before antibiotics, that was a serious business.

There a young night-nurse touched me in more ways than one, caressing my uptight, pink-fuzzed scrotum and teasing my uncircumcised little penis tenderly erect.

This was by no means the same as self-masturbation. She cradled its virginity in the palm of her hand, silently pumping and squeezing to induce absolute bliss.

"You'll be okay now," she murmured, wiping me off and tucking me in again. With those four words alone, she slipped away.

This remained my secret. I never communicated it to anyone, until now. But sex is too sacred, enjoyable and indeed liberating a subject for me to avoid or blur away.

Nurses in general do not get half the credit they deserve. I owe that one a heartfelt vote of thanks for her tender "sexual abuse," which suited me perfectly.

I'd been momentarily released from an ivied brick prison of institutional nightmare.

Loomis was wired for sound. Alarm bells kept ringing to remind us of impending classes and meals. Tardiness or absence piled up "demerits," resulting in confinement to campus, even on weekends. More serious infractions were punished with humiliating and painful "paddling."

Cigarette smoking and "indulgence in alcohol" called for expulsion, yet I dared to practice both wicked ways.

The school's splendid art library, donated by the Carnegie Foundation, lay stashed away in the powerhouse because our jut-jawed, fiercely puritan Headmaster, Nathaniel Horton Batchelder, feared that its many images of nudes might possibly—

"Distract the boys from higher things."

Our sage and kindly art teacher, Madame Cheruy, thought me "promising." Hence, unbeknownst to "Mr. B.," she presented me with a powerhouse key.

During my three years at Loomis, thanks to Madame, I thoroughly perused every art book at the powerhouse in blessed solitude. That was quite an education in itself.

For starters, consider Albrecht Durer's 1514, engraving called "Melencolia 1." It shows a dark angel sitting motionless with folded wings, majestically hunched upon a stone slab, as if magnetized. She's surrounded by architectural tools, alchemical implements, and tons of geometrical solids which center on a truncated rhomboid.

Behind the crowded foreground scene, a bat arises in flight, while the haloed 'giant dwarf' of a dying star stops everything cold. Melancholy casts a steady pall over intellectual existence. The livid whites of the angel's eyes flash warning—

"Mine is NOT the path!"

Durer followed "Melencolia 1." with a second etching called "Saint Jerome in his Cell," and presented both to his closest friends. The first is chill, cluttered, and anxious, whereas the second is warm, open, peaceful, and happy.

Jerome sits writing. There's a tiny inkwell at his elbow, a delicate upright crucifix before him, and a lectern to hold his book at a convenient angle. Otherwise his table is bare. Like an accomplished helmsman on the bridge of some space-ship, he seems absorbed in his working voyage.

At the top of the steps upon which we stand looking into Jerome's studio, a guardian lion and a small companionable dog lie dozing together.

Above, in the immediate foreground, hangs a plump, leafy gourd. An hour-glass plus a broad-brimmed hat, occupy the far wall. A few books sleep beside the wrinkled pillows on the shelves, as does the saint's "reminder of mortality," the weathered human skull on the windowsill.

For me, the hat and hourglass behind the saint represent the "Given." Namely, space and time. The skull suggests "Reason," plus finality, or mortality if one prefers. The lion and the dog bespeak "Great-heartedness" alongside "Faithfulness." The gourd swells with "Fruition."

In short, the picture's thrust is fast-forward, from the given through reason, great-heartedness and faithfulness to final fruiting.

Although Madame Cheruy never discussed her private life with me, I've since come upon evidence that she'd conducted a passionate affair with the consummate American artist Edward Hopper during his formative Paris years (1915-1918) when they were both in their twenties. Witness the profoundly tender drawings and the etching of her in a fur hat, which Hopper created way back then.

Madame's own drawings of cathedral interiors, each incorporating four or five separate light sources, struck me as magical, by the way.

My sexual potential was easily stirred, but never by Durer, whose pictures thrilled a not-yet-manifest aspect of myself. I never dreamed that Jerome had translated the Bible into Latin, or that I might eventually turn to literature.

But that's odd, because I used to compose love letters for wealthy classmates to copy, sign, and mail to presumed sweethearts back home. I charged a dollar per letter, my first easy money from free-lance writing.

Mr. David Newton, the dryly quizzical English literature teacher whom we boys called Newt, subjected us to a deliberately tough survey course which I enjoyed.

The romantic poets in particular moved me profoundly and opened the eyes of my imagination to a brave new verbal universe. I hope and trust that this process still occurs in English classes everywhere. When you lack poetry you're missing one of life's major blessings and guides.

Please remember this for your own children and grandchildren.

It strikes me that *"Kublai Khan,"* by Samuel Taylor Coleridge, must have sparked my first personal attempt at verse.

PARADISE LOST

Lonely, slender, slicked with steam
in my pleasure dome of dream
a damsel plucked her dulcimer.

Things get nicer than they seem.
I sang the tune; she didn't scream,
so I guessed I'd lucked out with her.

She dandled my outstanding thing
cool-handedly, to make it swing
until some inner force took wing.

My perspective widened then
but I can't say where or when.
Such ecstasy escapes my pen!

I asked the dusky damsel why
do music, love, and laughter die?
She swirled away like a smoke-ring.

 I proudly submitted that effort to "The Loomis Loom," our school literary magazine, which Newt supervised. He naturally elected to suppress my "Somewhat embarrassing item."
 Being rather proud and vain in my secret heart, I've never yet taken rejection lightly. So I asked Newt to reconsider.
 "Don't fret," said he. "Just pull your poor self together and give us a different sort of fantasy with no dang SEX involved!"
 That led to a second effort: the following nonsense number, which also failed to pass muster—

MASTERNAUGHTS

Donchu Speaknosex abides
in upper space with seven brides
who despise adolescent boys
and snatch away our favorite toys.

It's dangerous but what the heck?
As Captain Ahab told the whale
in Herman Melville's dreadful tale:
"Don't you dare be MOPING, Dick!"

The final exam Newt laid upon us included this astounding item: "Please list England's kings from medieval times to the present."
Never having bothered to memorize that interminably extended list, I offered—

YE OLDE ENGLISH KINGS

Among the monarchs I remember
from way back in September
are Ethelred the Unready
Harold fairly Steady
Canute B. Wetfoot
O'Rollem the Rash
Arthur Snap Garter
Hairless Balderdash
Lester Chestnuts Afire
and the foul usurper: F.U. Sire!

Well, Newt felt himself obliged by strict rules of the testing game to rate my entire academic year's efforts at an ignominious "B"!

Although I scarcely knew her, I suspect that Newt's patient, childless wife understood her husband well, and even scanned me correctly.

I guess she told her spouse he ought to offer something by way of an apology for the insulting grade he'd laid on me. Anyhow, Newt chose to part with his Everyman *"Biographia Literaria"* volume, authored by S.T. Coleridge, which doubtless bored him anyhow. His inscription astonished me—

"With admiration and great hope!"

During the summer months, I puzzled my way page by page through the whole book, with steadily growing amazement. Coleridge pinpointed the fact that—

"Objects, considered AS objects, are fixed and dead."

Imagination, he added, is contrastingly vital. If it were not for Imagination, our universe would spin without significance! As the poet put it—

"The primary Imagination I take to be the living power and prime agent of all human perception, and as a repetition in the finite mind of the eternal act of creation in the infinite. "The medium by which spirits understand each other is not the surrounding air but the freedom which they possess in common as the ethereal element of their being, the tremulous reciprocations of which propagate themselves even to the inmost of the soul.

"Where the spirit of a man is not filled with consciousness of freedom, all spiritual intercourse is interrupted not only with others but even with himself."

In full foliage, Coleridge was an Aeolian harp of a man, alert to the winds of heaven. His *"Ancient Mariner,"* for instance, still rocks with rhythm, rhyme and revelation.

His marriage was a disaster, however, resulting in early separation. Then, fortunately, in 1799, he fell happily in love with golden-haired Sara Hutchinson (William Wordsworth's wife's sister). According to the Coleridge authority Richard Holmes, Sarah—

"Never quite went to bed with him. Instead she did secretarial work, accompanied him on walks, nursed him when ill, and tried to prevent his taking opium, which led to their eventual estrangement in 1812."

"Never quite went to bed with him" during thirteen long years together? Oh, yeah? Commonsense persuades me that the pair must have relished secret sex.

The same goes for William Wordsworth and his sister Dorothy, who lived together always, and had toured Europe, early on, as husband & wife.

But I mean no offence to Mr. Holmes, whom I much admire for his dedicated, fascinating effort...

The aging author of *"Biographia Literaria"* languished lonely, poor, addicted to opium, bloated, and snubbed. "A ruin," as T.S. Eliot observed.

He still dared to meander, however, as his onetime worshipper William Hazlitt acidly commented—

"Into the world unknown of thought and imagination. As if Columbus had launched his adventurous course for the New World in a scallop without oars or compass."

Some say there's nothing much left to explore these days, unless it be deep space. But let's take a hint from S.T. Coleridge, that immortal "ruin" of a brave poet, who preached personal exploration above all.

Every great voyage of discovery involves losing one's way to enter upon a better one. Take the case of Columbus himself, who thought he'd reached India. Columbus had a compass; Coleridge possessed imaginative awareness...

Movies, Booze, Jazz, and romantic Sex meant most to me as a teen-ager. Romantic Sex would have come first, naturally, if it were not so difficult to obtain. Booze began early in my case, when I kept a bottle of Hennessy cognac stashed in my laundry bag for secret sipping at Loomis. Liquor has always been to me as the chimp

Cheetah was to Tarzan. I mean mischievous, laughable, yet there to rescue one from the Pilgrim Slough of Despond.

From 1930 to 1950, movies were the world's most influential medium, offering million-dollar slices of fantasy for nickels & dimes, an irresistible deal. Consider Busby Berkley's—

"GOLD DIGGERS OF 1933"

When Berkley's well-drilled girls
exhibited their winsome curls
coy smiles and enticing thighs
to our bedazzled, bulging eyes
it extended the slide trombone
of each incipient gentleman

Born way out West in Omaha, Nebraska, the bawling, squally boy named "Frederick Austerlitz" was destined to grow up scrawny and become an ecstatically tapping, twirling, grinning and gliding icon of male elegance.

As Fred Astaire, he was the star property of whom Samuel Goldwyn remarked—

"We pay him too much, but he's worth it."

This internally angry, industrious, smoothly courteous and ever determined performer danced his songs and made his effervescent dances to somehow sing along.

Ginger Rogers accompanied him in "Flying Down to Rio," "The Gay Divorcee," "Roberta," "Top Hat," "Follow the Fleet," "Swing Time," "Shall We Dance?" and "The Barclays of Broadway." All still worth seeing once again, and sharing with your children.

FRED TO GINGER

Twirling, swirling, sweating, cursing
leggy, loose, and long-rehearsing.
Getting better understanding.
learning to be lightly landing.
Quickly picking postures purer
what a PARTNER Ginger, you were!

Peeking into my elder sister Torka's Silver Screen magazine, I learned that Hollywood's premier musical comedy couple were not lovers after all.

What a weird mystery for my adolescent self to brood upon. Let's say Fred got off on the wrong foot. In that case, how would Ginger Rogers have responded?

GINGER TO FRED

During dance-melt, you told me later
we should let these tootsies cater
minus socks and patent leather
stark naked to one another.
Has a beau aimed lower ever?
That just froze this feather boa.
All of my ten toes went: "WHOAH!"

When the sensationally ingenious American playwright and novelist Thornton Wilder was residing abroad, he sent this breathlessly hyphenated comment to his friend Mabel Dodge Luhan—

"In Europe, go to see a Ginger-Rogers-Fred-Astaire movie. Watch the audience. Spell-bound at something terribly uneuropean. All that technical effortless precision; all that radiant youth bursting with sex but not sex-hunting, sex-collecting. All that allusion to money, but money as fun, the American love of conspicuous waste, not money-to-sit-on, money-to-frighten-with.

"And finally when the pair really leap into one of those radiant waltzes the Europeans know in their bones that their day is over."

I couldn't ride, shoot, fence, box, dance, sing, charm, seduce, or detect, half so convincingly as did a score of Hollywood's male stars on-screen. Nonetheless, I tried to act as if I knew how, in my cool, assured yet somewhat suspicious Humphrey Bogart style.

STAR LORE

When Bogey fingered Mary Astor
as the "Maltese Falcon" blaster
Every moviegoer shed a tear.

"Casablanca," where he lingered
more in sorrow than in Ingrid
was the apogee of his career.

So, although you long to hold her,
fluff the lady off your shoulder.
Leading men are hotter, colder.

I used to croon a lot, both to myself and to the few girls who would listen. Chief among my male idols was Bing Crosby. (Sinatra came along later.)

HOLLYWOOD WARBLER

Bing gargled with Rheingold,
his baritone tingled.
His ears were outstanding.
his pitch was so pure.

Known as "The Groaner"
though never a loner
he winged it with Hope
and went home with Lamour.

When jazz was hot, Bing was cool, miles ahead of his time.
"Learn to croon," he advised: "You'll eliminate each rival sooooon!"

FIGURES ON A SCREEN

Extra virgin, cold–pressed
duly powdered, fancy-dressed
Olivia de Havilland performed
an innocent princess at nineteen
in the pirate epic "Captain Blood"
with bravely dashing Errol Flynn.
The glamorous couple had it made
with seven more big-time hits ahead.

Retired to Paris decades afterward
Olivia wrote Errol that he'd been
the best of all her leading men
but forgot to post her letter
so the jump-around actor
who was indeed superb
in every sense of the word
died minus Olivia's accolade.

Once at a Springfield, Massachusetts supper club I caught Fats Waller. Spinning the piano-stool, he settled his bulk on it, looked around, and cried—

"*Is you all on?*"

My date was a very attractive girl whom I scarcely knew. She'd helped my under-age self get admitted. When Fats invited requests, she sang out:—

"*Blackberry Jam!*"

Raising both hands, palms spread at shoulder-level, Fats arched his Byzantine brows to create a comically intense expression of surprise.

"The gal in brown is not so dumb," he exulted. "One never knows, do one?"

HOT WALLER

>Fats' left-handed boogie-woogie beat
>rumbled low-down, bumpy-sweet
>while the ragged dragon-flight
>of his lightly flickering right
>sparkled with savage desire
>like an Apache signal fire.

Between sets, on his way out back for a smoke, Fats brushed close by us.

My date leaned sideways to detain him, palm to paunch. She asked for his autograph, and Fats responded with a brief, hugely stooping smooch.

"Dat's MAH autograph!" he chuckled. Smiling broadly to himself, he waddled off.

She blushed, glowingly.

I froze, meanwhile, and then came unfrozen with a start, realizing that Fats had manifested spontaneous majesty.

Back then, "Negroes" and "Whites" were supposed never to mingle, yet Waller had abruptly desegregated "the gal in brown."

Plus, by extension, my half-baked self.

I guess now that my date was probably "passing," concealing her partly Afro-American slave heritage, as millions did in those dangerously racist days. If that's true, then Fats would naturally have intuited her story.

At one o'clock in the morning, when Boston's Southland Club had emptied except for a sprinkling of us wild enthusiasts, Count Basie called for anyone who felt like it to try singing with the band.

I had the gall to stand up. Having hearkened to Jimmy Rushing ("Mr. Five by Five"), I dared not sing. But might I offer a sonnet from Shakespeare?

"Why, sure!" said the Count.

Jo Jones brushed the skins in comradely fashion, and Lester ("Prez") Young slipped in sidelong saxophone hues and cries, whilst I moaned, intoned and even hollered into the mike. I was terrible, but it was beautiful.

Duke Ellington's compositions naturally meant a great deal to me. "There are two kinds of music," he once declares: "Music that sounds good, and whatever you care to call that other stuff."

For him, music was all that mattered, and full-out collaboration created the best of it. No man ever had a better band, or treated its members with more consideration, year after year, than did the Duke.

Once in middle-age, I found myself sitting next to him. It happened at a New York Opera performance of *Der Meistersinger*. Following the finale we rose, smiled at each other, shook hands, and departed on our separate ways without a single word spoken.

He'd returned an impulsive stranger's handshake in good faith, as if I were an equal. This hand has clasped Mr. Ellington's hand.

4. Down in Black Mountain

During the 1930's, thousands of rightly frightened, mostly Jewish, Europeans found refuge in America and started to provide the tidal boost that would soon elevate our culture to unaccustomed heights.

Among them came Josef Albers, a lapsed Catholic and former teacher at Walter Gropius' Bauhaus school of architecture and design. Hitler's Nazi regime had closed it down and dubbed Albers a dangerously "degenerate" artist.

Escaping with his wife Anni (who belonged to a distinguished Jewish family of publishers) Albers landed up at Black Mountain College, amid the Smoky Mountains of North Carolina.

Starting in 1936, at age seventeen, I had the good fortune to study with him for two years there.

Black Mountain was an historic experiment in higher education, as bold as Charles W. Eliot's reforms at Harvard half a century before. Our college consisted of about a hundred students and fifteen professors, all equally blessed with freedom for learning and/or teaching whatever and however we desired.

"Trahit sua quemque voluptas" (Each towed by his own fancy), as Virgil put the case.

John Andrew Rice dominated our supposedly democratic politics. A roly-poly, pipe-puffing, charismatic Carolinian, wickedly adept at persuasion, and a loosely defined law unto himself, he had founded the college just a few years before, and assumed the position of "Rector."

Rice was hot; Albers cold. Rice was educated; Albers cultivated. Rice was forceful; Albers formal. Both men were romantic idealists.

But Rice's ideal was uninhibited Mutual Inquiry, whereas Albers' ideal was disciplined Artistic Experiment.

The mountain setting was lovely, and the life-style austere. We performed our own chores and helped on the college farm, forest, and road. No grades or credits were given. I myself eagerly pursued Art, Theatre Workshop, French Literature, and Philosophy.

We had only two rules at BMC, and those were conveniently contradictory. First: No indoor sex for singles. Second: No violating "Don't Disturb" signs. Quite an improvement upon Loomis!

Albers greeted us new students with—

"I sink not von off you can drrraw a strrraight line!"

That didn't sound hard, until he turned to demonstrate what he meant at the blackboard. Stepping sideways, he chalked a line precisely parallel to the floor, twelve feet across!

Within a week we could do it, too. "Control ist freedom!" he told us. Meaning self-control, of course.

Next came a circle, an ellipse, letters, numbers, a cup and saucer, a rhododendron, fellow-students' faces, and finally their figures (clothed).

Facility failed to satisfy Albers. He drove us to draw with either hand, followed by our feet, with drippy Japanese ink brushes gripped betwixt our toes.

A pumpernickel-nibbling stickler for self-discipline, Albers wasn't just teaching art. Although art is expression, to a degree it connects with science, being primarily a matter of experiment. So when creative endeavor begins with exercises for developing self control, it may grow to become an investigative process in its own right.

Speaking of investigation, a seriously disturbed student named Richard Porter went around asking whether any of us possessed a handgun. He required one, Dick explained, for the purpose of suicide.

A refugee German/Jewish psychoanalyst named Sol Moellenhoff served on our faculty. The man's aristocratic, smiling face was crisscrossed with saber-scars acquired by fencing minus the customary wire mask.

Had he been cruelly hazed by Nazi fellow-cadets, or did he possess a reckless dueling streak?

Sol advised us that if anybody had a gun, by all means lend it to Dick! Why? Because the boy was not so stupid as to shoot himself. Brought face to face with his own silly behavior, he might even begin to get well again!

One student did have a gun, and lent it in good faith, whereupon Dick committed suicide.

Dr. Moellenhoff called a conference of the entire college, and told us—with tears in his eyes—that if anyone felt guilty about what had occurred, he ought not to. Because, after all, "Guilt feelings are sick."

I came away convinced that we're fools to suppose we can read other people's minds, and idiots to imagine that we can help our friends and relations out of every difficulty.

Nonetheless, at age twenty-one I myself would dare to marry an especially lovely victim of what has since come to be known as the "bi-polar syndrome."

What dreadful things we do go through. Bi-polar and post-traumatic stress must have plagued humanity for some two hundred thousand years, unrecognized by science until after World War Two...

I believe Josef Albers' own art was primarily inspired by the poet Goethe's presciently psychological *Theory of Color*. That was originally written to contest Sir Isaac Newton's universally accepted opus: *Optics* (1704).

Using a prism to intercept a single streak of sunshine which issued from betwixt his curtains, Newton projected a rainbow-colored blob upon the shadowed wall. Thus he demonstrated that white light contains all colors, and darkness none.

Newton's experiment seems so very simple, even primitive. Yet nobody had ever thought of it before. He thrust darkness into outer darkness, as it were.

He set the stage for the "Age of Enlightenment," with its periwigs, powder, lace ruffles, huffy arguments, coffee, rough logic-binges, and little pinches of snuff followed by handkerchief-waving, dismissive sneezes.

Optical science keeps on advancing, however, and it has since been ascertained that in fact darkness embraces a very broad ultra-violet color spectrum all its own.

The ideological elevation of light over darkness exerts a skewing effect on human thought in general. We forget that light and darkness go together. Their interaction naturally generates colors, and mirrors our emotions.

In childhood, I had a dream about colors. It began with the nearly colorless hour of dusk. My elder sister Torka, our dog Pippo, Mom, Pop, Grandpa and Grandma Cook, had all piled together into our brand new Star touring car, whose radiator-cap was a glassed-in thermometer.

Waving and laughing they drove away, leaving me alone in charge! At age seven, could I handle it? As I mounted the porch steps, my clothes vanished. I stood surprised, naked in the cool breeze.

A clean sheet hung across the porch railing, ready for me. Wearing it in toga-style, I rang my own doorbell.

Opened by angels, the door swung inward. I stepped out upon a rock plateau which overlooked forests, hills, rivers, meadows, valleys, farms, roads, towns, and even the surrounding ocean. None of their prismatic hues looked at all familiar from my exalted perspective.

That was when my father wakened me. Not his fault, but from my viewpoint a terrible blow. It was a school day, Pop announced, so I should get dressed right away.

I told him I'd been involved in a beautiful dream, with colors which I'd never before seen.

"Describe them!" he said.

I shut my eyes, prepared to try, but no colors came. Then it seemed that somehow I embraced a blond school friend named Mimi Moog, and we practiced experimental kissing while horizontal in mid-air. We landed on the grass with a bump, and I came fully awake at last...

Colors vibrate, interpenetrate, expand, contract, reflect, bleed through and transform one another. Everything depends upon the relative intensities of light and darkness which imbue each hue. The mathematical possibilities involved are endless, which makes color an open-ended proposition.

A cubic yard of air contains about fifty trillion, trillion atoms. It's a thin sea, so to speak. Contemplating a clear daytime sky, I gaze through moist, glistening atmosphere into black space beyond. Hence I perceive cerulean.

When the setting sun gets richly red as it approaches the horizon, that's because of obscuring droplets, dust, and other dark matter in Earth's lower atmosphere.

Closing my eyes for sleep, I remember to observe the multi-colored sparkle that occurs.

There's obscuring darkness inside each of us, plus light-waves and shifting color patterns as well. If not, could we dream in color?

The "primary colors" employed by Renaissance painters' included Green, by the way, right alongside Newton's scientifically determined Red, Yellow and Blue.

The "secondary" colors Purple and Orange were more sparingly employed.

Black and White remained least called upon, except in signage and literature, where their juxtaposition works wonders of clarity,— as you can see right here.

By selection and juxtaposition alone, Albers created interactive choirs of communal colors, usually three, and four at most, never mixed but squeezed from their paint tubes and nested squarely together.

Such works should be seen one at a time. When you contemplate a single late Albers for an hour or more, its glimmering will finally billow the curtains at the windows of your psyche, opening unexpected vistas...

My favorite professor once confided to me that his own start had been difficult. As a Bauhaus student, back in the 1920's, Albers had rebelled against his strictly doctrinaire, cultish instructors, and been expelled by Walter Gropius.

"I was so MAD," he said. "I went down to the dump and KILLED all the bottles I could find!"

Returning home with a sack full of broken-bottle glass, he arranged the fragments on masonite panels covered with bright white gesso, creating deep-textured gray, brown, blue, and green abstractions.

A Berlin gallery exhibited them. Walter Gropius saw and loved the show.

"We misjudged each other," he told Albers. "Please come back to the Bauhaus."

"No, thank you," Albers told him.

"Not as a student. Instead I badly need you to redesign and conduct our Foundation Course! I've lost its director. He was too old, anyhow."

The foundation course that Albers gave at BMC included what he called "Effect-making." The idea was to produce objects calculated to "astonish" our peers. We sat in a circle on the floor to appraise each other's efforts, while Albers observed us from a chair.

My first effort was a battered, broken old farmer's boot, which I'd found somewhere and polished up to the point where it became mirror smooth—reflecting forgetfulness of how hard earthy workers toil.

That elicited no interest whatsoever.

Subsequently, I offered up a porcelain beer stein brimming over with rainbow-colored cotton batting.

Our circle sat silent, obviously unimpressed once again.

Then a pal of mine named Everett Herter arose to flip away the cotton and expose the snippets of colored paper I'd inserted underneath.

Furious, I kicked Ev's interfering rear, so that he fell face-down into my offering, and Albers exclaimed—

"*JAWOHL!*"

"By Saint Andrew's dandruff!" as Miranda ("Sandy") Busch of Baltimore exclaimed, I'd "Made an Effect" after all.

Sandy was a knockout, but not for me. Lithe, blond Martha Chalice, of Winnetka, Illinois, on the other hand, was the kindest person I've ever known.

Recently graduated with high honors from Smith College, Martha served as personal secretary to John Andrew Rice. Here's a verse I composed back then regarding our connection—

COLLEGIATES

"Not content to squeeze a breast
I wonder if you'd get undressed
and hopefully expose the rest
at my reverential request?"

"Unhand my bosom, witless twit
now that you've grasped half of it
and abandon 'hopefully', dear
when you propose to enter here."

"Sorry about the gaffe
I'm very sure.
My diction was
indeed impure."

"And yet the southern comfort bit
upon which I'm obliged to sit
is becoming quite pulsatile!
So you've got a done deal."

"Holy mackerel, this is swell!
I thought I'd come up short.
May I present Sir Cockerel
of Good King Arthur's Court?"

    Toward the middle of my first academic year at Black Mountain, Mr. Rice called me into his office—
    "Eliot, I've had my eye on you, and reached a negative conclusion."
    "What, sir?"

"Despite your excellent background, you are nothing but a wing-smoking, corn-likker-drinking, jitter-bugging, brainlessly grinning, girl-crazy mutt!"

"Thank you, sir. It's true that I'm crazy about your secretary. In fact Martha and I often laugh—"

"That's enough. I'm not renewing your scholarship for next year. Black Mountain will do better without you."

"Huh?"

"GOODBYE!"

Well, I was doubtless an aggravating fellow. Trudging upstairs to Albers' studio, I told him what Rice had said.

He listened impassively. Then, wearing his usual straight face, Albers assured me that my brief interview with Rice—

"Never happened!"

That meant two things. First, my scholarship was secure. Second, Albers was becoming a power in the school. Not that he had political skills, but because of his Promethean integrity.

Although reassured by Mr. Albers, I developed a bit of panic about Mr. Rice, who could be brutally vengeful. Might he try to extort tuition money from my parents? They couldn't possibly afford that. So I sent them a Western Union telegram—

PAY NOTHING STOP

After brooding over my economically brief, but stupidly mystifying wire for an hour or more, Mother decided (as she told me years later) that I must have: "impregnated some poor, innocent girl down there."

The next thing I knew, she turned up at Black Mountain for a week-end visit, having driven all the way south from Massachusetts.

She was hospitably greeted by Albers, and Rice made no complaints to her. I soon explained the cause of my unfounded fear and dumb wire. Mother's visit passed off well.

A memorable moment occurred over Sunday afternoon tea on the college verandah. Enjoying our spectacular view of the Blue Ridge Mountains, Mom spontaneously turned to Albers and asked—

"Aren't you tempted to paint all that beauty?"

Far from bristling at what a lesser artist would have taken for bourgeois naiveté, Albers smiled and replied: "Madame, I would never dare to try!"

During my second year at Black Mountain, Albers gained a feisty ally. Bauhaus-trained Xanti Schawinsky arrived in flight from Fascist Italy, with his beautiful blond bride Eurena clinging to his arm, and his *bocce* balls hung in a net-bag.

Xanti had brought along a prize-winning Italian poster painted by himself, showing two eggheads in a restaurant. The eggs were faceless and identical, except for their positioning.

The waiter's egghead nodded, pointy side down, which gave him a highbrow appearance, whereas the customer's leaned backward, pointy side up, which made him look to be a jowly glutton. The work plainly suggested that a note-taking posture beats a greedy one. Also, that serving beats commanding.

Might Xanti's poster have caught the evil eye of Italy's jowly dictator? Whether or not that's true, Mussolini issued an edict severely banning employment of foreign Jews. Thus, *Il Duce* happened to propel Xanti our way.

Until his arrival, our idea of "community" had been to convene at Roy's Roadhouse, four miles from college, and dance "The Big Apple."

The Pulsating Pole, as I dubbed him, beamed with communal enthusiasm. Under his direction, we built a *bocce* court and played *bocce*. We also mounted theatrical shows, with six-foot ears, eyes, lips, and noses cavorting to Stravinsky recordings.

Xanti proclaimed that none of us were geniuses. We accepted that, while privately regarding our individual selves as exceptions. We boys, I mean. For girls in those relatively barbarous times, the question did not arise.

"You Americans are too serious," Xanti once told me, "It's because you haven't suffered!"

He had a point, but the Great Depression was in full swing, and lots of suffering occurred right down the road in Black Mountain township, where hundreds of "poor white trash" sharecroppers competed with yet more oppressed blacks. As Bessie Smith, put the case in her distinctively belting song style—

*Down in Black Mountain
a chile will slap yo face.
Babies cry fo liquor
an all the boids sing bass!*

One dull Saturday, Xanti instigated a dress-up party, urging everyone to come to dinner in costume. Mr. Albers was too austere to dream of taking part. But John Andrew Rice grabbed the opportunity to make what he thought would be appreciated as a Marx Brothers sort of gesture.

Our Rector blackened his toothbrush mustache, combed his hair slantwise across his brow, donned a brown shirt, and pinned on a Swastika arm-band. Strutting dramatically late into the dining-hall, he greeted us with Hitler's casual, catcher's-mitt *"Heil* Me!" salute.

Being at Alber's table, I watched him react as Rice entered. Far from smiling, he sat beset by a sudden hell of appearances, not so much disgusted as shocked to the heart.

For Rice, it was *Heil* and Farewell. The following autumn, after I myself had departed from BMC, our unreflective Rector found himself caught in Clintonesque dalliance with a juicy student.

His pet dachshund had betrayed him, by dolefully hanging out, night after night, beneath a "Don't Disturb!" sign on her corridor door.

Some things don't change. Men will invariably seek disaster in milady's chamber, and women will always be excoriated for permitting what happens naturally.

Mr. Rice endured dismissal, and banishment forever, from the revolutionary institution that he himself had dreamed up, brought to turbulent birth, and steered through the first of its few precarious years on earth!

Nowadays, kids can go to college, in the sense of getting knowledge, practically free. So marble-halled pomp and mortarboard circumstance hardly matter anymore.

Now's the time for fresh, free-spirited, inter-education of the kind John Andrew Rice so bravely pioneered.

5. Indian Summer

Following my second and final year at Black Mountain, I drove out to the Southwest with my mother and little sister Patience Anne. The Archbishop of Santa Fe, who adored Mother's books, had invited her and Patience for a summer month's stay in a guest house on his palace grounds.

That left me free to explore the Navajo Reservation in the family Ford V-8. I had the extreme good fortune to make a month-long, meandering tour throughout a beautiful expanse of mountains and deserts, the size of New York State.

Happily crooning to myself, I drove along the jarringly corrugated dirt roads, of what was still fairly "Wild West" territory.

The Reservation's widely scattered "trading posts" were concession stores where white merchants traded coffee, sugar, flour, and levies (now called blue jeans), for Indian blankets, pottery, and jewelry. Having stopped for the night at one such place, I found myself in a poker session.

The game proved to be over my head and too rich for my blood. So I wandered out to the kitchen and talked with the trader's wife.

She was a darkly beautiful, bitterly unhappy person who would now be identified in mixed company as a Native American of the Ute nation.

One thing led to another; we slipped out and drove off together. Soon we stopped beside a small table-rock, or mesa, and scrambled up a rift in its side to the flat top under the stars.

There we fully enjoyed each other's company. That is, until a pick-up truck came barreling along the road, with its headlights bouncing up and down at every bump. The truck slowed as it approached, and pulled over to park beside my car.

"It's him!" the woman moaned. "My devil-damned husband."

Peering over the side, I watched three men get out and approach the rock. I fully expected to feel a rush of fear, but that didn't happen. Quickly, with more elation than panic, I rolled a boulder to the top of the rift by which we'd climbed up. If the trio dared come after us, I'd send that boulder crashing down upon their intrusive craniums.

"Please, no!" the woman begged. I ignored her.

Crouching to stay invisible, and actually smiling to myself, I watched the men spread out at the foot of the rift. They were talking casually amongst themselves. Was it in English, or Navajo? I couldn't quite make out the words.

GOOD QUESTION

Can I trust myself to be
virtuous in any way
under pressure?
You don't say!

All three men unbuttoned their Levi's, jutted their hips and pissed against the rock-face. Then they turned around, ambled back to their car, and drove on down the road out of sight.

Coincidence could not be excluded, but I assumed that the men had recognized my car. Also, that they guessed where I must be. In Wild West parlance that meant one thing: I "had the drop on them."

Our visitors presumably contented themselves by leaving their "territorial signatures" on the rock-face, in wolf-pack style

Immediately after their retreat, I started trembling like a yellow aspen leaf. "Let's get back to the trading post," I said.

Twenty minutes later, we were there. The woman nipped around to the back, while I walked boldly in at the front door and—with apparent calm—rejoined the game. No one appeared to have noticed my absence.

This incident was a stark initiation for me. It showed that I'm a human rattlesnake, a deadly creature when crossed...

An afternoon sunbeam has just slanted into my studio. It lights up a silent swarm of dust motes. Sitting still at my desk, I witness hundreds of golden flecks, each one floating fitfully amid its neighbors' spins and counter-spins.

This brings to mind the hovering, light-filled symbol in Rembrandt's miraculous dry-point called "Faust in his Study, Watching a Magic Disk."

The Scottish botanist Robert Brown was one who gazed with sudden understanding upon just such an image as the one confronting me. Brown was the first person to notice, back in 1827, the universality of the phenomenon which circulates within the present javelin shaft of sunshine.

Tiny particles suspended in moist air or in a fluid always jiggle around each other, causing visible ripples. "Brownian Movement" has been observed in water droplets sealed for geological eons inside quartz crystals!

Between people, of course, collisions are commonplace. I must have delivered a thousand and one clumsy, hurtful bumps over the years.

Never through malice, I defensively insist, but mostly on account of my obvious inadequacies!

ABhyuttagdbd9 Wait a minute. I can't let this account degenerate into a tearful tome, such as *"The Sorrows of I. Wannamaker,"* or *"Why Me?"* by Hugo Figure.

Taking my clue from the fellow so impressively profiled on our nation's nickel, I supposed that American Indians must be a melancholy, heavy-burdened bunch. Of course I was wrong. Beneath their brightly beaming, tightly smiling semblances of good cheer, my own Yankee kinfolk were far gloomier.

The Indians I met often looked severe, yet seldom acted that way. Not light-hearted, they seemed surprisingly harmonious all the same.

Following the time when I turned recklessly lustful and then murderous, I began to be kindly treated on the Reservation!

Did the highly intuitive Natives sense that I might be a fairly acceptable Paleface after all? I guess so.

The legendary Spanish/American "Indian Trader" Lorenzo Hubbell graciously took me in for a while, and he brought me together with an old priest of the dead-secret Hopi religion.

I had the honor of chauffeuring the priest between his tribe's mesa-top villages, and while I drove he taught me a religious dance-chant that I can still sing.

Thanks to him, I witnessed a long, long Green Katchina Rain Dance, plus the downpour that followed.

I also helped celebrate a Hopi wedding, and painted a watercolor of the bride in her ceremonial buck-skin costume.

The girl's people were so poor that all they could muster for her wedding reception was oilskins unrolled on the dirt floor by way of furniture, plus artificially colored water and tortillas.

Later on, for three eye-opening days and nights, I camped alongside an old Navajo medicine-man's home in pine-forest, high country.

My lean, wrinkled, rather remote host spoke no English, nor did his heavy-set, calmly hospitable wife. Fortunately for me, however, their three sons did so, having suffered through years of compulsory "Bureau of Indian Affairs" boarding school.

Since I was an obvious ignoramus, unarmed and quite alone, the family regarded me as a responsibility. Their "savage" culture required no less.

They accepted my company and invited me to their dinners, where all I could contribute was soda-crackers, canned sardines, and cigarettes.

We got along fine, in a joking way. They called me *Dagga Ch'ung,* which means "Dirty Beard."

Teasing nicknames were a Navajo custom. One of the boys had a nickname picked up at school: *"Don't give a shit!"*

I never saw a more peaceful, warmly comforting structure than the family's single-room, bee-hive-shaped "hogan".

Built of cantilevered logs chinked with mud and turf, their dwelling centered upon a round fireplace beneath a round smoke-hole in the dome.

Folded Navaho blankets formed a circular divan around the walls. Stars glittered in the smoke-hole at night. The rough-textured cedar dome interior glowed womb-like by firelight.

As each day began, the family emerged to perform their customary morning worship, which welcomed four deities in turn.

APPEARANCES

Blue
dawn
boy

White
dawn
boy

Yellow
Dawn
Boy

Fiery
father
Sun

The boys told me what it was all about, and I delighted in taking silent part. That was the first religious experience in which I felt myself to be an actual participant. Catholic Mass, which meant so much to my mother, had never even begun to interest me...

Later on, I detoured off the Reservation to take in the Grand Canyon, and splurged for a night at the fancy El Tovar Hotel.

I found a roadhouse in the village, happily swinging with drinkers, dancers, and jukebox jazz. There I fell in with some vacationing stenographers on the loose.

While I was dancing with one of them she asked if by any chance I had a personal dream.

"What sort?"

"Some one thing, not necessarily important, that you're just yearning to do."

"Yes." I said. "My dream is to paint a picture that's almost as beautiful as Paul Gauguin's creations."

"Paul WHO?"

"Gauguin."

"Never heard of him."

"A Frenchman."

"Oh."

"He was an artist who wound up in Tahiti, did his very greatest paintings there, contracted syphilis, and kicked the bucket about forty years ago."

"You mean he's dead."

"Yes."

"Shall I tell you my dream?"

"Please do."

"Well, it's to get myself laid at the Canyon's very edge, doncha know. I mean, it would be fun overlooking the whole darn thing."

"This can be arranged!"

"Hold on. It's just a doggone dream of mine."

"Happy to oblige."

"Not so fast, Mister. Why the deuce would I pick on you?"

"Dunno."

"Me neither. Jiminy cricket! It's all my fault, I talk too much."

"I admire freedom of speech."

"Yeah? You talk pretty free yourself!"

"I do apologize."

"Not your fault. How the dickens did we ever get into this?"

"Because we've got lots in common. Would it be okay for me to stick another quarter in the jukebox?"

We had nothing in common except reckless American youth. Never having met before, and never to meet again, we got together out of space/time into a narrow time-slot under the wheeling stars.

HIGH-JINKS

Perched upon a ledge
in our most precipitous Park
I heard a distant rooster crow
and a lonely watchdog bark.
Then, to be honest, I took
the Congressional Medal
of Honor, Junior Class
for midnight, uptight
conjunction with
an extremely
spunky
lass.

This event gave me a fear of heights, which would persist for the next dozen years or so—a small price to pay. I've never before mentioned the incident to anyone except my present partner, who capped it with a brief personal account of her own.

That has already been anthologized twice over, but even so I feel drawn to repeat most of her story here:

"I was seven when my great-grandmother reached ninety. She was a beautiful woman with large, violet eyes, exquisitely groomed white hair and magnificent hands, veined and transparent, which she enhanced with antique rings.

"She gave me one, an oblong amethyst set in heavy silver, which I love more and more as I get older.

"She wore brocade dresses with lace petticoats. The shoes on her little feet always matched her velvet hair ribbons. She liked talking to me and I loved listening.

"She told me once about a love affair she had 'on the edge of the Grand Canyon. She'd been younger then,' she explained, 'seventy-four.'

"'On the very edge,' she repeated in her crystal-clear yet most soft voice. 'It was very romantic. I looked straight down the canyon walls—a thousand miles below. We were passionate and unafraid, being young.'

"I believed the story and so I also believed that life is extravagantly beautiful, slightly risky, and continuously love-filled. Also precarious and a bit sandy. Not for the faint-hearted. In a word, mythic."

Jane then relates that on our first trans-continental drive she and I stopped for a night at the El Tovar.

There was just one accommodation available, we were told, a pricey suite in the old building, which we gratefully grabbed. Her narrative continues—

"The first thing was a hot bath. It took some time to fill, but soon the heat was loosening the tensions of the day. After a while I remembered the sunset. The window was right there by the tub. I hardly had to move to pull back the curtain and look out.

"Sky, orange and gold, shot through with giant splashes of green and purple. A star. A half moon, green in the golden air. I looked over to the far side of the grandest canyon of them all.

"The edge was still visible. My eyes climbed slowly down to a silvery ribbon running in the already black of the canyon bottom. I got up on my knees to see better, and gasped.

"Grabbing a thick towel I tumbled out of the bath and ran into our bedroom. The bed was set right against an enormous window. I jumped on it and threw open the curtains. Sure enough, the bed, too, was right over the canyon. I understood immediately that this had been Great Grandmother's room all those years ago. Speechless, I beckoned Alex."

So much for Jane's account. I must remember not to quote my beloved again, until her life-changing first appearance to me, back in the year 1950...

While I went haring around Indian country, Mom completed her best-known "Catholic novel" in Santa Fe, beneath a shady tree in the Archbishop's garden.

Her story goes that in December, 1531, ten years and four months after the Spanish Conquest, a middle-aged Aztec Indian farmer named Cuatitlatoatzin heard voices like those of songbirds calling from Tepeyac hill.

An Aztec maiden, standing as in a shell of pulsating color and light, awaited him on the hilltop. "Where were you going?" she asked.

"Noble and dear lady, I was on my way to Tlatelolco, to attend the Mass that ministers of God show us there."

"Littlest and dearest, it's in my honor that the Sons of Saint Francis offer Mass."

Juan waited respectfully.

"For I am Mary, mother of God."

"I know!"

"After Mass, make your way to the Bishop. Tell him I want a church built right here, as a refuge for everyone to enter at their own free will."

The bishop naturally took Juan Diego's message with a grain of salt. "Go back," he ordered, "and inform your visionary Lady that we require a sign to prove her identity."

Trembling, Juan did so, and the Virgin at once agreed to the Bishop's request. She caused roses to spring up and bloom from the crest of Tepeyac. Juan cut them, bundled them up in his long rough cotton cape or "tilma," and carried his evidence back again to the Bishop's palace.

But the flowers failed to convince anyone there. That is, until the Bishop noticed the tilma in which Juan had carried them.

It was lined with the Virgin's own image!

I'll conclude by quoting Mom's own final passage—

Her mantle is the inimitable green-blue of the sky at dawn—a color seen nowhere else in nature or art.

"As, in that dawn sky, stars appear to be melting visibly away in the day's new light, so, through the folds of the Virgin's mantle, faint stars are dissolving."

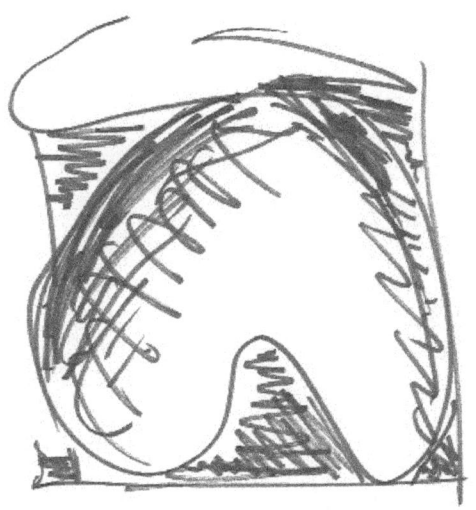

Book Two: Women Then

Man's Better Half

    The Girl Was Courage

    Spirit of the Elements

    Anthony & Vanessa

    Fear of the Dark

    Good Looker

    Pavan for a Princess

1. The Girl Was Courage

When you look at the drawing which heads this section, in seems clear enough at first. Then the shapes appear to waver just a bit, becoming partly unreadable. That's on purpose, because—like most men—I find women fairly difficult to decipher.

Is the reverse as true? Do women often despair of reading men?

Among my father's brightest students at Smith College, and Mom's best friends, was an attractive, intensely serious and pious girl named Elizabeth Hart.

When I lay deathly ill with scarlet fever she came to our quarantined house and prayed for me, hours-long, standing in a snowstorm beneath my sick-room window.

This occurred long before the American invention of antibiotics during World War Two. Mother attributed my "miraculous" recovery to Elizabeth.

After receiving a master's degree in literature, Elizabeth chose to become a cloistered Carmelite nun, much to her wealthy parents' distress.

In later years, we corresponded some. She took an interest in my books, and produced a few devotional ones herself. When she was appointed her nunnery's Mother Superior, I took the opportunity to go and converse with her through a grille.

The mature Elizabeth Hart struck me as keen, virtuous, humorous, and happy to be all three, but perhaps a trifle matronizing…

Here's something I've never before confessed, let alone put in print. Not for fear of censure but because it was so indefensibly stupid.

Once upon a time, not knowing any better, I dared to proposition my gorgeous elder sister. Torka responded with—

"Ye gods and little fishes!"

Although she would eventually bear two children to a devoted newspaper-publishing husband, Torka was shy, pious, and temperamentally chaste, like our mother.

She stood well within the "Thanks, but no thanks" ranks, whereas I myself leaned eagerly the other way.

What dictates such extreme differences?

My sister very gently talked me down. "Anyhow," she concluded, "sex isn't HALF what it's cracked up to be."

"It ISN"T?"

"No, disappointing, in fact."

TRIAL BY JURY

Sex is disappointing.
Right, or wrong?
Ten seconds to respond
before the gong.

Silence ensues.
The Grand Jury's hung.
Perhaps Miss Pussycat
has got its tongue?

A disinclined minority
objected all along.
By now, they're probably
a billion strong.

The Parisian lady who took the *nom-de-plume* George Sand (1804–1876) wrote twenty-four plays, seventy novels, and an estimated 40,000 letters.

To signal and celebrate her personal independence, Sand wore fashionable men's attire, anticipating the film star Marlene Dietrich by about a century.

Her labors entertained while serving a social purpose as well, educating—

"Poor, dear stupidity, which I do not hate, and which I look upon with maternal eyes."

Sand mussed the hair of Alfred de Musset, for one, driving that poet half mad with her *"si belle, et si pliable"* charms. Musset executed a poignant sketch of her bundled up against the winter's cold, puffing a long-stemmed opium pipe.

One might expect romantic bliss and misery to cancel each other out, creating a calm refuge. Not so, as most couples become aware.

ADJUSTMENT

Lovers' tiffs are mainly due
to minimal dichotomies.
Luckily, we can unscrew
and mitigate a lot of these.

Frederick Chopin, whose noble features Eugene Delacroix so dramatically portrayed, was Sand's last, longest and greatest love. Seeking the lonely Polish composer/pianist out at home, she dropped her mannish pants, assumed a moonish role, astonished, and assiduously seduced him.

FRENCH TOAST

George Sand's blushing stern
whose sweet cheeks gleamed wet
with the great author's sweat
led Chopin to improvise
a poignant Nocturne
extolling her fair
pink derriere
upturned upon
his Persian prayer carpet.

"*La Belle Époque*" was a roughly three-decade stretch leading up to World War One. Our American sage Mark Twain ironically dubbed it: *"The Gilded Age."*

The poor suffered as usual, while the rich got much richer than ever. Music, Literature and High Fashion flourished. Modern painting climaxed with a burst of fireworks.

Wealthy friends once persuaded the American artist Frederick Remington to accompany them on a European trip.

They hoped their bumpkin buddy might bring his painting up to date by confronting the "School of Paris."

Faced with Monet's expansive oils at the *Orangerie,* Remington grumbled, stamped about in his thick boots, and finally rumbled—

"I've got a couple of maiden aunts back in Upstate New York, who KNIT better pictures than these!"

DAYLIGHT

From rising time, Claude Monet shows
the sunshine streams with lilac flows
lemon gleams and breathing rose.

From noon to dusk her lambent power
shades toward amber, hour by hour
seeding nightfall's shadow flower.

At that point it was only beginning to be understood that space/time is infinitesimally grainy, comprising entities to which the theoretical physicist Max Planck gave the name "quanta." Each particular quantum adds up to a playfully rushing brush-stroke, one billionth of a trillionth of a trillionth of a centimeter short!

On a postcard from Paris to a family friend, Remington wrote—
"*No, Honey, I'm going to do America. It's new. It's to my taste.*"

There was in fact no time to lose. Scientific cosmology had become too appallingly awkward to handle, and religion resembled a disembodied grin.

Irreversible erosion of the American Frontier followed hard upon the heels of our Civil War self-slaughter. No sooner had we buried our multitudinous acres of war-dead, than our once-Indian Eden began being mucked up for good.

Those events semaphored a steep decline in American confidence. Like the vanishing of the Cheshire Cat in *Alice Through the Looking Glass*.

ROUGH RIDER

His paunch was greater than his purse.
Hence Remington seems crass to us.
We're fond of cats; he rode a horse.
Until he got too fat, of course.

It's fair to say the gent had zest.
We suppose reserve works best.
Fred chose to bare his hairy chest.
We troop to church; he headed West.

Within a single generation, the Wild West would be replaced by cinematic horse-operas, and kidded in gritty ditties. Such as, for example, the following fragment which I seem to recall from some old vaudeville show —

Way out West upon the plain.
That's where men are men.
They never have a bath
when they need one.

They don't TAKE
one, even then!

Remington's "The Scout; Friends or Enemies?" presents an Indian brave on horseback in the winter dusk, peering toward some distant campfires.

The scene is deeply spacious. Snow-fragrance fills the air and my nostrils expand to take it in.

At first, I identify with that solitary Indian scout. Then I imagine myself huddled beside one of those distant fires. Might that be a Covered Wagon encampment?

Finally I'm playing "Cowboys & Indians," while feeling as "old" or timeless as the snow itself.

PALEFACE CAVALRY

Astride a glorious rocking horse
I rode to war with Jennie Doe
Cornelia Cook and Cousin Paul.

As captain of our cowboy force
I fought the noble Navajo
to a draw when we were small.

My dappled mare, our battle-course
The other kids, where be they now?
Around the bend with this old fool.

Edith Wharton, Henry James, and Stephen Crane, all three voted with their feet in the opposite direction from Remington, preferring cultural life abroad.

Wharton used to pop across the English Channel from her estate near Paris to cheer up her old friend James in Essex. She enjoyed sweeping him away on Rolls Royce rides to sites of literary interest.

Edith's chauffeur sat glassed away from his passengers, who were fond friends, and may well have been holding hands under the mink lap robe.

The pair usually talked a lambent blue streak, but now as they tooled smoothly along through leafy Somerset, silence fell between the two.

HOT ROD

As Henry eyes the sliding scene
from Edith's gliding limousine
he spins a turn-about daydream
concerning King Arthur's Queen.

Guinevere was a childless one
dear to God, monarch, and men.
Especially the blameless knight
passionate young Lancelot.

At Avalon, one evening late
she unlocked her wicket-gate
to entertain the champion
in long, close conversation.

When word of that reached Camelot
the Court concluded that they must
have betrayed King Arthur's trust
unless the Queen agreed to clutch
a red-hot rod, and clearly swear
that Lancelot never touched her!

Thunder rolled, as freezing sleet
sloshed across the open Court
to quench the Trial Iron's glow
in steam, as the Queen bent low.

Reduced to normal temperature
the rod rose in her grasp demure.
Quite innocent, pure to the core,
eyes twinkling, Guinevere swore.

Stephen Crane spun *The Red Badge of Courage* at only twenty-three, from imagination plus considerable research. It so happened that he had access to a stack of magazines which carried photos showing battlefields littered with honored and/or dishonored dead, plus accounts by surviving veterans.

The battle that rattles his pages seems a succession of sounds and images, not words. It's a passionate panorama splashed with poisonous flame.

I staggered away from the novella having been drawn into the ancient fairy-tale—

"Boy meets Girl. Boy loses Girl. Boy gets Girl."

But this time the Girl was Courage, and her fiery kiss had awakened the Boy to iron reality—

"He knew that he would no more quail before his guides wherever they should point. He had been to touch the great death, and found that, after all, it was but the great death. He was a man."

The rising novelist H.G. Wells commented—

"Crane will be found to occupy a position singularly cardinal. In style, in method, and in all that is distinctively NOT found in his book. He is sharply defined; the expression of certain enormous repudiations.

"He is more than himself in this. He is the first expression of the opening mind of a new period."

Crane's cool, simple prose would eventually inspire Ernest Hemingway's hopeless clarity and gestureless depth, which influenced thousands of aspiring twentieth century authors.

Yet Wells could get screwed up at times. For example, he cruelly quipped that Henry James's novels made him think of:

"A hippopotamus striving to pick up a pea!"

James might have replied that such critiques reminded him of a rhinoceros attempting to gore a butterfly.

But that was never his style. Instead, he wrote his previous friend—

"It is art that MAKES life, makes interest, makes importance, for our consideration and application of these things, and I know of no substitute whatever for the force and beauty of its process."

How's that for a classy, perceptive comment? Like a smoke-ring, thoughtfully blown...

In the next generation came D.H. Lawrence, a rash, bushy-bearded, fine-grained coal-miner's son from England's miserable Midlands.

He pick-axed psychological limestone and winched up blue basalt boulders for the public to contemplate.

His partner, the German aristocrat Frieda von Richtofen, had impulsively married a tomb-cold British academic.

Soon she abandoned her husband to wander far and wide with Lawrence.

FREEDOM FRAU

Nobody's
chattel
she
rattled
society
causing
rank
tattle
by
frank
impropriety

The pair began by hiking through the Alps from Bavaria to Italy. At one point, Lawrence lustfully tugged Frieda toward an empty wayside chapel.

"No thanks," she told him, laughing. "We'll be much more comfortable consorting in a haystack!"

Lawrence's final novel, *Lady Chatterley's Lover,* was firmly based on Frieda, and long banned for its "sexually explicit" contents. The book energized whole generations of sneaky readers, including myself...

Katharine Hepburn was a slim, upper-crust tom-boy type from Connecticut, whereas Spencer Tracy happened to be a reckless, thick-bodied alcoholic from Milwaukee, with a guilt-ridden Roman Catholic background.

Both were dedicated stars (and co-stars nine times over) of a cynical industry that crackled with ersatz liaisons. Yet they stayed happily married in all but name, remaining lovers right up to the time of Tracy's death.

Imagine the pair in their mid-20th-century prime, vacationing at Lake Tahoe.

Playful Kate insists upon a midnight skinny-dip, and she dives smoothly in. Sparkling phosphorescence encircles her re-emergent face—

SPLASHIFACTION

"Habeas corpus
COLD!" Kate calls.
"Jump in, baby.
Freeze your balls!"

His misdemeanors
to expunge
Spence ventures
the icy plunge.

Quite a sobering
chunky-dunk
for one dearly
beloved hunk.

2. The Spirit of the Elements

Twisting art and science together, Leonardo da Vinci formed a pointed tight-spiral projection, like a unicorn or narwhal horn, to lay in the lap, and also in the mirror, of Nature.

By morning light, this old master might set himself to counterfeit with his paintbrush the chiaroscuro "smoke" of shadow-play, through which flickers the ephemeral "fire" of human flesh.

Come nightfall, believe it or not, he might design a flying machine, or sketch his precise concept of a human fetus in the womb.

Here's what Britain's controversial and refreshing art historian Michael Daly has to say about Leonardo—

"He was born in the late Middle Ages filled with superstition and fear. He grew up leading the way into the Renaissance. He dissected corpses to provide the most accurate information we've had until relatively recent times.

"His work as engineer, geologist, botanist, and astronomer cannot be disconnected from his work as an artist. Fidelity to nature is a Leonardo trademark that can be used to determine the authenticity of his work."

I agree. "The Madonna of the Rocks" at London's National Gallery is consistently unnatural, true, but the Louvre Museum in Paris displays the same subject, painted with perfect fidelity to nature. Ergo, Paris has the real Leonardo.

Giorgio Vasari's up-close classic called *Lives of the Artists* contains this account of Leonardo's most famous painting—

"*For Francesco del Giocondo, Leonardo undertook the portrait of Mona Lisa, his wife, and left it incomplete after four years of effort. While doing her portrait the artist hired people to play and sing, and jesters to keep her merry.*"

That's puzzling, to say the least, because the Mona Lisa appears to have been fully finished, with extremely tender care. What's more, the artist held firmly on to the painting for the rest of his long life.

Except for Pieter Brueghel's deathless image of the pregnant Virgin arriving at Bethlehem, and Piero di Cosimo's "Madonna & Child with a Dove," not one of the other iconic figures in world art that I've seen is secular.

They all have to do with divinity. But the "Mona Lisa" (or "La Gioconda" for Lady Giocondo) represents a living, breathing, vulnerable human being, like the rest of us.

The picture would eventually become a popular icon, discussed by millions over the years. A hit song of the 1950's, superbly performed by smoky-voiced Nat King Cole, enshrines its abiding drama—

> *Are you real*
> *are you real*
> *Mona Lisa*
> *or are you*
> *just a cold*
> *and perfect*
> *work of art?*

In his recently published biographical novel called *Leonardo*, my old-time pal Curtis Bill Pepper offers a totally fresh concept of the "Mona Lisa." Leonardo's painting does not portray that lady at all, Bill suggests, but the Virgin Mary!

Well, I'm not about to quarrel with Bill. When we lived close by each other in Roman Trastevere, he and his abstract sculptor bride Beverly were my best friends.

Let me quote his key passages—

"*He would portray her in the Valley of Creation. Amid its primordial waters, with the veiled haze of distant mountains, she would appear again across the centuries. Her flesh and bones ageless as the valley's fluvial earth and rocks, her eyes staring far beyond the plains of Judea.*

"*The mother of Jesus, the marginal Jew, was waiting for other marginal souls to speak to her—her hands folded upon her pregnant belly, her lips appearing to move in the brief eternity of a surfacing smile.*

"'*There you are*', *he said, but it didn't help. Her eyes remained upon him, waiting for more. Nor, he realized, would it end there.*

"*This was going to happen to many others who walked into her silence with a sudden awareness that this woman had always known them. Known who they were, their secret dreams, and why tomorrow would always be temporary. That was how it would be for them, even though they didn't know the lady was Maria, or why she was there in a picture frame.*"

When one encounters La Gioconda, or the Black Virgin's image—or both together if you will—at the Louvre, it appears much smaller than expected.

But if one looks long enough it keeps growing larger and larger. Her face looms with loving grace, just as one's mother's face must have done when one was a baby.

Can you imagine Leonardo as a helpless infant at the breast? Not easy!

"*You can't take it with you!*"

That's what they say, but is it necessarily the case? While dying in Amboise at age seventy-five, with the King of France sitting at his bedside, Leonardo hugged the Mona Lisa to his fluttering heart.

Why did the painter embrace this crowning work on his deathbed? I believe he must have done so in devoted memory of an adulterous, four-year-long relationship.

ABOUT HER SMILE

They tell us Leonardo was
dispassionate and queer.
Mona Lisa smiles because
she has a more informed idea.

Painting at its height suggests invisible effects. Sculpture cannot. This brings me to the polar difference between Leonardo and his contemporary rival, Michelangelo.

Roman Catholic doctrine maintains that, however dynamic and beautiful the human body appears, it's still the soul's dungeon. Michelangelo firmly embraced that idea; he felt his own flamboyant spirit to be enslaved, chained to the body.

His carvings of the Slaves, so-called, intended for Pope Julius's tomb, illustrate the point. They writhe in dreamy pain, as if invisibly bound into the marble blocks from which they've been chiseled, but not released.

Thanks to recent scientific developments, the whole world has now begun to exhibit a certain transparency. Things no longer appear so concrete and opaque as in the past. We're conscious of less Matter and more Energy, less Things and more Events.

Since the body/soul dichotomy has ceased to convince, the old view of the body as a dungeon for the soul no longer carries conviction.

I myself maintain that the subjective/objective dichotomy also has outstayed its usefulness and ought to be discarded at long last.

If Michelangelo's faith pointed backward, Leonardo's did the opposite. Passion for physical reality, plus intuitive outreach, led Leonardo up to the doorposts of modern science, which pictures the human form as a momentary nexus of elemental forces extending through huge tides of cosmic space/time.

For him, however, art and science were not a bit separate, but one and the same. As he wrote—

"If you disparage painting, which alone imitates all the visible works of nature, you disparage a most subtle science which by philosophical reasoning examines all kinds of forms on land and in the air; bathed in light and shadow. This science is the true daughter of nature.

"My subjects require for their expression not the words of others, but experience, the mistress of all who write well. I have taken her for my mistress, and will never cease to say so.

"Man, who with continual longing and full of joy looks forward to each new spring, new summer, always to new months and years, never seems to realize that what he's really wishing for is his own destruction.

"But this yearning is the quintessence, the true spirit, of the elements, the spirit that finds itself imprisoned by the soul, and always longs to return from the human body to Him who sent it forth in the first place.

"Investigator, do not flatter yourself that you know the things that nature perform for herself, but rejoice in knowing the purpose of things designed by your own mind.

"The ambitious who are not content with the gift of life and the beauty of the world are given the penalty of ruining their own lives.

"Observe how much grace and sweetness are to be found in the faces of men and women on the streets, with the approach of evening in bad weather."

3. Anthony & Vanessa

In 1999, I went to Antwerp for the opening of an exhibition to celebrate the four hundredth anniversary of the birth of Anthony van Dyke.

I spent my writing time at the beautifully restored *Rubenshuis*, sitting on a bench in the old master's garden, with its low hedges, little gates, blackish trellises, straight paths, white and yellow flowers, and yellow-billed blackbirds calling sweetly back and forth.

Peter Paul Rubens adorned his garden with baroque statues of Minerva the Roman goddess of wisdom, and Mercury the guide of souls. He also set a little temple of Hercules, the only pagan hero to achieve godhood, in its midst.

Hercules wore a lion skin, with the deceased creature's head hooding his own. The champion's acute, observant face gazes sympathetically from under the kingly beast's muzzle.

If Rubens had Herculean breadth, body, and balance, van Dyke possessed his own swift, sad, nervous, and intensely sympathetic sensibility.

A slight, self-conscious, princely figure of social grace but uncertain health, he began as Rubens' favorite apprentice, and became the Lowland father of portraiture's fabulous "British school."

Van Dyke achieved his furthermost heights at the Cavalier Court of England's King Charles the First, where oppressive taxation, highly conspicuous consumption, and extreme sexual license prevailed.

The painter married Queen Henrietta Maria's favorite Lady in Waiting, yet he kept a mistress named Miss Lemon, believe it or not, and made her so jealous of his female sitters that she tried to bite off his thumb! I do mean thumb, the right one with which he gripped his paintbrush.

Eventually, the warty Puritan Parliamentarian Oliver Cromwell overturned Charles's toplofty regime, and savagely beheaded the King.

Not a few of the proud dandies whom the artist had portrayed in all their finery, with sword at hip and little "van Dyke" beards, were fated to lose their lives defending the doomed monarch. The Court's favorite painter himself passed away at forty-two, on the eve of Charles's downfall.

Among the riches in the Antwerp exhibition, "Venetia, Lady Digby, on her Deathbed" went straight to my heart. This image seems breathed and misted out upon the canvas, rather than painted.

When Venetia expired in her sleep in 1633, at age thirty-three, her husband Digby called upon his friend van Dyke to portray her. Dead at the artist's own age, she lay as if in dream, with her warm, earthly bloom gone cold and yet still enchanting.

Who was she, and how did she die?

Venetia Stanley Digby had a contemporary named John Aubrey, whose engaging and invaluable book called *Brief Lives* reveals the inside story—

"*She had a most lovely and sweet-turn'd face, delicate darke-browne hair, a perfect, healthy constitution; strong, good skin; well proportioned, much inclining to a Bona Roba. Her face, a short ovall; darke-browne eie-brow about which much sweetness, as also in the opening of her eie-lidds.*

"*The colour of her cheekes was just that of the Damaske rose, which is neither too hott nor too pale. She was of a just stature, not very tall. She was a most beautifull, desireable Creature, and being maturo vivo was left by her Father to live with a tenant and servants at Enston abbey in Oxfordshire.*

"But, as private as the place was, it seemes her Beautie could not lye hid. The young Eagles had espied her, and she was sanguine and tractable, and of much Suavity (which to abuse was great pittie).

"Among the other young Sparkes of that time Sir Kenelme Digby grew acquainted with her and fell so much in love with her that he married her, much against the good will of his mother. But he would say that a wise man, and lusty, could make an honest woman out of a brothel house.

"She dyed in her bed, suddenly. Some suspected that she was poysoned. When her head was opened there was found but little braine, which her husband imputed to her drinking of viper-wine; but spiteful woemen would say 'twas a viper husband who was jealous of her that she might steale a leape."

Had Venetia conspired to "steale a leape" with van Dyke? The painter was one of her husband's closest friends. It's possible that Digby intercepted a glance or a note that gave their game away.

His favorite hobby was chemistry. Did he "abuse the suavity" of his all too sanguine and tractable bride, by poison?

Might Digby have known that van Dyke was due to arrive next day? Did he prepare to greet the painter with crocodile tears and an innocent-seeming but cruel command?

"She's dead, Tony! Go and look. No, wait. You've got to paint her there in her bed, this morning, just as she lies—dreaming of God knows what!"

Five years after van Dyke's deathbed portrait of Venetia, came his superbly monumental "Eros and Psyche." That picture illustrates the following tale from a Latin classic: *"The Golden Ass"* by Lucius Apuleius.

Psyche, whose name means "Soul," longed to marry Eros the god of love. But Eros's mother, the goddess Venus, insisted that Psyche undertake three apparently impossible tasks to prove herself worthy.

With timely help from the sympathetic animal world, Psyche accomplished the first two tasks. But Venus's third and final challenge was the most daunting of all.

"Carry this cosmetic jar down to the Underworld," the goddess told the girl. "You must persuade Persephone the Queen of Hades to put some beauty-ointment in it for my private use."

"Why?" Psyche asked. "Nothing could make you any lovelier than you are already!"

Venus smiled coldly: "Well, Jupiter is giving a ball tonight, and I wish to be at my most attractive. Bring my jar back with the magic salve I require, and I'll let you marry Eros!"

The power of Psyche's love was such that she performed almost all of this suicidal mission. Emerging with the precious jar in hand, to see daylight again, Psyche offered up a prayer of praise and gratitude. Then, pausing on the Upper-world's threshold she thought—

"I'd be a fool not to steal a dab of Persephone's beauty ointment for myself before delivering the rest to Venus. Eros will love me all the better for it!"

So she opened the jar. Out crept a dank vapor of drowsiness, a stygian sleep. Falling, she lay supine, with the jar between her cold fingers. The irony was that Psyche, like Venus herself, required no beauty treatment.

Eros, god of love, was unique in this regard: he loved but once! Isn't that a suggestive piece of information?

Just now, Eros found himself unable to bear Psyche's absence a moment longer. Bursting out through the narrow window of the room where his mother had imprisoned him, the god followed the nose of his desire, which soon brought him to Psyche's side.

Carefully, tenderly, he brushed away the deathly sleep from her body and shut it up safe in the cosmetic jar again. That done, he brought his beloved back to life by the small prick of an arrow.

A Tree of Life, thick with whispering foliage, fills the top two thirds of van Dyke's crowning work. Beside it rises a storm-stripped, passionately writhing second tree. Limp from head to toes, Psyche lies where the trees' roots join.

Alighting from the left, Eros draws the deathly drapery back and away from her lolling head. He's a nakedly radiant figure of speed, agility, passion, and keen concentration.

It's van Dyke who leans in with hand outstretched to dispel the cloud of death and bestow return of life upon his beloved. Four years short of his own death, the artist revives and rejoins Venetia.

5. Fear of the Dark

Before our Civil War, New Orleans was America's most cosmopolitan city, with strong French connections. The metropolis boasted two separate but equal aristocracies: the French speaking, mixed-blood Creole one, plus the Anglo-Saxon. Each had its own opera house, for example, plus its own symphony orchestra. Virginie Avegno was born there.

When her American father passed away, her French mother brought Virginie home to Paris.

Soon married to a prominent banker, she became Madame Gautreau, the celebrated high society figure whom John Singer Sargent was fated to portray.

Sargent and his friend the novelist Henry James were American aristocrats, raised mostly in Europe. The two are often classified as "closet-gays." In their day, however, "Epicene epicureans" would have covered the ground.

As everybody knows at last, we're all double-sexed in some degree, blessed with infinitely varied percentages of male and female genes alike. This makes human sensibility a mysteriously unsettling spectrum which glimmers with contradictions galore.

Sargent's portrait of James displays the author's plump face in sepia shadow crossed by a down-slanting spate of light that seems to illuminate some bumble-bee buzz beneath the bald-domed brow.

There's no available evidence that either man had carnal relations with anyone, whether male or female, so I suspect that they may both have been impotent. But that fairly common affliction does nothing to diminish one's fascination with sex.

Sargent's *"Egyptian Girl,"* and *"Mrs. Charles E. Inches"* convey deep interest and wondering delight in the sexual auras of women.

What's more, James's *"Portrait of a Lady"* (which really should sport "Mrs. Inches" as a frontispiece) plumbs the charms, powers, and problems pertaining to humanity's more vulnerable, less physically powerful, and therefore put-upon half.

Ezra Pound commented, "What I have not heard is any word of the major James, of the hater of tyranny; book after early book against oppression, against all the sordid, petty, personal, crushing oppression, the domination of modern life.

"What he fights is 'influence,' the impinging of family pressure, the impinging of one personality upon another."

That sounds right to me; how's about you? We've all been bullied, one way or another, and done some ourselves.

I still recall my own sorrowful shock when a particular partner accused me of "emotional bullying."

She was correct of course, but the possibility had never even crossed my thoughts.

"Portrait of a Lady" has a most appealing protagonist named Isabel Archer, who "affronts her destiny" by getting trapped in a truly horrible marriage.

A former suitor from America begs her to break out of that domestic disaster and abscond with him.

The man's soul-kiss, as described in the book's final edition, was—

"Like white lightning, a flash that stayed, and spread again, and stayed; it was extraordinarily as if, while she took it, she felt each thing in his hard manhood that had least pleased her, each aggressive fact of his face, his figure, his presence, justified of its intense identity and made one with this act of possession. So she had heard of those wrecked and underwater following a train of images before they sink. But when darkness returned, she was free."

Meaning, free to do no such thing...

Sargent himself was born to American expatriate parents in Florence, Italy. Writing from Paris to a lesbian, Florentine friend named Vernon Lee, Sargent confided—

"Do you object to people who are blotting-paper color all over? If so, you would not care for my sitter.

"But she has the most beautiful lines, and if the lavender or chlorate of potash lozenge color be pretty in itself, I shall be more than pleased."

Gowning Madame Gautreau's sinuous presence in a black satin evening dress, and isolating her refinement as if in a tall mirror, Sargent breathed a cigar-smoke-thick, blotting and besotting aroma of sexuality upon her.

Her seductive steaminess does not appear in the least deliberate, however, nor even self-conscious. So Madame's sexiness alone cannot possibly have put sophisticated Paris in a snit.

Yet when Sargent showed the portrait at the annual Salon Exhibition of 1884, his booming career suffered sharp setback.

He'd not identified his model by name. Being a celebrated upper-crust figure, however, she was recognized at once.

Hot off his easel at the Salon, Sargent's canvas must have seemed deliberately provocative.

High-collared Parisian gentlemen, and ladies in their own décolleté gowns, doubtless read the painting as a reminder that aristocracy need not imply pale skin.

Mutterings of shock and horror fluttered the Salon's *vernisage*, after which Sargent's subject and her mother stormed tearfully into his studio.

"My daughter," Madame Avegno screamed, "is LOST on account of you!"

Sargent had been regarded as a golden boy in Paris. Now he found himself snubbed, more or less driven from the city that he called home. At Henry James's suggestion he moved to London and started over.

Since Madame Gautreau had bitterly declined to purchase her portrait, Sargent slapped a mystery title, *"Madame X,"* on his masterpiece and sold it to Manhattan's Metropolitan Museum, where it got systematically swabbed down by way of "restoration."

Chlorate of potash-lozenge is not dirt, not for artists anyhow, but art conservators can't tell the difference.

Despite its obvious desecration, the image has always appeared miraculous to me.

Sargent conferred glorious, unquenchable life upon his red-blooded, elegant Creole clothed with the sun,—that loose-limbed, starkly aristocratic Dark Lady of Everyman's dreams.

6. Good Looker

I was standing on the corner of Elm Street, half a block from our Northampton, Massachusetts, house, at age four or five, when a nice old neighbor known to me as Mrs. Sprague, stopped to ask what I thought I might be doing there.

"Waiting," I explained, "for a Smith College girl to come along and tie my shoe-laces."

That's what Mrs. Sprague reported to my mother, anyhow.

I've always been lucky with respect to members of the opposite sex whose paths intersected mine. But were they all that fortunate to find me?

At nineteen, I fell for the first girl to enchant my previously self-centered psyche. We met in summertime, at the Cummington Massachusetts Center for Art and Music.

Diane (pronounced DEE-Anne) was four years younger than myself. Bittersweet and lissome as a panther, she had wide green eyes, which often filled with tears, and hair like smoke of incense.

During our school get-together meeting, I could barely restrain myself from looking around at her.

Next day, I drew Diane aside and frankly confessed my confusion of the evening before.

"That's because I was posing for you alone," she told me simply, in her soft, confiding voice.

Diane's father was the merchant prince David Nemerov, who owned and ran Russek's Department Store on Manhattan's Fifth Avenue, as its "Fashion Director."

Her mother Gertrude was in fact a Russek, whose predecessors had made a fortune from the fur trade.

Raised in Park Avenue grandeur, or "protectively dunked in a mink-lined teacup," as she put the case, and saddled with a strict French governess, Diane had dreamy good manners, stubborn independence, and immeasurable melancholy crossed with sensuous delight.

In an autobiographical essay for her Fieldston School magazine, she dryly commented—

"I'm not born yet."

The Nemerovs had packed their alarmingly alluring daughter off to Cummington in order to separate her from an instinctively elegant, severe young suitor named Allan Arbus, who worked at Russeks.

Her chosen summer school project was an oil painting she called "The Angel Gabriel."

It wasn't meant to look like Allan in the flesh, she confided to me, but he was the subject. She imagined him as a tree king or chlorophyll Pharaoh, and slicked his skin with a pale green tone.

"How would you paint me?" I asked.

"Um. As a rock formation."

"Why"

"My Gabriel happens to be Vegetable. You're volcanic Mineral."

"I am?"

"Yes, and I'm an invisible Animal!"

"Not so," I told her. "I can't agree to your EVER becoming invisible!"

Our physical connection began with back-rubs, and remained fairly tentative at first. Thanks to Diane's genius for sensation-sharing, it was also unforgettably intense and fun.

One day Diane used her "Big Red" Parker fountain pen to imprint the word "bone" on my left wrist.

"Why this?" I asked. "Could it be a comment on my always getting one with you?"

"Nah. You're LIKE a great bone, with a sad smile."

"Oh, how I love talking with you!" I said. "Nobody else understands."

"I KNOW!" she told me, and that was true. She understood me better than I did myself.

PASTORAL

Half undressed upon the grass
by oval, golden sunbeams laced
within a budding chestnut grove

This urgent youth and virgin lass
talked of awful problems faced:
Family, Teachers, Art, and Love.

Allan had given her a silver slave bracelet, which she wore with religious devotion. One afternoon, she removed it to show me the engraved inscription he'd composed for its inside curve.

I can't remember how that went.

The incident slipped from our minds until dinnertime, when someone asked what had happened to her bracelet.

"I forgot!" she said. "It's out near Wilbur's Rock."

"Let's go back and find it right now," I offered, getting up at once. "Before dark!"

Diane was much loved, so half a dozen friends took part in our suspenseful but ultimately successful search.

The story of the bracelet swiftly spread. It doubtless scandalized Sidney Cox, whose Theatre Workshop sessions we'd often cut.

His longstanding friendship with the great but terribly temperamental and star-crossed poet Robert Frost was our teacher's main claim to fame. Frost once wrote in a letter—

"I said to Sidney Cox that I was non-elatable. While I wasn't exactly fishing, I hoped he might see I wanted to be contradicted. Which is of course not to say that HE is elatable."

Contrastingly, Diane and I were "elatable" for sure. First by beauty and second by love play. Hence we intensely enjoyed each other's company. We didn't "go all the way," however, until later years, and then on just a few occasions.

Patricia Bosworth's womanly, sympathetic biography, *"Diane Arbus"* (1984) relates the full story of our extremely traumatic, long-belated romance, with compassionate grace. Since it's already on record, and painfully "close to the knuckle," as they say, I don't suppose I'll ever address the matter in print myself.

Gloomy, puritanical old Cox doubtless complained of our "strange behavior" to the school's Director: Miss Frazier. She was a maiden lady in her sixties, who had grown up on the property, inherited it, and put it to good use as a summer school.

Miss Frazier's manner struck me as "distant," and mine may have looked the same to her. In youth, one barely perceives the people who run things.

The following morning, Miss Frazier commanded Diane and me to come to her house at five o'clock for "A little talk."

The summons sounded ominous.

She began with Diane—

"I'm here to learn, my dear. Please be so kind as to tell me what you two egregious young people suppose my school is for?"

Diane responded with a calm, silent gaze. Nothing ever seemed to frighten her, but she obviously found the question unanswerable.

Miss Frazier turned to me—

"Well?"

"I don't know!" I said.

"That's nowhere near good enough."

"Hey, couldn't YOU tell US?"

"What's the putative reasoning behind that idiotic suggestion?"

"Well, then we might understand."
"Beside the point, young man."
"The point?"
"We're here to discuss YOUR relationship."
"Okay, it's true."
"What is?"
"Diane and I somehow connect!"
"Just how do you do that?"
"Pardon?"
"You heard the question. I'll not repeat myself."
"Uh. Hum. Jeeze…"
"Make an effort to articulate."
"Mr. Cox prefers tragedy over comedy. For its moral uplift, he says."
"Do you presume to oppose uplift?"
"I'm neither for it, nor against it."
"That's shilly-shallying."
"If you say so. In fact the whole business escapes my comprehension."
"I think you've got something there."
"Well, Diane and I are simply trying to explore this whole thing together. It's our own business, you know, so don't rush to—"

JUDGMENT

Her crinkled features glowed beet-red.
Would she expel us or explode instead?
"I'm disappointed in my staff," she said.
You're self-assured, fairly well bred
at ease where angels fear to tread
and as for me, I've been MISLED!"

Might Miss Frazier have once been young? Smiling tenderly at Diane, she murmured—

"Feel free to do whatever YOU like at my school!"

At summer's end, Diane gave me her painting of Allan in trade for a broken heart abstraction of mine.

The first letter I got from her concluded—

"P.S. I feel as if I could just take anything and know it and paint it MY WAY, but it doesn't paint half so well as I know it."

The Nemerovs generously invited me to visit them as a house guest during the week after Christmas. On that occasion I became close friends with Allan Arbus.

Also, with Diane's elder brother, the Harvard student Howard Nemerov, who proved to be painfully aware of anti-Semitism's universal curse on Jews and Christians alike.

Howard lived in genuine fear of Adolf Hitler's hugely looming threat. Talking with him was something of an education for my ignorant, non-political self.

On the final day of my visit, Mrs. Nemerov told me that if I had any hopes of marrying Diane, I'd better bury them.

"Allan is bad enough," she huskily sighed. "But I'll *never* let my daughter wed a *goy*!"

Later, I asked Howard what "goy" meant.

"That's Yiddish for 'Non-Jewish'," he explained. "Like when Christians call me a Yid, Hebe, Hymie, or Kike."

"They do?"

"Sure, but they don't necessarily mean to insult me. The same goes for my mother and you. She was just being as straight as she knew how. Mummy would be horrified to hear that up at Cambridge I'm dating a Radcliffe college chicksa. That means Christian girl."

At eighteen, Diane married Allan. Her one wish was to be his perfect partner. The couple set up shop as anxiously industrious fashion photographers. Diane supplied ideas, and schmoozed with models. Allan did the shooting.

Their work was featured in Glamour, Seventeen, and Vogue. Soon, "Diane & Allan Arbus" became a fairly big name in the industry.

There's a lot more to tell about Diane, but not yet. I'll return to her tragic and yet inspiring story in due course.

7. Pavan for a Princess

Anne Dick and I first met at an art collector's beachfront party on Boston's North Shore. She was gorgeous, witty, and pale blond. We took to each other, soon wandered off together, and consummated matters—

THE GOTTA SONATA

As Lorna Dune told Conan Doyle
and Popeye promised Olive Oyl
seaside sex tops treats in bed
like cherry pie to buttered bread.

When we bared our buns to dent
a sandy beach, on romance bent
under star-hung heaven's tent
and came in concert, sorrows went.

*"We can make our lives sublime
And, departing, leave behind
Footprints in the sands of time."*
So Henry W. Longfellow opined.

Although Anne belonged to "Boston Brahmin" old money society, she was instinctively bohemian, regarding snobbery as "vulgar in the extreme."

I was still hoping to develop a workable philosophy of existence. Having abandoned that ambition, Anne said we'd be lucky to settle for: "Personal adjustments to the cruel and inscrutable."

Anne's maternal grandmother, the dowager known as "Granny Tuckerman," reigned during the summer months at Appleton Farms in Ipswich, on Boston's North Shore.

Granny soon became aware that Anne and I had embarked upon a relationship, or what was then called an "affair."

I don't suppose that bothered her one bit, although she would have regarded it as unmentionable, like most things in life. She instructed Anne to bring me down from Boston for a week-end visit.

Everyone at Appleton Farms had known Anne since she was small. They loved her and made much of her.

Granny's head gardener and chauffeur, Hector Butts, occupied the gatehouse with his family. On Saturday afternoon, Anne brought me over there to get acquainted, and we were asked to stay for tea.

A thick mop of gray hair partly obscured Mrs. Butts' large, dark eyes. She freely admitted to being a witch, blessed or cursed with "second sight."

"Can you tell fortunes?" I asked.

"Well, I can't prophesy my own fate. Nor can I see the fortunes of folks I love, such as Miss Anne. But I'll read *yours* if you like, in the tea."

Taking my drained teacup between her palms, she gazed down into the configuration of tea-leaves left there. When she lifted her eyes to mine they seemed a thousand miles distant.

"I'll give it to you straight and quick," Mrs. Butts began.

"That sounds ominous."

"I simply tell what I see. First-off, you marry Miss Anne."

"Dead-right, so far!"

"Then you marry a second time. That's the real one. You travel all over the world, residing in different countries for years at a stretch. You make lots of money, and live to a ripe old age."

I gaped at Mrs. Butts: "Is that it?"

"Yep."

Shooting a fond glance at Anne, I responded with all the witless arrogance of youth—

"Someone else must have been sipping from my cup!"

"Why so?"

"First, I aim to stay loyal to Anne. Second, my only ambition is to paint a few beautiful pictures before I die. Nobody gets to travel, or be rich, that way. Anyhow, my personal gut-feeling is that I'll expire at the age of forty!"

"Nope."

"Why should your prediction be more reliable that mine?"

"Because tea leaves don't lie."

Can the eternal storehouse of potentialities ever be opened and entered in this present life?

Well, yes. Prophetic intuitions are not a bit uncommon. I've never made much money, except perhaps by 1939 standards, but apart from that Mrs. Butts was uncannily prescient.

On Sunday morning, Granny Tuckerman took me aside and spoke with dragonish severity—

"You've upset my women!"

"How?"

"By having NO pajamas for them to lay out on your bed!"

"Sorry about that."

"I, too, am quite upset. You came WITHOUT a hat!"

Stumped, I shuffled my feet.

"All the same, I want you back next week-end."

"Gee! Thanks, Granny."

"Come with a nice Borsalino fedora on your head, and appropriate night-clothes in your valise!"

"But—"

"No ifs, ands, or buts about it!"

Being somewhat scary for us both, Anne's and my engagement remained informal. Here's a verse I composed concerning her—

BEAUTY & THE BEAST

We two discordant lovers stood
silent, beside a snow-bound wood
amid the mad March wonderland.
She extended a kid-gloved hand—

"Please listen, Alex. Try and bend.
I'm so bewildered, understand.
Like a traveler in a strange land.
You'll always be my best friend."

"So, what the fuck?" I yelled at her.
"With any luck, we'll make a pair!"

"A big problem," Anne once warned me, "is that I'm sick a lot!"
"Female difficulty?"
"I suppose you could say that, in the broadest sense of the term, but I mean really, truly depressed."
"Do you get bed-ridden?"
"Rarely. Most times, it's on the couch!"
"Psychoanalysis?"
"I've had a few sessions with the Jungian analyst Merrill Moore. We mostly talked poetry, which happens to be his hobby. But in fact I meant MY couch, not to mention Crane's Beach, the Byrd garden by moonlight, and matinee sessions beside the stream at Appleton Farms."

I smiled: "It's hard to imagine *you* depressed. Your *wits* are just as perky as your *tits*."
"Here in Boston, we say 'bosom'."
"That's inappropriate. The Bible refers to Abraham's bosom, true, but men are men, and women are double breasted!"
"You don't say?"

"To form a proper concept of the matter, one should carefully consider TWO tits, at least. Aristotle in a lost lecture, and Ludwig Wittgenstein—"

"Nice of you to change the subject, but waves of misery do sweep over me. Some day, they'll carry me away…"

F. Scott Fitzgerald's novels spoke to Anne and myself like a wistful, naughty uncle.

This Side of Paradise, The Great Gatsby, and *Tender is the Night* were sad saxophone riffs of truth in fiction, perfumed with sex and pickled in gin cocktails.

The author's beloved Southern belle of a bride, named Zelda, desired to become a ballerina. She spent six years in psychoanalysis and eventually spun out of control.

Her distraught husband checked out facilities for the insane, and committed Zelda to one. As he later confessed in a letter to his editor Maxwell Perkins, Scott left his heart along one of those gravel drives that wind down and away from private hospitals.

Following nervous breakdown and a brave but dangerous spell "on the wagon" in Hollywood, Fitzgerald died of heart failure at just forty-four. Zelda herself expired much later, at a second "sanitarium"—what a word!—roasted behind bars in a roaring fire.

Might heavy doses of hard liquor have edged America's few supreme 20th century authors out upon spirit-flights of an uncanny sort, such as shamanistic drum-riders practiced in prehistoric times?

Yes, I believe alcohol provided the wavering edge of mystery, risk, and pain, that those major players required.

THE BEST & THE TIGHTEST

Scott Fitzgerald
William Faulkner
burnished Ernest
Hemingway
grief-stricken
Eugene O'Neill
John Cheever
James Jones
Sinclair Lewis,
Thomas Wolfe
 and Jack
Kerouac
wallowed in
forgetful drink.
unfit to write
a twit might think.

Mindlessly obedient to the culture of our time and place, Anne and I also drank plenty. Not doing so was regarded as anti-social. Besides, we enjoyed it, or thought we did. Practically all our set drank, smoked, danced and partied, in a manner that would appear crazy today.

I valued my worst hangovers; such devastating clarity! But that was too intense to bear for more than a few hours. I'd soon falter, and resort to "hair of the dog that bit me," or "re-administration" in the medical lingo of today...

After some time, Anne brought me together with the rising poet Robert Lowell, known to friends as "Cal." Brooding, Bostonian, hugely ambitious, he resembled a handsome Death.

Back at St. Mark's School, he'd played football with more enthusiasm than skill, charging blindly until he felt his head explode in sparks. Cal was like that; he made things marble-hard for himself, and others.

When Anne was a debutante and Cal was a Harvard student, they'd been intimate in his rooms at the university's Eliot House. That "wasn't done" back then.

Their scandalous, half-deliberate indiscretion lead to a quarrel between the Dick and Lowell families, both of which vetoed Cal's plan to marry Anne.

Having furiously knocked his filthy-rich father flat, Cal departed to reside with a southern pal, the poet Allen Tate, who arranged for his acceptance at Kenyon College.

To console herself for his absence, Anne composed an essay which the prestigious *Sewannie Review* published. It strikes me as the single most convincing interpretation of Shakespeare's culminating work, his tragicomedy: *"The Tempest."*

She suggested that proud Prospero and his daughter had been murdered, the King's ship had sunk with all hands on board, and the magical island was in fact Purgatory! In other words, a between-the-lives location where the main characters could repent at long last, and be reconciled!

The Eliots and the Lowells were not related, yet Cal called me "Cousin" in his lordy Shakespearian style. At a clambake on Beverly Beach, he once complained—

"Do quit blathering, Cousin."

"Did you say blathering?"

"None of us WANTS your comments on Matisse!"

"Then, what should we talk about?"

"Poetry!"

"That makes YOU a minor poet, Milord."

"Oh?"

"Major ones have wider horizons."

Rudeness was a common feature of the social scene back then. They tell me things are less pretentious and somewhat kinder now.

During World War Two, Lowell's indignant public condemnation of our fire-bombing cities landed him in jail for a miserable year.

His protest proved truly prophetic. Our nation took the lead in spreading terror from the air, causing more civilian casualties than one cares to think about, and opening an especially dreadful chapter in the dismal history of war.

So, if Cal seemed somewhat crazy, the world was not all that sane either. Nor is it yet.

Jail-time for outspoken moral decency braced Cal to endure worse incarcerations during the ensuing years, when he began to suffer spells of delusion laced with terrible anger.

Psychiatrists pronounced him "in danger of destroying himself and others." Hence, experimental injections were administered to dye Cal's seething brain-fluid electric blue.

Convulsion-inducing shock treatments were employed, as well. That's an incredibly cruel non-cure, comparable to blood-letting, via black leeches, in a previous era.

It's not generally realized, by the way, that doctors deprived our first President George Washington of almost half his blood-content in hopes of overcoming the old hero's pneumonia, the day he died.

OF ROBERT LOWELL

That lofty Beacon Hill aristocrat
was also a pure, poetic alley cat
whom no critic could corral
with horrors to rehearse.
I liked the man better than
his yowling back-fence verse.
Courage was the essence of Cal.

Granny 'Tuckerman's self-consciously grandiose and yet paradoxically minuscule universe was about a thousand miles removed from that of my Eliot grandparents, who practiced neo-puritan "Plain living and high thinking" at their Revere Street mansion in neighboring Cambridge.

Samuel Atkins Eliot, Senior's "bride," as he always referred to Grandma, had raised seven rambunctious children and launched them all on interesting careers and/or marriages.

Her heavy-lidded look and formidably forthright manner awed almost everyone, myself included.

Having been a worry for Grandma Eliot, I assumed she disliked me. That is, until I accidentally discovered that she'd anonymously mailed me the only valentine I ever received.

Came the day when Granny Tuckerman invited my grandparents to tea at her Beacon Street residence, in order to discuss Anne's future and mine.

They accepted, as a matter of courtesy. But Frances Hopkinson Eliot informed Granny straightaway that she herself disapproved of my "strange interest" in Anne.

"Alexander was to the manor born," Granny retorted, "but WE rescued your grandson from the GUTTER!"

"Oh. Come now."

"He never even had a *hat*! Nor suitable night clothes, for that matter."

Drawing a gold watch on its chain from his waistcoat pocket, Grandpa Eliot got to his feet.

"It's late," he declared, "and there's a committee waiting at my church."

"Late, is it?" Granny sniffed. "Alexander, you must show them your fedora!"

I stepped out to pluck it from the hat rack in the foyer, and paused before the hall mirror to give the brim a casual slant. Returning, I assumed a hopefully nonchalant pose.

"Very nice, I'm sure," Grandma Eliot decided, heading for the door. I snatched off my hat, but she did not look back.

A year from the time we met, Anne bravely gave me her hand in marriage.

Granny Tuckerman hosted the Anglican ceremony and champagne reception at Appleton Farms,

Afterward, we drove a borrowed Chevrolet northeast along the Maine coast, for a brief honeymoon.

Anne composed a nuptial verse en route, and recited it in the car. Something like this—

ANNE'S SONG

We're driving so fast and free.
Sea to sky, and sky to sea.
You and I, the wedded "We"
although in fact I'm only me.

It's fortunate we dovetail well.
An hour from now, at our hotel
I'll wax nostalgic, looking back.
Comfort me with applejack.

Like the ocean, women lie low.
Men pursue the moon you know.
They come; afterward they go.
Ask any girl if that's not so.

As part of an impulsive pair
with half my life ahead to share
I cannot say if I should flee
our Chevrolet, but let that be.

The mixed-media artist Cynthia Stillinger has sent me a hollow egg constructed by herself, as an Easter present.

Peeking through its beaded opening, I perceive near at hand a nest which cradles two miniature bright crimson eggs. In the background looms a proudly paternal white rooster, with a red coxcomb.

Elizabeth Bishop wrote—

> *That crown of red*
> *set on your little head*
> *is charged with all your fighting blood.*

Brevity, bullying, illness, depression, and warfare grease the downside of this roller-coaster existence. Levity, love, sex, the arts, and beauty most of all, spark the upside.

As William Carlos Williams noted—

> *so much depends*
> *upon*
>
> *a red wheel*
> *barrow*
>
> *glazed with rain*
> *water*
>
> *beside the white*
> *chickens*

I had to earn a living, but how? I was determined to do so in some enjoyable and idealistic fashion. No "nine-to-five" moping-&-coping for this poor devil, if I could possibly help it.

So Anne and I started a cooperative gallery called "The Pinkney Street Artists' Alliance," in our Beacon Hill apartment. The roster featured such still unrecognized colleagues as Alphonso Ossorio,

Richard deMenocal, King Coffin, Arthur Lougee, and Lawrence Kupferman.

Since we lacked all shrewdness, our business venture was comically rash. The gallery didn't lose money, but neither did it make ends meet. Hence, after eight months' effort, we moved to Manhattan, where I undertook a hateful occupation.

Namely, selling five-dollar lithographs by Thomas Benton, Grant Wood, and John Stuart Curry among others (most worth thousands now) plus eighteen-dollar "Geletone" color reproductions of contemporary paintings, at the Associated American Artists' Fifth Avenue showrooms.

Finally, sickened to death by the selling game, I applied to "The March of Time" newsreel company for an "assistant to the producer" post.

(Before the advent of television, M.O.T.'s monthly twenty-minute documentaries rounded out the bill in thousands of movie theaters.)

The newspaper ad asked aspirants to appear on Friday morning between eleven and twelve o'clock. I got there on the dot of nine, instead.

The receptionist informed me that I had a two-hour wait ahead. At that point, luckily, the company's imperious producer Louis de Rochemont entered and happened to overhear.

"Hello, kid," he said to me. "Want to take a look at yesterday's rushes? Come on along to the projection room!"

We saw the rushes together. When the lights went up, he asked what I thought.

"Unsuccessful," I told him frankly, and proceeded to outline my personal views.

"Well," de Rochemont decided. "You're an arrogant young fellow, ignorant as hell, but obviously honest, and I need somebody honest around here. The yes-men are killing me. Welcome aboard!"

Back then, filming "on location" was still a technically clumsy and complex process. To my own surprise, I much enjoyed learning on the job and improvising solutions to our frequent dilemmas.

Our productions always closed with a truism, solemnly enunciated in stentorian style—

"Time, Marches On!"

We laughed about this, but it never occurred to us that the assertion might be suspect.

Einstein's "Theory of Special Relativity" (1905) never called time's inexorable march into question. But then Erwin Schrödinger (1887-1961) developed a statistical theory according to which the order of events is what determines time's behavior! His *"Mind & Matter"* lectures at Trinity College, Cambridge, in 1956, conclude—

"Time is our most severe master, ostensibly reducing the existence of each of us to severe limits. To play about with such a master's program seems to encourage the thought that the whole 'timetable' is probably not quite so serious as it appears at first sight. And this thought is a religious thought. Nay, I should call it THE religious thought."

ONCE & FUTURE BLOOM

While out for my walk yesterday
I heard a dead gray dandelion say
"Bend down, mister. Kiss your sister. "
Plucking her, I puffed a spate
of silver seedlings to their
olden, ever golden fate.
Life renews, come what may.

While I always recognized the gallant gleam of Anne's spirit, I did so in an insufficiently cherishing manner. For example, when summer came to Manhattan I actually felt pleased to pack her off and live alone.

That was "the thing to do," of course. Surrounded by her classy friends and relations on Boston's North Shore, she'd be happier, I fatuously imagined, without me hanging around.

Closing my eyes, I drift back to midtown Manhattan on a muggy July night in the 1940's.

Although the great mass of Anglo, Negro, Hebrew, Irish, Latino, Polish, German, Italian, Greek, Chinese, and Japanese New Yorkers are home asleep, the metropolis herself sleeps not.

Late-night workers and dilatory home-goers slink, slope, hurry, stoop, waggle, and strut on by. Along the lamp-lit sidewalks, high-heeled prostitutes, both light and dark, strike stimulating poses.

Bag-ladies drag their pinched, reluctant feet from trash barrel to garbage can and back again.

Out-of-towners leap about, shouting each other down.

High above the pavement, about a million windows alight.

Behind the bright glass, students cram, scrubwomen dust and mop, clerks file, invalids sweat with pain, crooks conspire, dirty folk shower, and lovers make whoopee.

Thousands of solitary people doubtless sit drooping, out of sight, with a cup of coffee cooling before them or a cigarette in hand.

But I was never lonely. Gazing back, I recognize myself as a boozy jazz buff and blithely irresponsible family man.

At Greenwich Village's Stuyvesant Casino, the chairs were bent-wood, the tables big and round, and the beer served ice-cold in frosty pitchers.

Old Bunk Johnson's Dixieland band was a relic of the "Roaring Twenties," with wrinkled "Baby" Dodds on drums.

Their New Orleans music set us dancing until the floor, which actually had springs built into it, rocked beneath our flying feet.

The jazzy abstractionist Stuart Davis, whose "Report from Rockport" I much admired, sat puffing a cigar and sipping ice water with bulldog-sober composure. He was "on the wagon" at the time.

My dear friend and counselor, the kinetic sculptor Len Lye, circled the scene on what appeared to be six or seven egg-beater revolving legs .

There were women also, who saw fit to accommodate me.

I'm not ashamed of my behavior, which was typical of our crowd at the time. To offer a single example, I assumed that Anne was still consorting with Cal Lowell on occasion; not that she ever mentioned it.

We kept such delicate matters to ourselves, and rightly so, I think.

Hair-on-fire jealousy blows nobody good.

Among my summertime romances was an irrepressible Irish-American named Deirdre.

She once assured me that when a totally honest woman happens to pass the Public Library on Manhattan's Fifth Avenue, the impassive stone lions who flank its steps arise at last and roar approval in royal unison!

I believed her, naturally, and I also believe that when a ship with a fairly honest man aboard passes the Statue of Liberty, she drops her torch in astonishment.

I'm only being honest when I say this, like the Cretan of classical times who confessed that all Cretans are liars.

WHENCE WE CAME

At Deidre's austere
lace-curtained lair
four flights above
Sheridan Square

I spread apart
her slender thighs
the Dew Drop Inn
to scrutinize

Whose curly crop
of light brown hair
curtained a mystic
trysting area there.

She once remarked
when we were done:
"Can't you understand
sweet lover-man?"

"I could have been
a cloistered nun
with Christ instead
of having fun

 "So our steamy
summer liaison
is treason against
God in Heaven!"

When the Japanese bombed Pearl Harbor, I made a quick switch from M.O.T's outfit to the newly formed, Manhattan-based, Film Division of the Office of War Information.

Thus I managed to avoid being drafted, while contributing my documentary film know-how and tiny talent to the nation's "War Effort."

Yes, I soon began to feel guilty about that.

Allan Arbus would soon be swept into the U.S. Army Signal Core, and sweat through furious Burmese jungle combat.

Howard Nemerov was already serving against the Nazis as a volunteer Canadian Air Force pilot. He would fly a hundred and fifty-seven missions all-told, first in British Spitfires and later in American bombers.

My boyhood friend Harry Maynard volunteered for the American Air force. He flew reckless, endlessly recurrent reconnaissance missions over what Winston Churchill hopefully dubbed, "The soft underbelly of Europe."

War distorts the look of everything and plays havoc with human values. At a low stretch in my emotional life, I wrote Harry to say that I might enlist after all. He shot back the pithiest message I've ever received—

"If you do anything so stupid, I will drop a bomb on YOU!"

About a dozen major European artists were in and out of town back then, displaced by the war. I happened to encounter the coolest of them all, Marcel Duchamp, at the home of the chess-master David Hoffman.

They played chess, whilst I kibitzed.

When David mentioned the fact that I painted abstractions, Duchamp drooped his eyelids and slyly remarked—

"The trouble with abstraction is, it doesn't get beyond the retina!"

"Do you suggest," I asked, "that abstraction offers no food for thought?"

He let the question pass, so I added: "Your 'Nude Descending a Staircase' has been described as a sneak punch in the public's face. Also as an explosion in a shingle factory."

"Old games."

"That's true, but I believe your picture pushed cubism into free-fall and cleared the way for non-objective painting."

"I hope NOT!" Duchamp declared. He'd forgotten to punch his game clock.

I kept right on as usual: "Social-protest, patriotic, religious, pornographic, sentimental, or commercial images impose upon individual will. They deliberately manipulate emotions and opinions."

"Isn't manipulation what YOU do? Making films for the Office of War Information—"

Waving my arms, I cut him short: "Christian, Hindu, and Buddhist religionists rely on images, as did the pagan world in general, but Judaism and Islam are more austere."

"Religion bores me."

"Jews and Moslems alike favor abstraction on religious, iconoclastic grounds. So Josef Albers and Piet Mondrian have plenty of precedent for propagating the non-objective tradition of purity in pictures!"

"You're puffing," Duchamp observed.

"Pardon me for puffing, Your 'Nude' carries magic packets in the pockets that she only seems to lack."

"What pockets?"

"Every angle and gland. She's flipping light in all directions. I see her as the captured queen in a chess game, forced to quit the board!"

At that point, David executed a swooping knight's move to whip victory from Duchamp's momentarily distracted grasp...

Very few of my pictures had proved saleable, and I couldn't bring myself to make art a hobby. So I practically ceased painting.

Instead I did a lot of museum-going, which was free back then, as it ought to be still, plus gallery-hopping. The Wheye, Willard, and Bucholz gallery proprietors were kind enough to let me browse for hours at a time. Not in business for the money, they could tell that I, too, really cared.

Most people have a few haunting images in their heads. Why this one or that, instead of something quite different? Among the paintings I dwelt upon back then, Phillip Evergood's seashore figure called "Juju as a Wave" springs to mind. Juju comes delicately dancing along a sandy beach, with distant wonderment in her eyes.

The lady is not conventionally beautiful, no, but truly so, because adored by the artist himself—as one can tell.

My favorite Manhattan gallery was "An American Place," which occupied a modest office suite in a mid-Manhattan skyscraper. I usually found the proprietor, old Alfred Stieglitz, sitting peacefully alone.

I'd been lucky enough to encounter a native Cree counselor at Camp Mohawk, Madame Cheruy at Loomis Institute, and Mr. Albers at Black Mountain.

Now came Stieglitz, whose radical initiative had inspired my own abortive "Pinckney Street Artists' Alliance" back in Boston.

His gallery was a cooperative outlet for a few close associates, including his beloved wife Georgia O'Keeffe alongside Marsden Hartley, Arthur Dove, Paul Strand, Charles Demuth, and John Marin.

Hartley, to start with, was wildly uneven, and yet the color-life in his best stuff can enhance one's personal perceptions. His "Dogtown," for example, invests a rural ruin with cathedral weight and dignity.

The cool green hill setting, the sun-stroked, bare-bone dance of the fallen barn beams, and the gray gravity of the granite stones, plus the levity of the cloud trio overhead, all play together as if to say, *"Be well, like ourselves!"*

Arthur Dove's watercolors and mixed-media works convey precisely the same message. Dove was careful not to reach awkwardly far, nor to ponderously describe. He mingled childlike spontaneity with the religious conviction that everything's much better than okay.

John Marin once wrote me a letter maintaining that his whole oeuvre was a matter of handwriting. He manipulated brush and wash to mirror, not the shapes so much as the half-hidden rhythms in nature.

"Red Sun, Brooklyn Bridge," for instance, goes Paul Cezanne's architectonic watercolors one better by introducing abstract dynamics. His crimson sun splashes down.

Stieglitz himself was a great artist, I mean one of the immortals. The little old gentleman used to greet me kindly and converse with me at leisure, mulling over whatever questions my vaguely seeking self introduced.

The main thing Stieglitz taught me was that art's purpose is to: "Get the spirit of the truth."

Yes, but less than one in a thousand professional painters, photographers, sculptors and architects fill that bill, and I was already beginning to suspect that I myself would never be numbered among the gifted few.

For me, Stieglitz and O'Keeffe were America's most distinguished couple. So I summoned sufficient courage to ask the master why they were no longer together.

"Health reasons," he said. "She needs the New Mexico altitude for her lungs. My heart couldn't stand it."

That was a white lie to protect my innocence. His marriage to Georgia had always been "open," with scattered side affairs, and it stayed above water. But I've since learned that Stieglitz had embarked upon romance with a worshipful disciple forty years his junior, named Dorothy Norman.

O'Keeffe had suffered a nervous breakdown over that, and begun branching in fresh directions of her own.

Most photography captures the dramatic glimpse, whereas Stieglitz dealt in reflective stillness.

While contemplating one among the many cloud studies he called "Equivalents," for instance, it's possible to sense ethereal currents threading the shadowy surface.

The placid, lightly floating cumulus clouds that we take pleasure in perceiving overhead are very much alive on the inside; cool and yet boiling with molecular turmoil.

Similarly, our bodies host storms of bio-electrical activity. This brings me to Stieglitz's photos of Georgia.

During their first full year together, she'd posed for him, mostly naked, holding still through three or four minutes a shot, three hundred and twenty-nine times. Spreading a batch of those photos out for me one day, Stieglitz said,

"Don't get your fingerprints on these. They're precious to me. I must take my nap. So when you leave, just snap the lock on the door."

Caressing her long, elegant contours without so much as a touch, Steiglitz exposed this woman's awesome depths. Kansas-born, farm-raised, she had a prairie sensibility open to fructifying winds of heaven.

If that sounds extravagant, my words pale in comparison to the correspondence between O'Keeffe and Stieglitz, which totals 5,000 handwritten notes totaling 25,000 pages). O'Keeffe wrote:

"The plains—the wonderful great big sky—makes me want to breathe so deep that I'll break—There is so much of it—I want to get outside of it all—I would if I could—even if it killed me."

After moving away to New Mexico, she decided:

"Eleven years have passed by. I see all its phases — all the days and hours & moments of ecstasy & pain — the growth of something very exceptional and very beautiful between us... All the wonder & beauty & life—and all the terrible ordeal."

Before leaving, I peeked in at the old man's tiny office. He lay supine on the leather couch, with his black cape pulled up over his face and one chalky hand trailing to the carpet. I felt a strong premonition of his death, which was not far off. Gulping, I slipped away...

Certain individuals' feeling/thoughts fall into hellish darkness now and then. Anne's poetic nature warred unceasingly with lurking depression

Not by any means her fault, but there we were.

Anne's case intrigued the psychiatrists at Manhattan's famed Payne Whitney Clinic. They persuaded my invisibly agonized bride to sign herself in for a free "Six-week Trial Cure."

That project foundered, however. When I arrived to collect Anne at last, the analyst in charge cheerfully admitted failure, and advised me to: "Spank her!"

"Why?"

"Because it's best that you do so."

Drifting half-way around the doctor's desk as he sat hunched over his *"Emergency!"* button, I came dangerously close to hitting him instead...

There's a particular Greek legend which casts a raking light upon the story of Anne and myself, so I'll include it here.

Toward the start of their ongoing career, the Olympian deities joined together to fashion an artificial woman.

Hephaestus the volatile, dark, volcanic master of refined artifice, shaped her.

Apollo, the lord of poetry, medicine, and music, painstakingly tuned her.

Hermes the sly prince of measurement plus thievery, put a touch of mischief in her.

Aphrodite misted her billowing blond hair with fragrant endearments.

Seeing that she was good, wise Athena named her "Pandora," the All-gifted.

Finally, Zeus the Cloud Gatherer allowed Pandora's divine makers to marry their creation to a somewhat stupid Titan named

Epimetheus, Greek for "Afterthought."

Next morning, Pandora got up first. Feeling curious, she wandered here and there around the numbskull Titan's palace. That's how she happened upon the small bronze jewel-box wherein he kept his troubles.

Beneath her fingertips, the box gave off a low buzzing sound. Gingerly, Pandora pried it open. To her horror, a myriad of whining, stinging insects which had germinated within swarmed forth. Swiftly they dispersed, spreading a woeful miasma around the world. Hope alone, the one butterfly, elected to linger.

"La esperanza moera ulitima."

Yes, hope is the last to die, but she's also the first to stay.

Thanks to Hope, Epimetheus forgave Pandora, and soon their daughter Pyrra appeared. She in turn became engaged to Deucalian, the son of Epimetheus' brilliant twin Prometheus or "Forethought."

Prometheus instructed the cousinly pair to build a commodious, waterproof box and spend their honeymoon shut up inside of it. The box should be seaworthy as a scallop-shell, he told them, for a deluge was on the way!

Zeus opened the windows of heaven and sent down the expected torrents. So the young couple took shelter inside their well-built cabinet.

After passing a timeless period of ecstasy wrapped in the sea-lapped Stygian darkness of their ovarian vessel, they finally felt the waters subside.

Their barnacled lockbox, or floating re-birth womb room had arched the flood and finally grounded upon a height of Mount Parnassus.

A bleak world awaited them, except for the radiant sun god Phoebus Apollo, who presided over Parnassus at Delphi. Standing tall, Pyrrha and Deucalion received the solar deity's first oracle—

"Throw your mother's bones behind yourselves!"

The couple understood. Gathering scattered fragments of Mother Earth's carapace, they tossed small stones over their shoulders. The flints flung from fiery Pyrra's hand turned into mortal men. Deucalian's quartz crystals became mortal women.

The fruit of Anne's and my marriage far outweighed all our troubles put together. Our daughter showered us both with unearned joys. She was born in Virgo, the holy Virgin's constellation, but we named her May Rose.

Like Pandora, Anne was marvelously formed and creatively gifted, destined to astonish and delight others, but not to be happy in herself. And I'm in the same boat as Pandora's blundering husband Epimetheus, whose only talent was for afterthought.

But May Rose Eliot Paddock resembles divine Pyrrha, the daughter of Pandora and Epimetheus. She remains a noble, pure flame if ever there was one, and a constant inspiration to her father.

Book Three: Artists Yes

In Praise of Excellence

Fast Company

Giant Frog

Lines in Sand

Color carver

1. Fast Company

For some young Americans on the make in the mid 1940's, journalism seemed a glamorous profession which required no special education. Hard scribbling, I figured, couldn't be too hardscrabble. After all, my literary idol Ernest Hemingway had made a go of it.

So, when World War Two approached its end, I applied to Time magazine for employment. I chose Time because its back-of-the-book critical review sections, which ran unsigned, seemed knowledgeable and refreshingly brash.

The Personnel people gave me various tests and eventually passed me upstairs to Time's Executive Editor, Dana ("Tack") Tasker.

Gruffly, with a momentary glance, Tack inquired what I thought I could do for the magazine.

"I'll write your Art Section," I said. "It runs only once or twice a month, which is unworthy of Time. I'll make it sing every week."

"Art doesn't often run because I keep killing the goddamn thing. I hate the guy who writes it. One of these days I'll make him walk the plank... You're a big fellow. Do you care for sports?"

"Naturally, but—"

"Our Sports Editor is on vacation. You can use his office."

"What for?"

"First, cut-ass up to the Sherry Netherlands hotel and interview Larry McPhail, the Yankees' owner. He's fired his manager. Find out why. I'll be working late, so have the story on my desk by seven tonight. If by any chance it's usable, I'll give you a three-week trial."

"Okay!"

Phoning from the Sherry Netherlands' front desk, I told Major League baseball's mighty Mr. McPhail that I was on urgent assignment from Time magazine.

"Come right up!" he said. "Do you favor scotch in the morning?"

"It's never too early, sir."

"Good. I'll have a highball waiting."

The baseball tycoon greeted me with strong drinks in both fists. We clinked glasses and toasted each other's health.

"I have only one question," I said.

"Go ahead and shoot."

"Why did you fire your manager?"

"That's easy. Off the record, he's an alcoholic!"

"Could you expand on the matter?"

Two hours later, I was back again at Time. But not for long, I gloomily supposed. Stepping into Tack's office, I bluntly confessed to having goofed—

"McPhail told me the reason all right, but off the record."

Tack sat back and laughed, "Don't fret. Weasel it!"

That was my first, and certainly most practical, lesson in journalism. The Yankees' manager, I easily weaseled, had "departed under a cloud closely resembling the D.T.'s." (for "Delirium Tremens.")

When I turned in my hand-written piece at Time's copy-desk, the supervisor glanced over, and gaped.

"We'll transcribe this as a special favor," she told me. "But from now on, give us typescript only!"

So the next day I taught myself to type. I've been hunting and pecking ever since.

I wasn't proud of my piece, but Tack loved it and immediately hired me, on probation, as a stand-in for the Sports Editor Marshal Smith.

Time writers had no bylines, and never appeared in print except on the masthead, unless as a neutral "visitor" or "viewer" if absolutely necessary. So we were unknown to the public.

Instead of recounting actual experiences, we were called upon to convey the "curt, clear, complete" Mind of Time itself, which was firmly made up anew every single week.

Having "pointed with pride" or "viewed with alarm," as the case might be, Time rested on Monday and Tuesday. Then the whole show marched inexorably forward again.

Our "group journalism" was a goofy charade for sure, yet a publishing triumph of religious proportions. Millions of middlebrow Americans faithfully followed and confidently echoed Time magazine.

The one thing I knew for certain was that art is nothing if it's not experience. The photographer/dealer Alfred Stieglitz, the philosopher John Dewey, the collector Albert Barnes, and the painter/professor Josef Albers, all four got that much precisely right.

Any work of art is best approached as a one-on-one interchange between either artist or viewer, and the object in question.

With that in mind, I set myself to become a conscientious journalist, not in the judging business, who shunned theories, distrusted missions, and reached for insights instead.

I saw myself as a non-intellectual non-expert, blessed with a hands-on background, and a controversial, exciting beat to cover. My ideal was to introduce artists to the public by pecking out paragraphs appropriate to their silent creations.

Not relying on Time's correspondents, I would go any distance to contemplate the actual art which I desired to discuss in print, and meet with its creator if at all possible.

The best way to become acquainted is via relaxed conversation. Hence I never carried a notebook or took notes, nor did I ask too many questions. I happened to be a whiz at remembering., able to recall crucial words and gestures for days or weeks if need be. Plus works of art, naturally.

I soon discovered that Time's Art Editor was the pioneer

documentary photographer Walker Evans, whose work I much admired.

Dropping by Mr. Evan's office, I shyly confessed that I coveted his job.

"SPLENDID!" Walker told me. "I assume you can put up with Tack the Knife?"

"Oh, sure."

"Personally, I detest him, and I hate writing anyhow, so I'm dickering with Fortune magazine to be their picture editor and Tycoon-of-the-Month portrait photographer."

"Thank God! I should have guessed —"

"Well, let's keep it secret for now."

Our company doctor took a dim view of me the day that I dropped down to his twenty-seventh floor infirmary with a wounded foot. Frowning, he inquired—

"How did it happen?"

"I stepped on a tack in my office."

"Just a tack?"

"Yes.

"Hmmm!"

"With my shoes off."

"Very interesting."

"Why?"

"You remove your shoes at the office?"

"Sure. Won't you please dab some iodine on this?"

"Not until I've asked a few more questions."

"I didn't come here to be psychoanalyzed."

"You seem unable to explain your odd behavior."

"I've got no time for this. Bye-bye."

"Wait... Well, go and be damned. This won't look very nice on your Personnel Record!"

When Walker closed his Fortune deal and I replaced him. Marshal Smith wished me well, but wondered—

"In Art, how can you tell who won?"

"You've got the hardest job," I replied. "In Sport, everybody and his little sister already knows!"

BRAVADO

> Friends asked whether I should seek
> to critique "Art" each passing week
> for such a lean, mean magazine.
> That was not for me to say,
> but I thought so, anyway.
> My task would finally take
> fifteen long years of joy and ache.

I'd been less than a month at my new post when American napalm bombing severely damaged Tokyo's Imperial Hotel. That masterpiece of the first order had been designed by the premier American architect: Frank Lloyd Wright.

Regarding the incident as an important story for Time's Art Section, I inquired whether Wright might return to Japan when peace came and supervise its reconstruction.

"Said Wright sadly: 'No.'"

So our Chicago News Bureau reported, and it's what I wrote. But my esteemed back-of-the-book editor arbitrarily re-phrased the matter in the down-&-dirty war-spirit which prevailed at the moment—

"Snapped Wright: 'Let the Japs do it themselves.'"

Henry Robinson Luce was rock-jawed, bush-browed and missionary-bred. The man owned and ran Time Inc from high above, in grandly tinkering style.

Now he summoned me and my Senior Editor to lunch at the company's private, top-echelon dining facility.

Mr. Luce entertained us genially and volubly, in paternal style. Then, while we were finishing our ice cream and coffee, he dropped his own bomb—

"Eliot, I happen to be friends with Frank Lloyd Wright. Not long ago he called me up about — guess what. Who the heck are YOU to dare misquote HIM?"

I stole a glance at my editor, who sat absently stirring his coffee.

"I've no excuse!" I said quickly. "That was the stupidest thing I ever did. It won't happen again."

Mr. Luce pushed back his chair—

"I think I like you! Let's get back to work."

"Close call!" I thought. But it strikes me now that Luce would have made inquiries right after receiving the architect's phone call. He doubtless knew the whole story before issuing his invitation to lunch.

Luce and my editor must have deliberately set me up, in order to determine whether I could respond calmly under pressure, and play the nerveless, firmly loyal, company man...

When Victory was at last declared, I happened to be working late.

Like thousands of others, I rushed out to join the joyfully swollen street throng. Snatching up the first lonely looking girl I saw, I danced around Times Square with her on my shoulders.

She was with friends, as it turned out, and we eventually wound up at the Greenwich Village pad of the fine black jazz trumpeter Frankie Newton, who very sweetly got out of bed to cook breakfast for us.

"You're happy," Frankie said to me, "and that's good. Your war is over, but mine is just starting!"

For a minute or two, I wondered what he meant. That's how simple-minded I was. The Cold War between White & Colored, Plutocrat & Proletarian, Exploiter & Exploited, had been seething for centuries and would soon build up a further head of steam.

Art was something else again, and American art, in all its furious variety, had overtaken the war-battered "School of Paris."

On our industrially booming, newly prosperous side of the water, thousands of Abstractionists, Expressionists, Regionalists,

Surrealists, Social-realists, and Romantics, pursued violently opposed agendas.

This brash, twenty-six-year-old failed painter and rank beginner in art criticism felt well situated to explore, while never presuming to explain, artists' efforts.

But the conflicting trends, so-called, never interested me. Neither did the "market," for that matter. Instead I could hardly wait to meet about a dozen individual American painters whom I believed to be people of genius.

First of all, for me, came John Sloan, whose "Wake of the Ferry" (1933) I'd contemplated at Washington's Duncan Phillips Collection, and which I regarded as the greatest American panting to date.

So, naturally, I phoned Sloan's Greenwich Village pad to request an interview. He proved to be a gaunt, peppery, bespectacled old fellow, with a wryly humorous Scots/Irish background—like my Grandpa Cook.

"My New York pictures," he told me, puffing his pipe for punctuation, "are no more 'Ash Can Realism' than a poem."

"Agreed," I said.

"Well, but you young people today have no idea how sweet—sweet and sad—this old town used to be. I mean, before Prohibition!"

I asked what he thought of photography.

"The camera," Sloan responded, "is mentally blind. We don't learn form optically, you must understand, but through our sense of touch!"

"Well, your stuff touches me personally, to the quick!" I told him, "and many, many thanks for your time..."

Intolerance, personal politics, rank opportunism, and the success/failure syndrome, stultified the art scene then, as always. It was saddening to discover that many artists despised us critics, along with each other, and even themselves! They didn't have anywhere near as much fun as they should have done.

Francis Henry Taylor, who directed Manhattan's Metropolitan Museum, had keen desire for important acquisitions, passionate concern for the collection, and near-zero interest in public relations. Taylor's total independence, plus his ingrained habit of resorting to French for confidential discussion, must have irritated Mr. Luce, who occupied a dominant position on the Met's Board of Directors.

Hence the man was eventually deposed, and replaced by a genial go-getter named James Rorimer.

When Rorimer succeeded Taylor as Director of the Met, I naturally interviewed him. He wore a bit of string tied around one finger, so I asked what it signified.

"Oh, that," he said. "It's a reminder."

"What of?"

"That I must not forget to have Harry Luce FIRE you from Time!"

Although I laughed at Rorimer's baronial jape, I was not altogether amused. I found myself courted and resented, in about equal measure.

My warm praise of Andrew Wyeth's painting called "Christina's World," which poignantly depicts a cripple clawing her way up a hillside, simply horrified Ad Rhinehardt.

"NOBODY," Ad said to me, "paints GRASS anymore!"

Andy, for his part, dismissed Ad's austere abstractions, as being "Null, AND void!"

The American public had always been slow to appreciate our native painters of genius. When President Harry S. (for nothing) Truman derided abstract paintings as "Ham & egg art by lazy people," millions cheered.

Moreover, our great museums such as the Metropolitan and Washington's National Gallery snubbed home-grown artists back then, as a matter of policy. The nation was far too timid, as yet, on the cultural front.

"Most museum directors are limp-wristed fellows who don't know how to drink or do anything!"

Thomas Hart Benton gave that pronouncement to a newspaper columnist. I quoted it in Time, commenting that Benton himself did indeed "know how to drink."

He bitterly contested my observation with—

"When I drink, it's never alone."

Since I myself indulged in solitary sipping, that retort struck home.

Benton was a far more accomplished painter than I myself recognized. He said it made him furious that "some dumb Dutchman," meaning Rembrandt, painted better than he did, but in fact he created some wonderful things.

Consider "The Rape of Persephone," for instance. Benton's supremely sympathetic take on the Greek myth portrays Persephone as a Missouri girl, perhaps a rural schoolteacher.

She's no pretty pin-up but a vulnerable plain-faced person, poised naked on the bank of a secluded swimming hole. Hades, King of Underworld, incarnated for the occasion as a horny-handed, cucumber-nosed old farmer, creeps up behind her...

European surrealism was riding high in the late 1940's, and Rene Magritte especially delighted me.

Like Agatha Christie's Hercule Poirot, Magritte was an uptight Brussels sprout. But he did his detective work in the polished walnut and pink plush interior of European dream life. Aboard his electric brain-train one might encounter a bottled nude, an open window on an easel, a sofa-size hair comb, or square-cut clouds.

I once asked Magritte, via our Paris Bureau: "What's the most important thing?" His reply—

"To be charming."

I was by no means persuaded. What might Missouri's bold, laborious, under-appreciated Tom Benton say in response to Magritte's philosophy?

The poet Robert Frost once noted—

"If you're looking for something to be brave about, consider the fine arts."

Yes, consciousness of one's own inner freedom is the first and last requirement for creative success.

That's the reason why such apparently opposed artists as Leonardo & Michelangelo, Ingres & Delacroix, Picasso & Matisse, Alfred Stieglitz & Walker Evans, Tom Benton and Jackson Pollack, Willem de Kooning & Edward Hopper, were partners in courage and brothers under the skin.

Edward Hopper was a non-charmer, quite without guile, but courageous through and through. I found him wintry and silent as a frozen stream, yet touching all the same, and I revered his work. He and Jo, his dear, chirpy sparrow of a wife, were invariably kind to me.

I've heard that a recent biography belabors Hopper for "abusing" Jo, which seems unfair. Jo did once complain to a lady friend of mine that Edward preferred what she called "the back door," but in fact the couple were much closer than most. They formed a mutually supportive, companionable pair, neither of whom could have done without the other.

Once, in an uncharacteristically confiding mood, Hopper told me—

"*Painting a design isn't hard. The same goes for painting a representation of something. But to express a thought in painting, that is hard.*"

Picking up one of his paintbrushes and dramatically pointing its dry tip at an invisible mid-air surface, Hopper went on—

"*The more you set down on canvas, the less is there. Why? Because you've LAYERED OVER the thought!*"

Jo stood glowing bravely in her husband's shadow. She helped me persuade Hopper to sit for his portrait: a Cover story in Time.

Then, at seventy-something, Hopper got a Gold Medal from the American Academy of Arts and Letters.

Recipients customarily graced the ceremony with an acceptance speech. Instead, the artist mumbled "Thank you," and sat down, much to Jo's distress.

Next day, I asked him: "Why so rude?"

His hesitant answer—

"Recognition doesn't mean so much. You never get it when you need it!"

True. During the first decades of his career, Hopper had been compelled to eke out a bare living by dint of mediocre story illustrations for magazines. In accepting his Gold Medal he had honored the Academy, not the reverse.

Hopper's most familiar masterpiece, "Nighthawks," hangs at Chicago's Art Institute. Recalling this to memory, I find myself near a city street corner at a midnight hour. I'm outside in the dark, gazing through the plate-glass window of a fast food joint.

Marooned at the bright-lit counter, as on a theatre stage, four figures animate the scene.

The counterman, clad in starched white, assumes an unobtrusively priestly, serving-while-observing stance. His three customers have nipped inside out of the vast, windy night—less lonely than the light—which sweepingly awaits their return.

The body-language of each participant projects a lost, bleak quality. They seem to cast about for God knows what, like an inchworm at the end of twig.

"We're born alone and we die alone!"

Although that's often said, it's inaccurate. One is born of one's mother, after all. She's there.

In peacetime, moreover, most people die with friends and family near.

Yet the sense of existing in solitary confinement, as if in a coffin, haunts millions.

The closest Hopper came to public confession, so far as I'm aware, was when he spoke of being a "self-seeker."

What constitutes one's self?

Is that the part which begins buzzing and emoting the minute one wakes up in the morning?

No, there must be something indefinable beyond that aspect.

Ralph Waldo Emerson made an observation, which applies well here—

"In every work of genius we recognize our own rejected thoughts. They come back to us with a certain alienated majesty."

Connoisseurs who label Hopper "pedestrian" are right, and yet wrong as can be. This artist balances quotidian overtones against a disturbing undertow which slopes toward one from way down the block...

On their very first date, by the way, Barak Obama took Michelle to visit Chicago's Art Institute. So they must have contemplated Hopper's familiar and yet intrinsically strange masterpiece together. They may also have heard Studs Terkel's pithy comment on the picture —

"Here are all the 'Open all Nite' beaneries you have ever experienced. Here is Everyman's lonesome valley."

Studs radiated sympathetic encouragement to everyone he interviewed on his Windy City radio talk show, myself included. Half a century ago, he interviewed the passionately dedicated black author and essayist James Baldwin, who offered an amazingly insightful prophecy.

Here it is, from Studs' final book: "PS"—

"If one could accept the fact that no nation with twenty million black people in it for so long and with such depth of involvement can actually be called a white nation, this would be a great achievement and it would change a great many things.

'If, for all these hundreds of years, white people are going around saying that they're better than anybody else, sooner or later they're bound to create a counterweight, which is simply to take the whole legend of Western history, changing one or two pronouns and transferring from Jerusalem to Islam.

"Just this small change can turn it all against the white world. And the white world can't call the Muslim leaders or anybody else on this, unless they're willing to face their own destiny."

Hopper bitterly accused me of "liking" Jackson Pollock. In fact I didn't.

Pollock's swaggering despair blinded me to his true qualities until after his half-suicidal death in a drunken car-crash. The man himself stood tall, however, among those whom I regarded as my Art Section's ongoing Cast of Characters.

He preferred his drip-stick to the paintbrush, and laid his canvas flat on the floor, suborning the force of gravity to convey an impression of energy on the loose.

Pollack's drippings actually project a paradoxically peaceful space-ballet effect. At their best, they suggest a not quite visible Br'er Rabbit or half-cracked Jackson who hunkers, hops, humps, spins, and leaps light-miles...

America's supremely sophisticated folk artist Norman Rockwell became famous for his *Saturday Evening Post* covers. Among the most acute was his painting of a partly bald bourgeois gentleman, with hat and umbrella in hand, contemplating a Pollack abstraction.

Square inch for square inch, Rockwell's Pollack rivals and may even surpass the revered original!

Pollack profoundly resented my dubbing him "Jack the Dripper," and that's understandable. Yet his dealer Sidney Janis actually thanked me for having given the artist a "memorable moniker."

In the New York Times one Sunday, critic S. Lane Faison, Jr. commented that Pollock—"Carries painting to a new extremity."

I ran the quote in Time, with a deadpan footnote—

* *Presumably his foot.*

Was I unfair at Pollock's expense, not to mention Mr. Faison's? Certainly. It's impossible, anyhow, for a person of feeling to be "even handed" about art.

Partial to my friends, I was by no means immune to arbitrary likes and dislikes. Hence I must have made some rotten calls. What critic hasn't? Yet, whatever those may have been, a kindly censor has erased every last one from my best recollection.

The magazine always stood by me. Never did any Time editor presume to question my aesthetic impressions. Nor did they second-guess Marshall Smith on athletes. Our editorial set-up was democratic to that extent.

It's true that Tack did publish one outraged reader's protest in our "Letters" column, with this tongue-in-cheek annotation—

"Time's Art Editor has been demoted to a smaller office on a lower floor."

My first view of Dong Kingman's watercolors, at the Wildenstein Gallery, made me woozy. He created calligraphic conundrums, cloud-soft jokes, and spotty, deep-colored images of things that seemed really there, pulling them from wide mandarin sleeves that weren't.

So I phoned and asked Kingman if he'd agree to a luncheon interview. "Naturally," said he.

An hour later, at *Le Chambord,* Kingman asked me to order first.

"Chateaubriand Bernaise," I decided, "with a nice bottle of Bordeaux."

Kingman ordered a glass of water, nothing more. Pulling a sketch pad from his jacket pocket, he nailed my "conspicuous consumer" aspect in a pen portrait.

A SONG FOR DONG

He furnished with fountains
the echoing mountains
and lectured on measure
to learned Pekinese.

His pigeons have light grace
achieved via white space.
Applauding for pleasure,
they circle at ease.

The best of his oeuvre
belongs in the Louvre.
Enjoyed at one's leisure
It's quite the bees' knees.

Dong's blatantly phallic moniker, diminutive stature, and underprivileged Chinese houseboy background, were not in the least burdensome to him. Blessed with low-angle perspective and an attentive, sunny, disrespectful disposition, he must have found me gluttonous, bibulous, pompous, and absurdly serious.

But nothing could prevent our growing fond of each other.

"Look at traffic lights," he once enthused to me. "Even when the streets are empty they keep on flashing green, yellow and red. Such dedication!"

"True," I said, adding: "But what is truth?"

Frowning with concentration, Dong replied—

"The TRUTH is that if the harpsichordist Wanda Lewandowska had married Howard Hughes, followed in due course by Henry Kissinger, why, she'd be Wanda Hughes Kissinger now!"

"These are deep waters," I said. "Tell me, who *is* Kissinger?"

Henry Koerner was the second artist to become a lifelong friend of mine. Broad chested and rather short, Henry exuded upright, eager vitality. One of his eyes rayed slightly askew, so he seemed to look at you twice at the same time—and perhaps he did!

It seems just yesterday that some hit-&-run Mercedes driver destroyed Koerner as he was bicycling out from his beloved Vienna to paint in the fields.

How I miss his phone-calls! They lit up my intellect and warmed my heart.

"This is Heinrich," he'd say. "I just completed another grrrreat picture! I'll describe it while it's still wet, so listen carefully…"

Koerner pretended that he owed everything to Sigmund Freud for his ideas, and to Adolph Hitler for annexing Austria.

Noting how his whole Vienna neighborhood rejoiced at Hitler's coming, young Heinrich had felt impelled to flee on foot across the Alps to Venice, where he found work as a singing waiter. (He had a lovely tenor.)

With an American great-uncle's help, Koerner soon emigrated to Brooklyn, and after Pearl Harbor he volunteered for the U.S. Army. By then, his parents and his brother had been snatched up and stuffed into the Nazis' gas ovens.

He crossed the Atlantic back to Europe on the luxury liner Queen Mary, which had been converted into a war transport vessel crammed chock-a-block full of fellow soldiers.

Waiting in line at the Coke machine, or to receive a plate of chow, or to use the toilet, he had endless opportunity for studying his comrades' brooding, bored, frightened faces, and that was enough.

Awakening to the floating enigma of human nature, Koerner embraced his destiny. Namely, to portray real people in personal depth.

Posted to Vienna, he discovered that his home neighborhood had been flattened by Allied bombs, all except the candy-store on the corner.

The proprietor still perched behind her cash register. She recognized Henry at once.

He was about to ask her something, but the old lady simply stared down from her stool and shook her head.

"I'd always hated her, anyhow," Henry told me.

When Koerner's acidly sympathetic drawings of rough life in the ruined metropolis were exhibited locally, they received favorable attention, including notice in the armed forces newspaper: Stars & Stripes.

That led to an Army commission. Koerner was assigned to sketch the Nuremberg Trials of Nazi war criminals. He produced an historic set of courtroom portraits, through which I first became aware of his existence.

My reviews of his first gallery shows in Manhattan contributed to Koerner's early fame. Later, however, when I persuaded him to paint cover-portraits for Time, he fell out of favor with the critical establishment, which regarded such work as merely "commercial."

In fact, he was radically experiential, portraying everyone strictly from life.

Koerner took a teaching post in Pittsburgh and married a violinist named Joan. They raised a family and developed what he called their Pittsburgh-Vienna Axis, spending the summer months in his re-built home city.

When Koerner came for consultations at Time, we used to wind up sipping martinis at Rockefeller Center's English Bar and Grille. One afternoon there I said—

"It's springtime for Henry, right?"

"Not good enough," he told me. "I need subjects to pose as I imagine them..."

One of his eyes wandered, and he went on: "Take the waiter in the corner, with the blue jowls. I want him on a tightrope, high over Pittsburgh!"

"That would be dramatic, especially for him!"

"See the big blonde sitting alone by the window?"

"Yes, and I'm rather attracted."

"Too late, your Horniness!"

"How come?"

"She and I are on our way to Austria. She'll dispose of her panty-hose, fluff out her flaxen hair, and slide down an icy slope for these eyes of mine alone! Do you understand what I'm saying?"

Soon after that conversation, Koerner undertook a dream-like process of artistic displacement, transposing folks who'd posed for him into inappropriate yet actual surroundings, painted "on location" according to his customary rule.

Thus he achieved the masterpieces of his final years, where one perceives many thing afresh.

Here I'll include Koerner's own thumbnail sketch of his career—

"As a boy in Vienna, at the Imperial Art Museum, I came face to face with the greatest influence on my artistic life: Pieter Breughel. Later on, at the Academy of Applied Art, I was confronted by the most abstract expression of mankind: the typeface.

"Only Brueghel, followed by Giotto and Cezanne, filled my being with adoration and envy. Those three artists penetrated to the core of existence. I broke through by incorporating in my work the findings of Cezanne. Then I was free to act out Martin Buber's idea of the Dialogue between the I and the Thou."

Willem de Kooning's first show, beautifully mounted by the pioneer art dealer Charles Egan, amazed me, and I "discovered" him without delay.

Holland-trained, and a natural draftsman, de Kooning made his pleasure in painting, plus his passionate enjoyment of life itself, abundantly plain.

Slapping on pigments with a firm and yet fluent hand, he let his disciplined, wild-on-purpose abstractions sing squeezily, accordion style, of concealed volumes crying to be released.

During our initial meeting over an expense-account lunch as usual, I asked—

"What's it like to be so talented, and yet totally obscure?"

"I don't mind," he replied.

"You don't?"

"Women support me!"

There's a deeply pervasive sentiment which associates Truth, Goodness, Wisdom, Nature, and the Muses, with womanly beauty. To me, that seems natural enough.

Nowadays, however, quite a few women proudly pad about as leopards in leotards, panthers in panty-hose, girdled American grizzlies, and wolves in she clothing.

Is this beautiful? Beastly, rather. But I mean no offense to the animal kingdom.

Many men, for their part, are well aware of being totally beholden to female powers, and find the fact extremely disturbing.

On the evidence of a very few pictures, Willem was one such. He abandoned abstraction for a year or more in order to externalize, and thus exorcise interior, female demons.

That infuriated the New Republic's influential critic Clement Greenberg, who was a constitutionally inclement champion of totally abstract art.

"You must never tell stories!"

So Clem instructed artists. We tell ourselves stories all the time, however, including the times we spend making or looking at pictures!

Like most great artists, de Kooning was a deep student of great art. His sharp-fanged, squat, monumental fury on canvas called "Woman 1." clearly echoes Albrecht Durer's famous etching "Melencolia 1." in a shriller key.

I personally believe his chosen title referred to the first and worst woman in Bill's own existence.

His mother back in Rotterdam was a waterfront bartender who doubtless handled her unwelcome wee Willem in hard-boiled and occasionally terrifying style.

As millions of children in every generation learn from tormenting experience, grown-ups can, and very often do, behave insanely.

Observe the mad, happily hating glare, and threatening lap, of "Woman 1." She hisses the Rotterdam Dutch for—

"Mama's gonna BEAT her bad boy GOOD!"

At a final stage in the months-long process of painting this image, de Kooning decided that it was too damned confrontational after all, and wearily consigned it to the trash.

Next day, at the urging of his insightful friend Meyer Shapiro, he rescued the canvas, and attached a narrow panel, splashed with radiator paint, to its left-hand side.

That set the image at a slantwise, more ghostly angle.

The picture's chilling impact made his fame, and rightly so...

In fact, de Kooning was extremely fond of women themselves. His warm, witty and ever supportive wife Elaine saw him through many an emotional crisis, not to mention his frequent extra-marital affairs.

Once, when he fathered a daughter on another woman, Bill told me—

"I wisht Elaine coulda had her!"

I much enjoyed going to art exhibitions with Elaine and Bill. One day at a Durand-Ruel gallery show of Claude Monet, he dismissed the pictures as being "Too milky."

"How about your own work?" I asked, and he responded cheerfully—

"Dot's right. Too milky!"

"Well, you've got a point," I said. "But don't you think the lactate look of these pictures derives from heavy cleaning on the part of restorers?"

"Nah!" said he.

Weeks later, at Manhattan's Metropolitan Museum, Bill gleefully pointed out various "hot spots" in the Met's otherwise marvelous Rembrandts.

When I suggested that those glaring patches, too, were caused by clumsy restoration efforts, he laughed. Which of us had it right? We made a bet.

Soon afterward, I spent an instructive weekend at the Worcester, Massachusetts, home of Francis Henry Taylor, who had long served as the Metropolitan's Director. I asked him to settle my bet with Bill.

Gazing sadly up at the ceiling in Roman profile, Francis rumbled—

"Our conservator ruined the Met's Rembrandt holdings."

Eventually, a prestigious committee of Rembrandt scholars reversed the decisions of equally distinguished but deceased colleagues, and summarily "de-attributed" dozens upon dozens of famed Rembrandts, including a number at the Met.

"Not genuine!" they decided. "No longer recognizable as genuine" would be more like it...

I once dropped into Washington's Phillips Collection for the pleasure of revisiting Renoir's 1881 "Luncheon of the Boating Party."

That historic masterpiece had been shifted from its central position to a dark side gallery as if in shame, and I could easily see why. The painting's blossomy colors had gone dry, droopy, and half awry. The seated foreground figure had turned corpse-gray.

Barging into Mr. Phillip's office, I begged him to explain the disaster.

"My fault," he said. "I sent the picture to our mutual friends. You're familiar with the restorers I mean. Best in the business, right?"

Mr. Phillips paused to wave away an imaginary fly. Tears misted the old gentleman's eyes—

"I'd asked them to iron out a small blister on the surface, and then forward the canvas to Paris for a show at the Louvre. Deciding that the picture required cleaning, they went ahead with that, and I foolishly let it happen."

"The crown jewel of your whole collection!"

"Was. The Louvre people refused to accept my ruin as a Renoir!"

"Hardly surprising," I said.

"No, but fortunately our friends had filmed their own insane cleaning operation. I forwarded a print of the film to Paris. There's another print here, which you're welcome to view. It shows *colors* coming *off* on the cotton swabs. But for God's sake, Alex, don't publicize this tragedy!"

Out of deference to Mr. Phillips I never did report on that. Nor did I mention in print the Metropolitan's defacement of its Rembrandts.

In fact, I failed to condemn our over-cleaning of masterpieces until much later, when desecration of the Sistine Ceiling occurred.

Conservators, so called, patiently inform us that their efforts are generally undertaken to "correct mistakes" committed by their predecessors. Hence, both the Met's Rembrandts and the Phillips' Renoir have doubtless been further diddled with in recent years.

At the world's major museums, conservators operate off-limits "wet labs" where they embalm humanity's painted inheritance with calm, relentless aplomb, like the morticians paid to pretty-up inert cadavers.

Approved methods feature *"inpainting"* which means brush-ups to fill wrinkles, brighten dark spots, freshen faded ones, and make pictures look "young again."

Masterpieces are spiritual as well as physical, like human beings in that respect. The decent thing would be to let them grow old gracefully.

What about the folks who undergo face-lifting and botox injections? It's none of my business, I agree, but people ought to be warned against "luxury cosmetology," or the surgical application of irremovable masks...

The "Dada" revolution, which eventually became Surrealism, originated at Zurich's seedy "Cabaret Voltaire" in neutral Switzerland.

Four people, sickened by the blood-soaked, mindlessly grinding horrors of World War One, started it. Namely, the German nonsense poet Hugo Ball, his wife, the raunchy singer Emmy Hennings, and the dancer Sophie Tauber who created her own masks, plus her cool set-dressing partner Hans Arp.

When Arp turned up at Fifth Avenue's St. Regis hotel, I phoned to ask if he'd sit still for an interview downstairs at the King Cole bar.

There, Arp and I ordered vodka martinis, served with a small dish of popcorn.

"I've only one question," I began.

"Really?"

"Your abstract sculptures and bas-reliefs strike me as bland, noncommittal, and beautifully harmonious. Yet the Dada attitude was always long on irony, shock and scorn. Just how do you reconcile your own creations with that?"

Arp dipped a finger in the popcorn dish and stirred it gently. Selecting a single kernel, he held it up.

"Look at this," he said. "You see how lovely it is?"

"Uh. Sort of."

"Unique as well."

"How so?"

"Like a snowflake, only rounded in various directions."

"True..."

"If I did this in marble, much enlarged, I'd have created something between a Malliol and a Brancusi!"

"I see your point," I said. "Whoever would have thought—?"

"So, my friend, we should be careful not to take beauty seriously."

"Oh."

"Nor art, either!"

Arp didn't actually mean to patronize me. Nor would I dream of scorning so distinguished a European visitor. Aware that he was hoping to lighten up the naïve young American sitting opposite him, I laughed politely.

A few days afterward, I received a phone call from someone who informed me, in orotund End-of-the-World tones, that he was—

"James Johnson Sweeney!"

A major modern art maven of that long-ago day, Sweeney had recently been appointed Director of Manhattan's Guggenheim Museum. I'd thought of requesting an interview, but never got around to it.

So now, assuming that one of my drinking buddies was putting me on for chuckles, I responded—

"Well, if so, it's not entirely your fault. So cheer up, Sweeney, and go FUCK your swinish self in person!"

Following a long pause at the other end of the line, the voice continued: "You're not going to like this, but I really *am* James Johnson Sweeney."

I laughed hysterically.

Hans Arp had alerted him to my existence, and Sweeney explained that he was always on the lookout for influential recruits to his chosen cause: Abstract art.

We made a lunch date, which led to warm friendship as time went by.

Jim's Upper East Side condominium featured large, arresting abstractions by modern masters, in a variety of styles. Not one conveyed the merest hint of any subject matter whatsoever.

The first time Sweeney visited my humble digs nearby, he glared slowly around at each picture on the living room walls, and confessed—

"Alex, I'm embarrassed. Unfortunately, I don't RECOGNIZE a single ONE of these artists!"

"The portrait of Anne," I told him, "is by Dickie de Menocal, from our Pinkney Street Artists' Alliance days. All the other paintings are by *me*, so I should be the one to apologize."

During the next few years, Sweeney was exceedingly displeased to see the Guggenheim Museum transformed from an upper Fifth Avenue mansion into an upwardly expanding architectural monument superbly designed by Frank Lloyd Wright.

I once asked the lordly old architect what had been his inspiration for that still astonishing masterpiece, and he replied—

"All I did was turn a Sumerian ziggurat upside-down, round it off, and hollow it out! In my personal creation, the spiritual world spirals graciously downward instead of aspiring jaggedly upward!"

The building can provide receptive visitors with a refreshing spatial and possibly spiritual experience, yes, but on the other hand it makes a precipitously dreadful and even disgraceful exhibition venue.

When I first dropped in on Sweeney at the new, rebuilt, Guggenheim, his secretary asked me to wait while the boss finished "talking to Europe on the telephone." So I wandered forth from his office suite into the museum proper.

Ten minutes later, Jim came bounding after me. "Good *god*, Alex!" he cried, in histrionic despair. "I never meant you should wait out *here!*"

Having been assigned to write a Time cover-story on the graceful, urbanely British leading man Rex Harrison, I began my task by attending the Broadway musical "My Fair Lady" in which he starred. I saw the show twelve times in a row, and the better I got to know it, the more enjoyable the whole production became.

"Sexy Rexy" was an obsessively dedicated performer. He used to endlessly, rehearse each little piece of stage business such as turning on one's heel, for example, while glancing at one's wristwatch, in order to get the timing precisely correct for the character he played at that particular point in the drama.

While interviewing the consummate actor Charles Laughton to elicit quotes for my story, I happened to mention Harrison's intensive rehearsal method.

"Of course!" Laughton told me. "Timing is the most important ingredient of performance."

Surprised, I said: "Really? I thought temperament—"

"No, that comes second."

"Just how do you mean?"

"*MISTER Christian!*" Laughton hissed, launching into one of his furious Captain Bligh set-pieces from "Mutiny on the Bounty."

His impromptu demonstration of temperament and timing alike socked me back in my chair, and seemed to rock the room itself! Unlike Clark Gable in the movie, I actually felt at sea for a minute or two.

Recovering, I asked: "Are temperamental actors hard to handle?"

"Not for me," Laughton replied with his broadly charming smile. "I was born in a briar-patch."

Speaking of temperament, the stupendous Red Sox baseball star Ted Williams was bitterly feuding with the press, plus his Boston fans, back then. Newspaper reporters excoriated the star for not humbly tipping his cap every time he hit a home-run and trotted around the diamond.

That's why Tack decided to spring a non-sportswriter on him. Flying to Florida, for cover-story purposes I spent a Spring Training week with Ted.

SLUGGER

Like an adolescent card
lurking in the high school yard
to grope some passing ass or tit
loose, relaxed, he'd wink, and spit.
Disdaining curves around the plate
knuckleballs and change-ups late
sinkers, splitters, sucker-bait
Ted had the wit to hesitate.
His weapon beckoned
on elliptical wait—

"Hurl a fastball
the kind I like.
Up and in
for Jesus'
sake.
Show me
crushable
Miss Right!

    I respected him as a fellow seeker in our mysterious world—like the artists on my regular beat—so we got along fine.
    The most impressive thing about Ted was his ability to make what Pindar, the ancient Greek celebrant of the Olympic Games, dubbed—
    "The right move at the right moment."
    Muscle and size are relatively unimportant. Ted decoded in milliseconds, and simultaneously translated to his half-sprung, swiftly uncoiling physique, the mingled signals which his cheerily leering eyes received.
    "I love to hit!" he once told me, and I replied—
    "Isn't that because you do it so well?"

"Yeah. I keep my eyes on the ball."

"You must have 20/20 vision."

"Better than that, my friend. Comes a fastball, I can even watch how the seams are spinning."

"Which comes first, seeing, or swatting?"

"This ain't no toothpick!" Ted replied, playfully and rather painfully poking my chest with his bat...

A genuinely great athlete, Williams reigned before booming commercialization and brutalization, powered by the steroids racket, imposed their insidious drag on American education, plus the health of our youth, not to mention ruining sports for some of us.

Track & Field, for example, used to be the prettiest imaginable spectacle, with beautiful-bodied young people performing impossible feats before one's eyes.

Recently, however, while watching an Olympic contest on TV, I was appalled to note that modern-day athletes come coarsened, as it were, by joyless work-outs plus plentiful infusions of performance-enhancing chemicals, be they legal or otherwise.

To use the only word that fits, prostitution desecrates sex and sport alike. It's tragic, I think. No self-reliance there. No pleasurably passing through the physical to discover spiritual value.

On my final night in Sarasota, Williams phoned to invite me home with him for dinner—

"I want you should meet my wife and kids."

"I'm terribly sorry, but I can't," I said.

"What? For Christ's sake, why not?"

"I wish I knew, Ted. It would be quite an honor for me, and I'm grateful, but..."

I've never told this story before. I was totally played out that night, anxious about my own family, intent upon the cover story I still had to write, and in no mood to celebrate as yet.

Sissy, in fact. Tack would have been disgusted...

The eclectic jazz saxophonist Sonny Rollins, who's now in his eighties, was superb at blowing his own right moves through right moments with musical colleagues.

Rollins once took two whole years off from professional life, incredibly enough, while his wife supported them both by secretarial work. As he told the critic Stanley Crouch—

"I left the scene to work on some things because I was getting all of this press and I was near the top of the polls but I wasn't satisfying myself and I didn't feel like I was satisfying the public.

"I wanted to work on my horn. I wanted to study more harmony. I wanted to better myself, and I wanted to get out of the environment of all that smoke and alcohol and drugs.

"In order to avoid disturbing anyone I went up on the Williamsburg Bridge and practiced."

This brings me to Charles Burchfield (1893-1967), whose watercolors engage with change and time itself as passing windows upon eternity.

The artist kept a poignantly poetic journal all his life. Here's a passage dating from May, 1945—

"God's greatest gift to me is the ability to be astonished each year by the incredible beauty of a dandelion. Surely no other plant is so full of the glory of God and his creation. It is beyond all comprehension."

Burchfield and his bride were pious Lutherans who'd raised a family near Buffalo, New York, on his modest income from wallpaper design. When I interviewed him, Mrs. Burchfield kindly sat in. I asked the artist—

"What do you make of Picasso?"

"I don't think he's just sincere."

"You've got a point there," I agreed, "but perhaps a painter of genius ought to be forgiven his aggressively ironic bent."

"Dedication beats pretension," Burchfield serenely informed me. "And pride goes before a fall."

True enough. To quote Pindar once again—

"Single is the race, single, of men and gods. But a difference in power keeps us apart."

Human power tends to drive those who achieve ultimate heights hopping mad. Modern specimens, starting with Stalin and Hitler, spring to mind.

For an old-time example, regard El Greco's portrait of Spain's Grand Inquisitor (ca. 1600) at Manhattan's Metropolitan Museum.

Attired in pink velvet vestments, this queenly figure, appears to be subjectively torn in two. One side of the Inquisitor shows composure, while the other writhes in silent rage. Behind those horn-rimmed spectacles, meanwhile, crazy questions blaze...

One morning, Alfred Stieglitz's widow Georgia O'Keefe called Time magazine's top brass and complained that I had the unconscionable arrogance to keep her waiting.

When I arrived half an hour late for a private preview of her Museum of Modern Art Retrospective, she greeted me gloatingly—

"I've fixed your wagon, my son. You're all washed up at Time!"

Confident that whatever complaint she'd registered had left my bosses unmoved, I laughed, and said: "Good try!"

O'Keeffe seemed to get a kick out of my cheerful reaction. She responded with a wry smile.

As we viewed her show together, picture by picture, during the next two hours, sympathy grew between us.

Her creations encapsulate deep and strong feelings in caressing, darkly brooding style. That goes for her early abstractions, her animal skull and pelvic bone pictures, her poetic evocations of midtown, nighttime Manhattan, her Southwestern landscapes, and finally her profoundly strange flower paintings.

Finally I felt able to pop the question that "Freudian" sophisticates were repeating at cocktail parties—

"Might these blossoms symbolize—?"

"No. They're flowers."

Well, they are, and then again they're a whole lot more than that. Brute symbolism would be less, however, and by no means better.

No true artist is content to merely symbolize. Nor to merely represent!

HESITATION WALTZ

Gertrude Stein's assertion goes
"A rose is a rose is a rose."
That's evident I suppose.
But then again, who knows?

D.H. Lawrence put the case as follows—
"The perfect rose is only a running flame, emerging and flowing off, and never in any sense at rest, static, finished. Herein lies its ecstatic loveliness. The whole tide of all life and all time suddenly heaves, and appears before us."
When I got back to my office, our Managing Editor Roy Alexander dropped by to say he'd received "a call from some hysterical bitch." Roy added that he hoped I would accord her—
"A proper critical roasting."
I once asked Roy why Time had no female writers. His carefully considered reply—
"Because women cry. You can't have that on a weekly magazine."
Time was more than half women, in fact, but the elite among them consisted of "researchers," who cried only to their writers.
I much admired my longtime researcher Ruth Brine, who never cried. Instead, she'd recite my frequent goofs aloud, giggling in her friendly style, and I'd correct them accordingly. Ruth was an exceptional person, by the way, but her story is not for me to tell...
I finally volunteered a cover-story to honor the memory of O'Keeffe's deceased husband Alfred Stieglitz, and proclaim that photography is indeed an art-form.
Although Stieglitz had propagated that simple truth for decades, it had never yet been accepted by the art-critical establishment.

Mid-twentieth century critics regarded "composition" as the foremost virtue of art. Paintings are composed, but they shoot photos don't they?

Well, yes, Walker Evens once confided to me that he would carefully frame in on the subject of his choice, take one step to the left, and shoot!

For my Photography story, Time's crack Cover artist Boris Artzybashev painted an acquisitively ogling humanoid Kodak on the loose. The editorial assumption was that I would be only too happy to justify Artzy's crowd-pulling picture with a joshing text.

But I had other ideas.

My story displeased the magazine's fiercely ambitious Henry Grunwald, who happened to be sitting in that week as our back-of-the-book editor.

Henry sent for me, and ordered in his own peremptory style—

"Reduce the Art angle."

"*What?*"

"This doesn't have to run in Art."

"Where the fuck else?"

"We might switch it to Business, or People."

"You might, might you?"

"Anyhow, give us a witty report on the new national hobby."

"What's that?"

"You know perfectly well. It's called 'Candid Camera' amateur photography.'"

I took a deep breath, stuck my fists into my trouser pockets, counted slowly, in silence, from one to ten, turned around, walked out and went home.

Although I took a taxi as usual, it might as well have been a—

HIGH DUDGEON

I felt fairly
sure I'd shot
my coveted
Time slot
but that
in any case
it's a lot
better
NOT
to "know
one's place."

Stout, squat, redoubtable Grunwald sat up all night, meanwhile, re-writing what he regarded as a rotten piece to suit himself.

From Henry's viewpoint, my effort to firmly establish the genius of Stieglitz and the dignity of photography was portentous and ill-timed, whereas the Candid Camera craze made commercially heady news.

This hairy stand-off may well have been crucial to both Henry's career and mine. We never held it against each other because—after a day or two of fuming—both of us understood that our quarrel was nothing personal.

It so happened that Henry loved the magazine as possessively as I did art, and vice-versa.

Resourceful, quietly forceful, Henry kept on rising to become Time's Managing Editor, and eventually Editorial Director of Time Inc.

He and his feudal Time-lords gazed smilingly down upon me as a red-bearded Bear of Little Brain, endowed with a grizzly temper and a strange heart where my cotton stuffing ought to reside.

2. Giant Frog

From the late 1940's through the 1950's, Red-baiting was the rage in our unaccountably nervous nation. When Salvador Dali proclaimed: "Picasso is a Communist; neither am I!" nobody laughed.

United States Senators stooped to snoop under the bed of "Modern Art," and jumped. Although I joked about such matters in my Art Section, I knew better than to dwell on them.

Back then, Time was something unthinkable today: a liberal Republican publication. Fiercely patriotic and idealistic in the old American tradition, our owner H.R. Luce devoutly cherished Culture, promoted Capitalism, opposed Democrats, loathed Communists, and coldly disdained radicals.

The two foremost "social-realist" painters on Manhattan's mid-century scene were Philip Evergood and Ben Shahn. While warmly reviewing their work, I was diplomatic enough to "weasel" and address its protest politics in an off-handed, even humorous, manner.

Not long before his death, Evergood sent me a kindly letter saying that he had always counted me among his strongest supporters. Oh, the irony! As I'd confessed in a free-lance piece which someone must have passed on to him, I accorded that great-hearted artist less than half the credit he deserved.

Walker Evans was close friends with Ben Shahn, so he brought Ben and me together. Like Evans, Ben practiced documentary photography. But he never exhibited the photos, preferring to use them as source material for his acerbic, powerful paintings.

I once headlined a favorable review: "More Mellow Shahn." At our next encounter, bulky Ben jovially backed me up against a wall, bellowing—

"*I haven't mellowed; YOU'VE mellowed!*"

Untrue. But since then, thanks to the kindly hand of time (with a small "t") perhaps I have eased up a little.

Much as I admired Shahn's and Evergood's art, I had to admit that the supreme revolutionary painters of the period were not North American but south of the border. Namely, Mexico's Big Three: Jose Clemente Orozco, Alfredo Siqueiros, and especially Diego Rivera.

Fortunately for me, a new Rivera mural unveiled at Mexico City's swank Reforma Hotel created considerable scandal, since it centered upon a banner reading—

"*DIOS NO EXISTE*"

I had no Spanish as yet, but Rivera's English was said to be fluent. So I seized the chance to persuade my superiors that Rivera was "Time-worthy" despite his atheist self. After some fussing, the folks in charge let me fly to Mexico and do a Cover story on the artist.

This was my first encounter with a true Citizen of the World. "One third Indian, one third Jewish, and one third Chinese," as he wishfully lied.

Rivera was in fact a schoolteacher's son, born on the Feast of the Immaculate Conception, December 8, 1886, of Aztec, Spanish, Portuguese, and Jewish descent.

Like many another traveler to Mexico, I soon developed a case of diarrhea, or "Montezuma's Revenge," as it was all too familiarly known.

"Never mind," said Rivera. "I'll take you to a beautiful wicked witch of my acquaintance, for an instant cure."

After driving some distance in his chauffeured limousine through the gathering Mexico City dusk, we got out to thread a maze of narrow alleyways on foot. Minutes later, we stopped beside a green door in a high wall.

Rivera pressed the doorbell. A butler appeared and admitted us to a walled garden, with a plashing fountain. From there we entered an elegant, snow-white studio.

Our laughingly dignified hostess wore a low-cut, cream-colored evening dress. She seemed a ripe, deep dish indeed, like a burnished brown clay casserole.

The lady ordered up a special cup of tea for me. When I drank the bitter brew straight down at her command, my intestinal churning instantaneously ceased. What might I have imbibed? The majestically sexy woman told me—

"Powdered cock's wattles, boiled with electric eel."

Was our hostess a witch? It's by no means impossible, But I'm certain that she was also Rivera's mid-life love, Lupe Marin, with whom he had two daughters and whom he'd abandoned for a fling with Edward Weston's former model and mistress, shapely Tina Mondotti.

Insatiably lustful and urgently romantic at heart, Rivera loved and left a good many women, notably including the Hollywood film star Paulette Goddard, while mostly managing to remain friends.

He had famously transformed the small chapel for Catholic worship at Chapingo into a secular shrine dedicated to Lupe Marin, who presides in a lunette above the chapel's interior doors. There she's a passively voluptuous figure with long black hair. Stretched out on the ground, she cradles a cactus plant in the hollow of one hand. Directly opposite, on what was once the altar wall, Lupe shows herself in full glory, pregnant, as if with the Sun itself. Finally, to bring myth down into history, Lupe reappears enslaved. A soldier, a priest, and a financier, fence the woman in.

At Chapingo, half a century ahead of his time, with Lupe's modeling assistance, Rivera conveyed tender reverence for Mother Earth herself. The artist was not only militant "Red" but prescient "Green" as well.

The Chapingo frescoes strongly reminded me of Giotto's Arena Chapel at Padua. I asked Rivera if that had been his inspiration. He nodded, and said—

"What a pity Giotto worked for the Church! The poor bastard had no choice."

"You both enhance the world," I responded, "with your warm-heartedness. But Giotto must have felt beholden to Catholicism, not the Church of Rome."

"Just how do you know that?"

"Well, aren't you beholden to Communism, rather than the Russian state?"

Rivera smiled: "You're talking useless sentiment, from outside the Worker's Struggle. Our war probably appears unreal to you."

"Unreal, no," I told him. "Hopeless, maybe."

The day after my diarrhea cure, I asked Rivera what he thought of Mexican folk art. "Let's visit a market," he suggested, "and see."

We spent half an hour wandering around a city square crammed with temporary booths and oil-cloth mats spread out on the pavement. Hand-crafted toys, leather-work, and silver-work adorned the mats, and the booths were festooned with hand-woven clothes.

At last Rivera stopped to chat with a white-bearded old fellow who sat like a rock on his oil-cloth. Half a dozen papier-mâché animal masks lay fanned around the artist's knees. They stared up at us, empty-eyed.

The monkey, the goat, the jaguar, the dog, the bull, and the fox, were plainly on a par with Aztec and Mayan fragments dug up by archeologists. They seemed to study my inquiring self.

Rivera discussed each mask with the artist. Then he purchased them, one at a time. Finally, he handed the whole lot to me, and told the mask-maker something that sounded like: "They're for my friend here, from New York."

"I'll treasure each one," I promised, "and so will my family."

Rivera impressed me so much that I made him an impulsive offer. If he were willing to cooperate in the creation of a definitive critical biography with lots of direct quotations, I said, why then I'd resign my post at Time in order to research and write such a volume.

That was idiotic, of course. Any such venture would have wrecked my career. Kindly keeping a straight face, Rivera declined, saying he required a Communist biographer.

One day at Frida's Coyoacan villa, Rivera generously shared their pre-Columbian ceramic collection with me. I would turn each statuette between my fingers for a few minutes of silence and then hand it back to him.

We seemed lost in the same dream, until he exclaimed: "I have to kiss Frida!," and bounded balloon-like up the stairs. A minute later he reappeared on the upstairs landing, and beckoned.

Black-browed, blunt-faced Frida Khalo was a marvelous painter too, although unappreciated back then.

Her panel called "What the Water Brought Me" offers a bathtub view, from the bathing Frida's own head, of her bare feet sticking up on both sides of the faucet. The warm tub water seethes with slippery objects and nude figures grouped around a volcano from which the Empire State Building projects.

Because of a girlhood accident to her spine, Frida was compelled to stretch out flat much of the time. I found her in that supine position now, with a darkly attractive companion. They lay naked, arm in arm, beneath a white linen sheet. Since there was no place else for me, I sat beside the women on the bed.

The stranger's slanted brow and high-arched Mayan nose contrasted sharply with Frida's rather feline features, while her burnt-umber skin complemented Frida's sepia complexion. There was something shadow-cool and serpent-like about Frida's guest, whereas she herself exuded a jaguar aroma.

Puckishly, as if to establish her priority on the scene, the stranger stuck out her wet pink tongue at me!

Ignoring that egregiously pretty provocation, I asked Frida for a quote concerning her husband. Could she say something suitable for publication by Time?

In barely halting English, Frida replied—

"Diego's a giant frog, with golden eyes, and I'm a small red bird, happy to hop about in his green shadow."

Presiding in the only chair, Diego smiled hospitably. The tile floor seemed to tilt down in the direction of his weighty presence.

"You have penetrated the innermost sanctum," he announced. "And so, my friend, it's up to you. Ask whatever you dare!"

Folding my hands in my lap to conceal its up-thrust, I replied—

"Thank you. Jaguars and serpents often appear together in pre-Columbian temple sculptures. The guidebooks tell us nobody knows why. But you must know?"

Rivera surged up from his seat. His boulder belly overshadowed us. Rubbing his sensitive small, plump, hands together, he explained—

"Jaguars are thunder, and serpents are lightning."

"Gotcha," I told him. "Right now I must get back to my hotel and put these nifty quotes on record!"

Commissioning Rivera to do a self-portrait for Time, I promised him that we would print it on the magazine's cover precisely as painted.

He chose to caricature himself, with page-bulging plasticity, as a beaming giant yam, flanked by a small Halloween pumpkin. Paper scraps swirled up from Rivera's sidekick of a pumpkin, to halo him in effect.

That inclusion referred to Time's recent Senior Editor Whittaker Chambers. None of us at Time suspected that he was a one-time Communist fanatic and spy for Russia, who had subsequently converted to equally extreme patriotic conservatism.

Whit was doubly cracked, in fact.

For fear that either Russian Communist agents or FBI sleuths might search his house, Chambers had hollowed out a pumpkin in his garden and stuffed it with documents from his spying days.

Then, to expose the State Department's prestigious Alger Hiss among others, he'd finally presented his pumpkin with its contents to Senator Richard Nixon's "Committee on Un-American Activities." At that point, Whit also stood exposed of course, and forced to surrender his position at Time.

Rivera's artful gag was published intact by us, as I'd promised. Since few people really look at pictures, the pumpkin went practically unnoticed, believe it or not, and my Cover story was enthusiastically received.

Emboldened by the success of my Rivera venture, I soon offered to write a Cover story on Pablo Picasso.

Dana Tasker convened a conference to consider my new proposal. Almost everyone present opposed it "on principle." Tack himself summed up the case against—

"Picasso's a Commie, he's immoral, and he hates us. The Spic won't even accept calls from our Paris Bureau."

"No problem," I said.

"No? Why not"

"Because he'll see *me!*"

Predictably, Tack howled with glee at my extreme presumption. Then, following a minute or two of thought, he decided—

"Okay. You can go ahead and try. First class all the way. Now listen up. If that Time-hating Pinko turns you from his door, don't come back here. Consider yourself *fired!*"

3. Lines in Sand

"I do not seek, I find," Picasso proclaimed.

What is to be found, first of all, in his tall, early (1903) image called *Boy Leading a Horse*?

By an invisible halter, boyish Picasso leads his delicately splendid, mist-trailing steed into dry, dusty-pink desert country. Perhaps the Twentieth Century? Might the horse represent Picasso's own Imagination?

Painted only four years later, in 1907, *Demoiselles d'Avignon* appears to depict Moorish prostitutes whose flamenco-streaked cadences and twisting gesticulations recall El Greco's attenuated saints.

But these creatures are more to be feared than revered. Their sharp-angled, proto-cubist shapes also relate to Native African wood sculptures.

Picasso badly needed women, and loved quite a few. Their attractions, pains, and vengeful passions, obsessed him. No other painter ever created so varied, extended and compulsively dark-toned a gallery of the subject.

He painted *Guernica* in Paris during the Spanish Civil War of the mid-1930's. This large pictorial protest refers to Franco's saturation-bombing of a Spanish Basque town called Guernica, by Nazi Air Force "volunteers."

(For those who don't recall the situation, I note that Nazi Germany gleefully abetted one side of that prophetic conflict, and Communist Russia slyly sustained the other.)

Swirling with crumpled newspapers amid black winds, Picasso's picture precipitates the viewer into midnight chaos containing just a few smashed plaster figures, a broken sword, an astonished woman, a grieving one with a slain infant, a horse in torment, and a bull in shock.

Illumination is provided by a kerosene lamp, plus a naked light bulb suspended out of nowhere in place of the sun. Also, a huge flash, as of a bomb explosion, coming from in front of the picture, where one stands looking. It's as if one's own little cranium just burst wide open....

I flew to Europe via Gander, Labrador (for re-fueling) ensconced in a British bomber which had been made over as a luxury airliner with sleeping-births, plus an all-night bar down where the bombs had previously nestled.

London was my first destination, because I planned to approach Roland Penrose, the wealthy anarchist painter, there. Picasso's biographer John Richardson relates that Sir Roland—

"Offered up his future wife, Lee Miller, the American photographer, to the artist when they all spent the summer of 1938 at the same hotel in Mougins."

Lee Miller had previously served as assistant and mistress to the Surrealist photographer Man Ray, who adored her. She'd also starred in Jean Cocteau's marvelous film, "The Blood of a Poet." Then, during World War Two, she gained fleeting fame as a photo-journalist. Her most talked-about shot, following Allied victory, presents us with an imperturbable nude Lee alone in Hitler's bathtub at Bergtesgarten, demurely sponging herself off.

Having been assured that the Penrose couple enjoyed helping people, I dared hope that they might provide me with an introduction to their intimate friend Picasso. Instead, they threw a garden party.

With her hair swirling loose and her svelte hips swinging in a clinging frock, Lee stepped shoeless, adorned with beetle-green toenail paint, amongst the guests. She lightly carried her infant son Roger (who was to become a noted mathematician) in her arms.

The mostly male celebrants were a shabby and badly depressed bunch. Not even our convivial hostess could animate those upper-crust representatives of victorious Britain's battered, impoverished and exhausted condition.

Lee wore a gold bracelet in the form of handcuffs, with both links clamped on the same wrist. When I admired it, she explained—

"*A nice anniversary present from Roland. He designed it, and Tiffany made it.*"

Might Lady Penrose have relished boudoir rituals of a sort that most women would regard as boring, not to say uncomfortable?

The psychologist William Moulton Marston, who invented both the lie-detector test and the famed comic strip *Wonder Woman*, opined—

"*Women are exciting for this one reason. They enjoy submission.*"

I beg to differ. Among the eighteen women with whom I've been physically intimate, one alone manifested a masochist proclivity.

Drawing me aside at last, Lee confided—

"*Pablo never reads letters or answers phone calls. But never mind. You must ambush the man at his secret Communist headquarters. Here, I've drawn you a treasure map of the place, with an X to mark the spot where he always sits.*"

Reaching Paris, I contacted a Minotaur-like Picasso crony named Oscar Dominguez, the latest lover of Countess Marie-Laure de Nouailles.

TRAVEL TIP

En belle Paree
mon cher monsieur
enjoy *Madame's*
derriere au poire.

Que voulez-vous
de plus encore?
Who could ask for
anything more?

    Oscar's delicate idea-pieces included a figurine of a pony entangled with a bicycle. "My next," he confided, "will be an all-enveloping super lion!"
    He had recently quarreled with Picasso, however, so no help there.
    Despite her title and inherited millions. Marie-Laure was motherly, cultivated, and modest. "Unfortunately," she confessed with a sigh, "Pablo has turned against us *both*."
    "May I ask why?"
    "Perhaps because Francoise hates my guts. Either that, or the monster personally objects to my growing fat!"
    The next contact on my Paris list was Broncia Talcoat, the hospitable toast of bohemian Montparnasse.
    We took to each other, somehow, and soon we were making love at her *Rue de Plaisance* studio.
    Having ejaculated thrice in a three-hour stretch, I told her—
    "No more please. I'm just dead!"
    "*Non, non, et non,*" she remonstrated, sitting up and pointing to explain—
    "*You've not yet fallen out of bed onto the floor!*"
    A fourth fuck followed forthwith. This had happened only once before in my life, aboard an American Southern Express train.

Days later, Broncia and I threw an expense-account bash to which she invited a host of art world friends. Purpose: to develop some fresh leads.

Our guests all agreed, however, that I would never get to see Picasso.

He consorted with millionaire collectors, international celebrities, radical French poets, matadors, and Catalan hangers-on, but never gave the press a look-in, regarding journalists as the slimiest possible form of scum.

While continuing to brush up my French on Broncia's pillow, I reconsidered my position, or rather the pickle into which I had fallen.

If I failed to interview Picasso, I could not return to *Time*. My journalistic career would crash. Plus, I dreaded disappointing Tack, the most irritating and yet secretly sympathetic editor I ever had.

Tack never once told me how he felt, but generously supported my personal reliance on direct experience of art and artists.

Picasso's roving eyes were famished black, I'd heard, like twinned tar-pits. I had only one hope left. Namely, to hit upon a means of attracting that avid gaze.

The most seductive girl at our party had been an American fashion model named Pati Hill. She worked for the Paris couturier Edward Molyneux, and her French was far superior to my college boy variety.

It occurred to me that Pati might do. Minus make-up, and clad in a pale blue satin slip, she could well resemble a "Blue Period" Picasso!

Contacting the girl again, I asked if she'd be willing to try out for the part. She laughingly complied. *Voila!* Pati was perfect, and ready to fall in with my scheme.

The next day, we flew to Nice. Just above the Maritime Alps, our eleven-passenger plane was struck and enveloped by lightning. It dropped precipitously. We were not strapped in. To keep Pati's momentarily weightless, flat-cushioned chassis from crumpling up against the cabin roof, I hurled myself athwart her.

Thereupon, heaving a deep sigh, she arched her pelvic region ecstatically up against me! Was that in fear for her life, or a demonstration of affection?

At dinner that night, I inquired about it.

"All I can say for certain," she responded, "is that the incident impressed my biffer state."

"Biffer?" I asked her.

"Yep. The state between two buffer states."

With its dark volcanic sand, the beach at Golfe Juan was perhaps the least fashionable stretch on the whole French Riviera. I possessed Lee Miller Penrose's sketch of the area.

Picasso apparently preferred it for sunbathing, plus occasional waist-high dips in the sea. Surrounded by a scattering of local children and their mothers, he must have felt relatively secure from snoopy interlopers.

Luck was with us. During our very first visit to the beach, Pati and I discovered the great man seated at ease on the warm sand with Francoise Gilot and little Claude.

Sauntering at my side along the water's edge in her abbreviated, smoothly clinging "Blue Period" costume, Pati kept pausing to stoop and bend for the ostensible purpose of collecting a seashell or ceramic shard from the sand, making sure, meanwhile, to flourish her shapely bottom in Picasso's direction.

"Don't look yet," she told me, "but he's going for it!"

Women always know. Picasso soon beckoned us over.

Oval-faced and classically beautiful in body, with her columnar neck and maternally full bosom, Francoise chose to snub Pati and me.

Getting up at once she turned away in her high-cut bathing costume, stretched, and stooped to gather up her infant son Claude. Coarse grains of black beach sand adhered to her firm pink posterior. My gaze clung too, as she doubtless felt.

With the baby in her arms, Francoise waded obliquely in amongst the glittering wavelets. At that point, she dropped her fleshly dimension and metamorphosed into a new, neo-classical Picasso—an astonishing incarnation of the *Cote d' Azure*.

To confess my connection with *Time* would have ruined everything, so I passed us off as American art students who naturally worshipped his work.

"I have only one question," I said. "What's the secret of your incredibly assured draftsmanship?"

Picasso nodded. He leaned over to regard the smooth sand at his knees. After a time, he incised the sand with a brief thumb line as straight as Francoise's frown.

He paused, and then, extending a forefinger, crossed the straight line with a curving one, like Francoise's rear.

Stumped, I stared at Picasso's diagram. A few minutes passed in silence. Sparkling sand-grains slipped down into the incisions he'd made.

ENIGMA

These two lines
incised in sand
by that wrinkled
sorcerer's hand—

How might they
perceive me?
As a question
mark maybe?

I raised my eyes to meet the cannon-mouth black of the artist's gaze. At last he spoke—

"When I draw a straight line, it's STRAIGHT, and when I draw a curve, it CURVES."

"*Merci,*" I told him gratefully. "*Je comprend.*"

Picasso had kindly underlined a creative principle that puts both passive precision and accurate representation in the shade.

I refer to mindfulness of one's own spiritual freedom, the most important element in human life and art alike.

4. Color Carver

Picasso's kindness had given me sufficient courage to phone Matisse's number at Nice. The old and ailing genius responded cordially.

"*Mais oui,*" he said at once. "I know your work, thanks to my son Pierre. He's sent me some of your reviews. Come right over, won't you? I have an urgent message to make public."

Matisse's longtime model, manager, and companion Lydia Delectorskaya, met us at their door. She seemed afraid that I might trip or faint.

Taking my hand in a warm grip, she led us to a pair of low chairs beside Matisse's sick-bed, and then drifted off to make coffee.

White-bearded, smiling cool welcome, Matisse reclined like a King Arthur of art, propped up against the massive bed pillows.

Thanks to some unaccountable increase of human laziness, he told us in his precise French, the whole future of painting hung in the balance.

"Young artists ought to work much harder," Matisse went on. "Above all, they should learn to draw!"

"*D'accord,*" I said. "Wasn't it Ingres who remarked that drawing is the probity of art?

"*Precisement.*"

"How about your own drawing?"

"*Comment?*"

"Does that come first, or is color more important?"

"One has to modify the colors to accord with the contours, and vice versa, for the sake of harmony."

"That's what you achieve," Pati offered. "Harmony."

"*Vous avez raison.* This has always been my chief problem. By definition, you see, incommensurables never balance out."

"In that case," I asked, "is aesthetic balance just an illusion?"

"Not at all. It's a free action. Understand?""

"I'm trying," I said.

"Well, since the cancer operation on my colon, I myself have been working with greater freedom!"

The cheerful heroism expressed in that remark astounded me. I couldn't think what to reply.

"We saw Picasso yesterday," Pati put in. "He sends you his love."

"*Tres bien.* He gave me a little picture recently."

"I noticed that as we came in," I said. "The owl strikes a sober note."

"*Vraiment.* It's an unconscious self-portrait. Or did you notice that as well? I sent him a Moroccan dress in return."

Pati beamed with surprise: "Why a dress?"

"I thought he'd enjoy painting Francoise in that. The skirt is so stiff with embroidery!"

Matisse had recently capped his career by creating a portfolio of colored paper cut-outs called *Jazz*.

Was he a jazz fan? I don't doubt that for a minute.

My own favorite among his cut-outs (which I gleefully reproduced in *Time*) was a concise coda to Pieter Brueghel the Elder's masterpiece: *The Fall of Icarus*.

Matisse's version frames starkly in upon a red hearted silhouette in free-fall. It suggests one's own shadow careening floppily down upon oneself through sun-struck cobalt sky.

Or might this represent the terminally ill artist?

As if he'd been reading my thoughts, Matisse reached over to his bedside table. Triumphantly, he held up his scissors and hand-colored paper sheets—

"*Michelangelo carved stone; I carve color!*"

"You do!" I said.

"*Alors!* One's best work should come last."

"True," Pati said, "but that can't be easy! Where do you find the strength?"

"God knows!" After a thoughtful silence, he added, "I'll soon surpass myself with the Chapel of the Rosary at Vence. It's actually something for my friends, the dear nuns there, one of whom nursed me through a crisis. Now, why should an old *fauve'* like me complete his career with so pious a flourish?"

He watched me cast about for some reply. Then, with a compassionate sigh, he said—

"You'll understand the matter very well, my friend, but only in your own good time."

How could I possibly tap into Matisse's acute gray-blue vision? It was now or never, so I asked—

"*Maitre,* what should I MYSELF do in life?"

His first response was what seemed a coldly searching glance. His second was silence. I waited, blushing I suppose, for two or three minutes. Then like music to my aching wilderness, came this vatic advice—

"*Do whatever you like. But keep your Naiveté. That will be all you've got, some day.*"

The French word carries no derogatory connotation. Instead, it suggests clear-eyed innocence and naked sensitivity.

Such things are regarded as okay for the kiddies but inappropriate for the prime of life, and simply pathetic in the aged. You can't successfully pursue business, politics, medicine, law, or war, in an innocent mode.

No, but naiveté helps one to participate creatively in the arts and sciences. Also, to interact with others, especially lovers and children. Plus, let's not forget, to enjoy life instead of fighting it to the death!

Unlike Picasso, Matisse could not cause astonishing concatenations of contours and colors to appear at the imperious command of his visualizing mind and painting hand.

Instead, he let them happen of their own accord.

The artist's "odalisques" have struck some connoisseurs as frivolously voluptuous. When you look long enough, however, the women he portrayed encapsulate curving gestures of the constellations…

Ideally, each of the two partners in a sexual conjunction feels at the very center of the space/time continuum, and communes with the other's equal centrality.

Exalted composure follows from such occasions, and cosmological calm of the ideal *après* sex sort imbued Matisse's oeuvre. The older he got, the more so.

Matisse created pretty much by instinct, and played his violin for relaxation. His drive was to generate, via contour combined with color, what he called—

"A soothing and calming influence on the mind, rather like a good armchair which provides relaxation from physical fatigue."

For Matisse himself, however, art was never a comfy chair; more like a bed of nails. In a letter to his daughter, Matisse once confessed that he felt condemned to blunder about a labyrinth whose ceiling exit never opened except on moonless nights—

"The little stump of a candle left by the memory of his predecessors casts no light on the way ahead, only on what lies behind. An artist is made so he can't go back without giving himself up for dead. He must go forward in whatever direction his efforts may carry him. For every generation, the ground behind you is quicksand."

Stubbornly conscientious, Matisse was subject to debilitating storms of emotion. Women obsessed him as they did Picasso, and an endless array of obliging beauties drew him into union.

The heritage he left us resembles a mountain range rising to snowy heights of voluptuary calm, purity, and levity. Upon his death at eighty-five, in 1954, an inexplicable sorcery also expired…

It's no secret that we're drowning in data-bloat, visual overload, slanted information, clotted expertise, and popover pretense. Horrifying images, dispiriting warnings, veiled threats and greed-inducing offers besiege our brains. So how can we keep mentally healthy?

Pollution, such as blood on one's hands leading to terrible retribution, was the basic ingredient of ancient Greek tragedy. Pagan religion remained more joyful than fearful, even so, and purification rituals customarily preceded its mystery rites.

For instance, the pilgrims privileged to approach Apollo's Oracle at Delphi began by bathing in the cold Castalian spring. Thus they gained the naked sensitivity required for what lay ahead.

Wouldn't renewal of innocence make us all the more vulnerable to pollution of the psyche? No, not necessarily, because innocence resembles hope. She's an elusive butterfly, with antennae of humor and sympathy.

There is no static essence in our brains, nor anything so glassy-smooth and serene as to reliably reflect the passing show. One's consciousness is not at all like Stendhal's "mirror walking along a main road." Instead, this resembles the path itself.

FLOWER POWER

Through the garden, ardently
a pollinating bumblebee
rumbles humming past my ear.

Roses blush, bluebells ring
Morning glories gladly sing
"Rimsky Korsakov was here!"

Returning to *Time* magazine, I composed a ten-page in-house memorandum for Tack, recounting most of my adventures. He proudly passed the piece on up to our ultimate boss, for comment.

Henry Robinson Luce contented himself with drawing a blue circle around my least fortunate phrase "words cannot explain," and brusquely noting in the margin,

"If words cannot explain, what the heck does Eliot think he's doing on *Time's* masthead?"

Perhaps I should have felt offended, or challenged at least. Instead I thought—

"That's a good question!"

Tack meanwhile sensed that Luce had lost faith in him. Feeling forlorn, doubtless, but not admitting any such thing, he moved over to a picture magazine called Look.

Eleven more long years would pass before I made my own final escape from Time's weirdly demanding and hugely rewarding clutch...

After Henri Matisse died, I returned to test his prophesy concerning the Dominican Chapel of the Rosary at Vence. Would I really "understand the matter very well," as he'd promised? In fact I was overwhelmed.

While designing and pushing through his final achievement, Matisse had found himself boxed in between deliberate obstruction from locally powerful Communist politicians, and aloof resistance by Roman Catholic officials.

Many false starts occurred. Financing came from the artist's own pocket, and he made a full-out sacrifice of whatever strength remained in his invalid frame. The old artist's crowning glory carries forward what our stone age ancestors created in their Basque-region cavern paintings.

Matisse's final masterpiece also revels in reverent animism. At Vence, however, the animals are colors!

Physically, colors remain a matter of vibration, like music, as Gauguin observed. But that's just their atomic substratum. They also have qualities, intensities, values, virtues, lives and even stories of their own.

In Christian iconography, for instance, the Virgin Mary often wears a red garment to signify her supportive Earth virtue. Her blue mantle, on the other hand, manifests Mary's subtly nurturing Air virtue.

Moreover, the gold backgrounds in surviving Byzantine mosaics, plus Greek and Russian Orthodox icons, represent a timeless and spaceless zone of activity.

William Butler Yeats once wrote—

Oh sages, standing in God's holy fire
As in the gold mosaic of a wall...
Consume my heart away; sick with desire
And fastened to a dying animal.

Born of sunshine, Matisse's colors slant in through the stained glass windows to cast abstract blue and yellow patterns down and around the Chapel's cool white interior. One sees those first. Slowly, one's eyes adjust to take in the black-line Madonna, Saint Dominic, and the graffiti-like, furiously poignant Stations of the Cross on the shining white tiles. Flooded with colored light, the tiles become space and the drawings sing out.

"God held my hand," their terminally ill creator exulted. "I've never drawn better!"

It has been said that when the nuns in charge of his culminating masterpiece asked Matisse if he would let them inter his body there, he felt devastated.

That would be natural enough. Surely he never dreamt of building his own mausoleum. His final achievement is a vessel of Surface, Space, Color, Contour, and Spirit.

Matisse's grave rests on a hillside donated by the city of Nice. There's a stone slab carved by his son Jean, under three trees: an olive, a fig, and a bay tree which grew up out of the ground all by itself, a decade after his burial...

My final visit to the Chapel of the Rosary occurred shortly after my mother died. I stumbled in, distraught, to kneel at the altar. Mistakenly supposing myself to be alone, I soon collapsed, groaning, on the floor.

The charitable Sisters rushed to comfort me. When I apologized for my behavior, they said it was no surprise. Once or twice a week, some visitor would break down!

Taking me into the vestry's shadowy quiet, the nuns drew forth and displayed half a dozen chasubles intended for wear while celebrating Mass on particular feast days. Matisse had designed them in cut paper, and the Sisters had executed each one in colored silks.

Weirdly enough, priests alone were permitted to don those magnificent works, hence the nuns simply held them outspread. The Easter chasuble was pure white, I recall, with a spray of gleaming leaf-forms in gold.

Observing that their chasubles aroused my intense interest, restoring me to good cheer, the nuns giggled with pleasure. Then the eldest opened a cabinet containing a crystal flask and a small glass. For medicinal purposes, she kindly served me a tongue-puckering gentian cordial, which recalled Mom's favorite flower.

HOW IT IS

The
pain
passes
but the
beauty
stays
on

Book Four: Mythosphere

Sweet Mysteries of Life

    Serenade for the Underpaid

    Three Poets

    Big Band Leader

    Soothing Laughter

    The Origin of Deities

    Portraiture on Purpose

    The Reciprocity Tightrope

1. Serenade for the Underpaid

Last night I was kept awake by a neighbor's dog who persisted in baying at the brilliant full moon. Swallowing my annoyance, I sensed a wistful, wild streak in him.

Genetic evidence suggests that canines first appeared on the central Asian steppe some fifteen thousand years ago, thanks to peaceful adjustments made between the wolf species and ours.

How did it happen? We'll never know, but I myself imagine fur-clad people huddled around a campfire, joyfully cooking up and feasting upon a lucky kill, whilst a few starving wolves just beyond the fire-lit circle howl their hearts out. Conceivably, someone suggested—

"*Why not toss the poor things some nice, meaty bones? It won't hurt us any, because we've got plenty, and it might even persuade the wolf deity not to hate our kind!*"

That could have been the start of our interrelationship.

A SHAGGY DOG'S STORY

In the beginning
was the wolf
I mean WOOF.
Later came
the WARP.

Arf, arf!

Being relatively short-lived and powerless, dogs stand in the same relation to people as we are to the gods. Companionable canines still shower us with such services as guarding, guiding, hunting, shepherding, pulling sleds, policing, soldiering, and sniffing out edible, useful, dangerous, or symptomatic substances.

Plus, most important of all, emotional support.

A woodcut artist named Andrea Aleiati created Europe's most popular 16th century volume, which he called *"Emblemata."* This features and extols the goddess Hope, because she springs eternally.

Aleiati favored crows in particular. They may seem to take a sardonic, mocking, croaking tone, but he presents them as divine emissaries—

"The crow is the most faithful of augurs because, when he cannot say 'All is well' he says 'All will be well.'"

Might human tongues, like canine ones, be lunar-fired? Did the appearing and disappearing, waxing and waning moon, help to generate languages on our planet?

Surely Saint John the Evangelist was a poet at heart. His Gospel opens with a highly paradoxical assertion, as follows—

> *In the Beginning*
> *was the Word*
> *And the Word*
> *was with God*
> *And the Word*
> *was God*

How could a "Word" be divine?

This vexing question takes me back to the Book of Genesis—

"And out of the ground the Lord God formed every beast of the field and every fowl of the air; and brought them unto Adam to see what he would call them. And whatsoever Adam called every living creature, that was the name thereof."

The Bible suggests that the very first specific words were Adam's, drawn forth by God the Word. I don't believe a word of that, but it sounds terrific...

If Herman Melville had interviewed a humpbacked whale on one of his voyages, we would now possess—

THE TALE OF A WHALE

Mother's humming
thrumming mind
informed me that
'd been designed
to traverse twelve
thousand miles
with her guidance
and perform
a low-down
Halleluiah
peculiar to our
cetaceous kind.

It's better to suffer the slings and arrows of outrageous critics than to endure the shame of never having expressed one's doubtless beastly self.

Hence, elk and their ilk utter haunted calls at rutting time, angry gorillas hand-drum their own sonorous bosoms, skylarks melodiously arise to greet the sun, and Gospel-singing crickets convene each summer to urgently address America.

INTERMINABLE OVERTURE

The jubilance of grasshoppers
is insistent enough to bore
suburbanites out of their
obscurely twisted
underwear.

"Oh, shush that shrill hubbub"
folks bleakly squeak
in their despair
"Lest we rush
back to town for
emergency repair!"

"Ah, there's the rub!"
as Hamlet said.
He'd flubbed the dub
at Elsinore
but married fair
Ophelia
a fabulous
masseuse in bed.

Assuming Herman Melville had also stepped ashore in Africa to converse with a passing land animal, then what?

ZEBRAIC THESES

Around here, things get kinda tough.
Sometimes I gotta gallop off.
Der Gotterdammerung ist gute.
You should remove that silly suit!

Zebras can't converse in German.
Just a few fine phrases, Herman.
Normally, we're Anglophone,
with a down-south whinny-tone.

Black on white, or the reverse,
we're conspicuous of course.
Brightly striped at every stride,
we often run, but we can't hide.

Hyenas hang around and snicker.
Ocelots lope a whole lot quicker.
Elephants have awesome noses
which they use as cooling hoses.

Lions gloatingly chomp on us.
Hippos prefer water lotus.
Peacocks pose; parrots chatter.
You folks resemble the latter.

Pliny the Elder, the classical Roman historian and naturalist, relates that once each year, in barbarous Gaul, when December was ending and the moon's reflective power approached full flower, Gallic Druids used to convene beneath a sacred oak bearing the mistletoe.

This bloom appears at midwinter, high amid the naked branches of oaks overhead. Here's a sometime plant that's taken flight, bird-like, to nest aloft in the coldest season.

Her dark green leaves and milky berries offer a brave example of self-shaping.

ON THE LONGEST NIGHT

A bearded High Priest robed in white,
climbs the Tribe's pivotal oak tree.
With a golden sickle he cuts free
its mistletoe food of the solar deity.

Afterward, a pair of snow-white oxen
undergo sacrifice for Father Sun.
They'll head south in spirit form
to draw the solar wagon home again.

When Earth's distant life-source is furthest removed from those of us in the northern hemisphere, it seems to hesitate at the Winter Solstice. Could we possibly help the sun turn back north in our direction?

Humanity's first big ambition has been entirely forgotten for a long time now. Yet Christmastime festivities do still occur on schedule.

HALLUCINATION

While driving over the Dordogne
one day when I was fairly young
I happened on a grove of oaks.

Tall, wet black, unbending folks
who snapped twig-fingers to defy
the frigid, furiously whining wind.

Getting out, I strolled about.
Huge icicles festooned the grove
and one fell crashing from above.

I spun around, tripped on a rock,
tumbled over backward
and collapsed in shock.

A troop of horsemen, eager hounds,
cast merry gleams around the scene.
Hunting horns made happy sounds.

Three monarchs clad in forest green,
with frosty beards and crowns of jade,
came riding, gliding through the glade!

    The mathematician, geographer, chronologist, and astronomer Claudius Ptolomeus superbly exemplified late Hellenistic culture.
    Ptolemy carried three extra strings (poetry, music, and astrology) underneath his specialties. Thus he resembled a fiddle of the resonant "Hardanger Fjord" variety. He proclaimed—

*I'm aware of being
mortal and ephemeral.
Yet when I contemplate
the spirals of stars
no longer do I touch
the Earth, but sit with
Zeus and sip ambrosia
like a fellow-deity.*

Ptolemy's compendium of classical cosmology was translated from Greek into Arabic as the *"Almagest"* ("Great Work").

Entering Europe via the Muslim occupation of Spain, and translated from Arabic into Latin, his Almagest became a literary Noah's Ark, which rode out the floodwaters of Europe's largely illiterate "Dark Ages."

That shaped speculative science all the way down to Copernicus, Galileo, and Johannes Kepler (1576 -1630).

After translating Plutarch's "The Face on the Moon" from Greek into Latin, Kepler theorized—

"The moon is a body related to earthly matter. Plutarch asserts this in many ways, and Aristotle's Arab interpreters force even him to this side. But the clearest evidence of the relationship between Earth and moon is the ebb and flow of the seas. I define gravity as a power similar to magnetic power, a mutual attraction."

Kepler composed the first work of science-fiction, which he called *Somnium* (Latin for "Dream"). Disguised as a magic night-flight, Kepler's Latin text envisions travel to the moon, what the moon is like, and how things look from there. The book anticipated America's "Moon walk".

Among *Somnium's* attractions are the verses with which he enlivened its footnotes during the final years of his life. Consider the following—

Charioteers dream chariots.
Judges dream disputes.
What we chase by daylight
waits for us at night.

Being well aware that his Italian correspondent and colleague Galileo languished under strict house-arrest for "Heresy," Kepler didn't dare go public with Somnium.

A stray copy of Kepler's text plunged him under suspicion, however, and Inquisitorial harassment plagued him.

Worse yet, it almost caused the burning of Kepler's mother as a witch! Why? Because he'd purported to quote the old lady as follows—

"There are present amongst us very wise spirits who, finding the noise of the multitude and the excessive light of other regions irksome, seek the solace of our shadows and communicate with us as friends.

"Nine of these spirits are worthy of note. The purest of them, the one particularly friendly to me, is called forth by twenty-one characters."

Kepler was just having fun. In a footnote to his posthumously published manuscript he expatiated—

"Was I referring, perhaps, to the Nine Muses? As goddesses to the heathen, they are spirits to me.

"Or did I mean the Sciences? Namely Metaphysics, Natural Science, Ethics, Astronomy, Astrology, Optics, Music, Geometry, and Arithmetic.

"As for the number twenty-one, that's the quantity of letters in the words 'Astronomia Copernicana.'

"Also, the number of possible conjunctions between pairs of planets, of which there are seven. And, finally, the number of possible throws of dice.

"The object of my Dream was to work out, through the example of the moon, an argument for the motion of the Earth."

To a moon-dweller the moon would appear to stand motionless, as the Earth seems to us. That's easy to agree with now.

For Kepler, however, it was a dramatic experience in mirror-still, heartfelt contemplation, where the reality of objects present to one's mind gains new meaning from human powers, such as the mathematical in his case.

Kepler was the first person to accurately map the orbits of the planets, proving them to be elliptical. To facilitate that process, he'd invented his own system of infinitesimals, a forerunner of the calculus. He exulted—

"The infinitely small is a divinely given bridge of continuity between straight and curved."

Kepler's Northern Renaissance contemporaries included William Shakespeare and Michel de Montaigne, who put up a sign in his tower studio that read—

"Que sais je?" (What do I know?")

The Provencal Frenchman's father was Catholic. His mother's people were Spanish Jews converted to Christianity, and his three siblings were Protestants. His German tutor, chosen for not knowing French, conversed with little Michel in Latin alone.

Trained in law, this paradoxically chivalric skeptic served France first as a courtier or "Gentleman of the King's Chamber" and later as the beleaguered Mayor of Bordeaux.

Throughout the religious civil wars which ravaged his region, Montaigne was a knightly peacemaker, trusted by both sides.

Imagine him on horseback in a mountain meadow, surrounded by fiercely earnest warriors: "Keeping the Dordogne Protestant is a high ideal, but do you really care to risk your lives for that?"

And later, safe in a Catholic commander's castle: "Converting everyone to Roman Catholicism is a high ideal, but do you really care to risk your lives for that?"

His estate produced a splendid wine called *Chateau Yquem*. Drinking such excellent stuff on a daily basis may well have been therapeutic for Montaigne.

"Yquem" reminds me that just in case French phonetics are unfamiliar to your ear, the name Montaigne rhymes with "Haunt Ahnya."

Montaigne devised the personal *"essai"* (for "Trial") form, which involved concentrating on his own mysterious psyche, and compiling free-spirited musings laced with classic Latin quotations.

Here's one of his typically Druidic riffs—

"When the vines freeze in my village, my priest argues from that event the wrath of God against the human race. We are almost all subject to this error; a mistake with important and prejudicial results.

"But he who sets before himself as in a picture the noble figure of our mother Nature in her full majesty, and who sees in her a universal and constant variety, who perceives himself in her—and not himself alone but a whole kingdom—as the smallest possible speck; he alone, I say, values all things according to their actual proportion."

Druid, Classical and Modern cultures alike echo through the strangely jolly genius of James Joyce. His lifetime (1882-1941) roughly coincides with the "Irish Revival's" span.

That literary and dramatic outpouring featured Oscar Wilde, George Bernard Shaw, William Butler Yeats, J.M. Synge and Sean O'Casey. Plus, if you like, Eugene O'Neal in America.

While still a student at Trinity College in Dublin, Joyce conceived the painful and yet simultaneously liberating notion that—

"God is a shout in the street."

His Jesuit professors were doubtless not amused.

Joyce stole the title of Albrecht Durer's most famous painting for his autobiographical novel, *"Portrait of the Artist as a Young Man."*

He had gladly abandoned Ireland, with its painfully provincial limits imposed by puritanical Catholic priests plus overbearing British authorities, to revel in relatively free Continental culture.

Strangely enough, Joyce's career was lavishly financed and promoted by five American women!

Ezra Pound cordially bowdlerized some of Joyce's *"Pomes Pennyeach"* to get them safely published in Harriet Munroe's Chicago-based "Poetry" magazine.

Harriet Weaver dared to serialize his *"Portrait"* in her small magazine called *The Egoist*.

Margaret Anderson and Jane Heap serialized Joyce's next book *Ulysses* (1922) in their *Little Review*, and got prosecuted for so doing.

A Manhattan Municipal Judge sternly ordained that no evidence be read aloud in court, because ladies were present! He then committed the defendants to cough up a fine or spend ten days in the pen for offending public decency.

Finally, Sylvia Beach, the American proprietor of the Paris bookstore "Shakespeare & Co," dared publish *Ulysses* whole in France.

It's a virtuoso performance of the utmost complexity, well worth perusing for its meticulous anti-metaphysical materialism, multiplicity of styles, and epic portrait of an all too human Irish/Jewish non-hero: Leopold Bloom.

Joyce devoted the last seventeen years of his existence to what he called *Work in Progress* and finally titled *Finnegan's Wake*. Pricked out with puns galore, this prodigious labor of love winks, blinks, tinkles, swings, and "speaks in tongues," unveiling the utter stillness which imbues the "Unspeakable Name of God," while glittering with New Testament fish symbolism.

Joyce's realizations had kept on deepening. He came to see that metaphysical oceans of an emotional sort surround and indeed wed the solid continents of human thought, inducing gratitude and penitence, plus, in his case, positively universal oodles of humor.

People take Joyce's mix-masterpiece too seriously, rattling an academic "skeleton key" in its non-existent lock, and then turning quickly away.

How many have enjoyed the book all through?

I did, but I'm no linguist so I never could have managed it sober. Instead, I would help myself to a hefty Jack Daniels nightcap, and relax in bed, letting Joyce's juicy genius pillow or billow me through to dreamless sleep, night after night, for months.

One passage in the book has the narrator playing an Irish tour guide. He begins with—

"Mind yer head comin' in,"

And at the end he warns—

"Mind yer feet goin' out."

While being guided through the grave mound at New Grange, Ireland, which preceded the greatest Egyptian pyramids, I heard those exact words spoken!

Our remote Paleolithic ancestors were superbly gifted astronomers and engineers. That's a fact, as pre-historians agree. New Grange's 250,000-ton mound was constructed of earth and stone to admit the rising sun's rays into its beehive dome for a few hours annually, during the week of winter solstice.

Well, I bumped my head at New Grange's low entrance, and then muddied my trouser-cuffs on the way out again!

I can imagine Joyce glancing aslant through his thick spectacles, and lifting his fine Irish tenor to explain—

"Didn't YOU come into this world head-first?

"And won't ye be goin' out of it feet-first?

"There, now!"

Many of us end "not with a bang, but a whimper," as T.S. Eliot remarked.

Extremely few cap their careers by celebrating the simultaneous flux of human existence, with its conscious/unconscious mind-play/love-play, which the passage of time cannot destroy.

Sophocles accomplished that with *Oedipus at Colonna*.
Euripides with *The Bacchae*.
Shakespeare with *The Tempest*.
And Goethe with *Faust, Part Two*.
In my lifetime, Joyce joined that supreme company. He died into his own culminating effort, and dyed it with his life-blood.

2. Three Poets

This morning brought a phone call from a woman who recited a verse and asked if I could identify it—

> *live always*
> *(my friend)*
> *as if you*
> *had world*
> *as if you*
> *had world*
> *as if you*
> *had world*
>
> *live always*
> *(my friend)*
> *as if you*
> *had world*
> *as if you*
> *had world*
> *enough*
> *and time*

"Why, yes," I told her, "and thanks for reminding me of a dear old friend who died not long ago. His name was Robert Lax, and he sent me that poem on a postcard back in the early 1960's. Bob's poem appears in an early book of mine called *Earth, Air, Fire, & Water*."

"What a relief!" she said. "It's in none of the Lax archives. I'm his niece, Connie Brothers. I first heard it when I was eighteen, recited by a boy in Florida."

"You've got a good memory."

"Yes, I never forgot it, but neither could I find the thing, so finally, I thought of you. Uncle Bob told me that he loved you and thought of you as a guide in his life."

"That's just the way I felt about him!"

"Strange. How could you be guides to each other?"

"Thanks to our differences," I said. "Bob was arch, pious and ascetic, as you must know. I myself was earnest, blasphemous, and shamelessly self-indulgent."

"In that case, what the heck brought you together?"

"Our saving sense of humor. Plus our shared affection for jazz, movies, and James Joyce."

Lax had studied Latin literature at Columbia, alongside his close friend Thomas Merton, who would soon become a controversial Trappist monk, and author of an influential mystic confession called *"The Seven Storey Mountain."*

Perusing Augustine and Aquinas in Latin led Lax to make a leap of faith, abandoning his intense Judaism to join Merton's church.

After college, Bob spent a lonely year at The New Yorker magazine, which published some of his poems. Then he moved over to Time magazine, as a stand-in for our fine Films Editor James Agee.

Lax invariably alienated thin-skinned, thick-headed sophisticates, while forming fast friendships with unlikely people.

For example, while doing volunteer work at a Roman Catholic settlement house in Harlem, he became chums with the local gang leader.

One Sunday afternoon, that genial dude cleared the way for Lax and me to shoot a silent 16-millimeter motion picture along a blocked-off Harlem "play street."

BLACK & WHITE

We shot nothing at all, except
sloping shadows worthy to be kept
of pot-smokers, hopscotch hoppers
groping shoppers, basket-ballers
plus one glassy green dragon
or was that an ice-wagon?

The view-finder on our borrowed, elaborate camera showed things upside down. So an intruding horse-team's jaggedly jumping shadow baffled me, until a flat-bed ice wagon shadow followed, rolling opulent ovals atop its emerald glow of ice blocks.

I was the movie technician, and Lax the eye on the loose. In fact he later bought a Kodak and became an early master of the snapshot.

Sadly, Lax's tenure at Time did not last long. I asked Hillis Mills, the amiable Texan who let him go, what had been the trouble.

"Waal," Mills drawled, "ah never could make out from his reviews whether or not Bob liked the dang movie!"

"Is that bad?"

"It ain't good."

"I would have thought that getting beyond mere 'Like' and 'Dislike' was the first essential step in criticism. But perhaps you were put off by his subtlety of mind—"

"Oh, be quiet!"

Lax had hitched a ride to Los Angeles. He sent me a postcard that read,

"Am writing swamp-cries for Maria Montez!"

That didn't last long, either. The Montez movie flopped, and Tinsel-town was too "crankingly square" for Lax.

His next job: Clowning in the Cristiani family's circus on a season-long tour of the U.S. and Canada. Lax also served as the family operation's movable bank. For safety's sake he carried the daily ticket revenues concealed in his droopy clown drawers.

The New Yorker, which paid top dollar and carried enormous prestige, commissioned Lax to write an insider's report on circus life. He showed me the piece before turning it in.

I said it was too good for the magazine, and that he ought to restructure the whole thing as a poem sequence.

Bob took my impractical, obviously foolish advice. *The Circus of the Sun*, designed and illustrated by Emil Antonucci, resulted. It's a beautiful item, which begins—

> *"Fields were set*
> *for the circus,*
> *stars for shows,*
> *before ever*
> *elephant lumbered*
> *or tent rose."*

Bob eventually settled for a life of holy poverty, enjoying it, on Patmos Island in the Aegean Sea. He used to walk with the toes of his big feet turned in, his long nose pointing down, and his bald spot shining like a tonsure in the sunlight.

The islanders proudly referred to Lax as their resident pelican!

With his wide, warmly perspicacious eyes, high cheekbones, and narrow beard, however, he looked more like a surviving Byzantine icon.

Bob's late prose writings reflect the beauty of his chosen home, plus the old pagan spirit that may still animate people of the Greek islands. Consider this oddly punctuated, small-cap excerpt from his 1975 journal—

> *"on the way to the boatyard I see a neat old lady in a neat old chickenyard. (chickens fenced in with a discarded piece of fishnet). the weather, she says. some weather, she says; its been raining for*

a week & will go on raining; oh well, she says, thank god for it; & let him send more; we do what we like & he does what he likes"

Descending a steep Patmos island lane one day, Bob stumbled and broke his front teeth on the cobblestones.

ASIDE

Some folks
smile at evening,
others do at dawn,
but the man worthwhile
is he who can smile
when his two
front teeth
are gone!

Eventually, the island's only dentist fixed Lax up with a porcelain bridge made to order in Athens. "No charge," the doctor assured him, "but I'd really like to be your friend."
When Bob told me that story, I recalled a similar incident.
Loping along Northampton's Main Street at age eleven, I swung my head around to see what movie was playing at the Academy of Music, and smacked forehead-first into a lamppost.
Along came Doctor Benedict Dunphy, who plucked me off the pavement and carried me upstairs to his office in the McCallum Building, where I regained consciousness.
"What in the name of Crikey," the doctor inquired of my dazed self, "made Ethel Cook Eliot, the pride and joy of Saint Mary's parish, produce a total *moron*?"
I should have thanked him for having salvaged me from the gutter and enriched my vocabulary, but that never crossed my mind.

WHERE LESS IS MORE

Verses
cobbled
by Bob
Lax
harmonize
and
ricochet
like the
ecstatic
alto
sax
of black
Sidney
Bechet

If Walt Whitman blessed American poetry with unprecedented latitude, Lax's deftly syncopated verses provide longitude via verticality.

This can be as narrow as one word at a time, slipping slowly down into one's psyche with the littlest possible splash. For example—

a
small
wave
says
a
small
thing
to
the
shore

Over a dozen Lax volumes have been published in Europe, where he's revered as a "concrete poetry" innovator.

Not here, however; not yet, anyhow. As the "New Directions" American publisher Jay Laughlin kindly explained to me—

"We decline to spend money on all that white space."

At the time of my last trip to see Lax, I was feeling weary and confused. So I asked,

"Bob, what do you think God wants *me* to do?"

With not a moment's hesitation, he replied—

"God wants YOU to ENJOY!"

"Hey!" I said. "That's the best advice I've had since I was nine years old, and Grandpa Cook told me to think something silly!"

I met Ezra Pound at a reception hosted by Harvard's English Professor Ted Spenser, in 1939. There I presumed to inquire why a poet of his eminence chose to embrace Fascism.

Pound responded: "How old are you?"

"Almost twenty, sir."

Laughing dismissively, he turned his back on me, so that was that.

Years later, during World War Two, Pound volunteered short-wave broadcasts from Italy, extolling the chesty (*ma non bene*) dictator Mussolini, cracking mean jokes, and raving on about "international Jewish bankers."

Collared by victoriously advancing American forces, he was cruelly imprisoned for some weeks in an open-air cage at a concentration camp near Pisa.

There, a charitable black M.P. whom he called "Mr. Edwards" slipped him a packing crate, saying—

"It'll get yuh off'n the groun."

Using the crate as a desk, Pound composed the first of his famed *Pisan Cantos*, which include the Edwards quote.

Ultimately, Pound was transferred to Washington to stand trial for treason! A capital offence.

Then the indefatigable, politically savvy poet Archibald MacLeish rallied Robert Frost, T.S. Eliot, and William Carlos Williams to Pound's rescue.

Aided by the National Gallery's Counsel Huntington Cairns, they persuaded American authorities that trying and executing their old colleague would constitute a miscarriage of justice.

So, what should be done with the embarrassing fellow?

It was decided to incarcerate Pound indefinitely at Saint Elizabeth's Hospital for the dangerously insane, letting "out of sight" be "out of mind," so to speak.

The satirical novelist Alan Harrington, an old pal of mine from Loomis days, collaborated with me on a radio script called *The Trial of Ezra Pound,* giving him a fictional fair trial of the sort we felt he ought to have received.

The producer to whom we submitted it responded with a scrawled note—

"Far too controversial for the nation's airwaves."

Some years ago, I happened to meet a psychiatrist whose father had been director of Saint Elizabeth's. He told me that Pound the prisoner always behaved like a jolly uncle to him, and been a huge help with his homework!

So much for the "dangerously insane" verdict.

The novelist William Faulkner was one of a very few to still stand up for Pound. He wrote—

"While Sweden gives me a Nobel Prize, my own government keeps our prize poet penned. We American writers should petition to set the man free now!"

Nothing came of that. But following twelve long years of incarceration, the aging and innocuous poet found himself summarily released as "cured." Meaning, let go with no regrets, and no apologies, either.

He slipped away to Italy. When an interviewer asked for his impression of America, Pound wittily replied: "An insane asylum!"

But he was a broken man, morose, bitterly silent for long stretches, pretty much ashamed of himself and his entire oeuvre. As he blurted out during one interview—

"I came too late to uncertainty!"

That was a profound personal insight, born of suffering.

When Pound's wife sank into despair of her own, his longtime mistress, the violinist Olga Rudge, undertook to care for him. They led a quiet life indeed.

On one of my visits to Venice, our paths happened to cross at a waterbus station. I ought to have signaled recognition and respect at the very least, but my lingering immaturity plus Pound's darkly forbidding melancholy prevented it.

The generous-hearted Jewish-Buddhist poet Allan Ginsberg soon tuned up, together with Gregory Corso, on Pound's Venice doorstep. The gay couple had undertaken their journey in order to personally apologize for America's shabby treatment.

"Do you need any money?"

That was Ginsberg's first question. No, was the answer, but Pound did consent to be taken out for dinner at a gourmet restaurant. There, Ginsberg praised the Pisan Cantos to the skies, quoting them a length from memory, and asked whether Pound would accept his blessing.

Pound brooded, nodded, and said: "Yes."

The poet then apologized for his former anti-Semitic stance, explaining that it reflected the mindless mindset common to his time.

True. From Europe's Dark Ages down to the moment when Hitler's industrial-scale Hebrew-slaughter finally stood revealed, that prejudice ran rampant.

The majority of Pound's friends and colleagues, including T.S. Eliot, Ernest Hemingway, and e.e. cummings, were anti-Semites.

PRAYER

May I overcome personal outrage
and look for common ground
like downcast Ezra Pound
in his detention cage
when a decent black M.P.
showed him the color of Mercy.

My father's library, which I inherited, contains an issue of *Playboy*. Not what you may think, but a literary rarity dating from 1919, the year of my birth. Its opening essay, by D.H. Lawrence, states —

"*The immediate moment is not a drop of water running downstream. It is the source and issue, the bubbling up of the stream. Here in this very instant moment up bubbles the stream of time, out of the wells of futurity, flowing on to oceans of the past.*"

Lawrence contradicts the classic view, which Marcus Aurelius articulated, that time is like a river sweeping everything away.

Who had it right? And what about these lines from *Burnt Norton* by T. S. Eliot?

"*Time present and time past
Are both perhaps present in time future,
And time future contained in time past.*"

Eliot's first masterpiece, published in 1917, was *The Love Song of J. Alfred Prufrock*. Its convoluted title conveys a Germanic "Probe-skirt" or "Prod-frock" echo.

Glum yet funny in its rum fashion, this work is a keenly imaginative young fellow's litany of old age woes and hidden rage. The protagonist ironically inquires whether or not it would be worthwhile—

> *"To have bitten off the matter with a smile.*
> *To have squeezed the universe into a ball*
> *To roll it toward some overwhelming question.*
>
> *"I have heard the mermaids singing, each to each.*
> *I do not think that they will sing to me."*

 T.S. embodied the Romantic sentiment which has imbued Western culture from Dante's time down through our own. Victor Hugo, the author of *Les Miserables*, deftly defined this as follows—
 "With Christianity, and by its means, there entered into the minds of nations a new sentiment, unknown to the ancients and marvelously developed among moderns. Humanity began taking pity upon mankind."
 Yes, pity saturates modern poetic diction. Witness William Blake's "Songs of Experience," and Allen Ginsberg's "Howl."
 Eliot once remarked that "Immature poets imitate; mature poets steal." He himself blithely raided Dante, for example, while composing "The Wasteland"—

> *A crowd flowed over London Bridge, so many,*
> *I had not thought death had undone so many.*

 Reading between those lines, one is treated to the percussive concrete music of a bumpily lumbering lorry, while also being reminded of Dante's original. There you have the poet's technical facility in a nutshell.

GENIUS IN LITTLE

Along a pebbled beach he strolled
alone, at eight or nine years old
skipping stones in solitary sport.
Who knows how far he walked apart?

There was something occult about
the boy: a streak exclusive, cold.
He never scurried back to shout
"Oh, come and see what I behold!"

But whether Tom could really hear
mermaids singing sweet and clear
among THEMSELVES, is not
in any reasonable doubt.

T.S. was Pop's contemporary, and a fifth cousin. What did my father make of him? I never thought to ask! But I can easily imagine Pop fuming over T.S.'s lofty dictum—

"Poetry, in our civilization as it exists at present, must be difficult."

No, it "must" not be any such thing. Difficulty has its uses, and civilization its discontents, but poetry is a free country.

Anyone can practice verse, and the game's true goal is not the grave, nor glory either, let alone lucre.

Millions of Americans like myself read, write, recite and listen to poetry, purely for the fun of it. You can too, if you like...

Ninety-something percent of my old friends have gone over the ubiquitous London Bridge up ahead, "undone," as Eliot put it, by death.

Among them slopes a grizzle-haired, blue-collared, cross-grained movie crew "grip" named Moochie, with whom I worked on some of my first film jobs.

I once asked Moochie to climb a ladder, carrying a large light-reflector, which could of course be dangerous. He reacted with,

"*I fuck YOUSE inny fucken ARSE!*"

Stunned by Moochie's savage indignation, I swallowed and then, for ten or twelve seconds of suspenseful hush on the set, pulled myself together.

Finally, to indicate my personal regard for the man as a colleague in our strictly stratified and ever stressful profession, I offered a smiling rejoinder:

"I fuck YOU in the ass, Moochie. So climb the fucking ladder!"

"Soitingly, sir."

Moochie later explained that he had felt compelled to test my "college boy authority."

We Americans are blessedly free to forget status, forgive each other's sins, and converse in friendly fashion.

Fortunately, that soon transpired between Moochie and myself. He used to entertain me with rueful, Rabelaisian tales of his misadventures as a "Nobody with Nothin'."

But no one is altogether bereft.

Because, after all, we still have time to spend, plus wonderful events to remember.

For instance, I'll not forget one night in my youth when I happened to be hurtling northward aboard a Southern Railway express train.

I sat slumped in the club car, morosely sipping a mint julep.

Along came an extremely attractive although rather matronly blonde, who proceeded to pick me up, and buy me more drinks.

Soon I was pouring my absurd ambitions and painful frustrations out to her.

When the bar closed, we retired to her Pullman sleeping compartment.

There, she shed her jaunty straw bonnet, ivory bracelet, pearl necklace, muslin gown, and panty-hose, item by luxury item.

LOCOMOTIVE ROCK

>Cloaked in silver gusts of rain
>our serpentine, madly hooting train
>clickety-clacked along the railroad track
>while milady's sweat-streaked, plump
>hot, pumping, pear-shaped rump
>gleamed sweetly back at me
>from our streaming wet
>ink-black windowpane.

Finally, I fell asleep in her arms for what seemed a blissful minute or two.

When I awakened she was fully dressed, powdered, and her valise packed.

The sun was shining and the train was slowing, entering a big city.

"This is where I get off," she said. "You probably took me for an aging playgirl."

"Gosh, no," I told her. "For me, the whole thing was a *miracle*."

"Well, anyhow, I'm the traveling fashion-buyer for an upscale department store. My husband will be meeting me in a few minutes on the train platform."

"I see."

"He's a weight-lifting, muscle-building male fashion model, extremely dear to me."

"Oh."

"We're seven years married, with no children yet! That's our only regret."

"Gee, I'm sorry…"

"I want you should peek out from this window and see us two together. Will you do me that favor?"

I nodded, unaccountably overcome.

Gracefully balancing against a screechy lurch and shudder of the train, she departed.

Watching through the window as promised, I saw the fine looking couple lovingly embrace, made for each other.

Auspiciously hissing, the train tugged, chug-chugged and steamed me on away forever.

I lay back hoping that my wondrous instructress would soon bring to birth the fulfilling infant for whom she yearned.

Thanks to my personal efforts, yes.

Or, if not mine, then some later, and equally lucky young fellow.

T.S. Eliot should have been so fortunate!

3. Big Band Leader

Benny Goodman first enchanted millions of teen-agers via his late-night "Camel Caravan" program on radio.

THE CALL OF THE WILD

Benny's fine-tuned
celestial clarinet
surging through
my crackly
crystal-set
Harry James's
trumpet rock
Gene Krupa's
compulsive beat
and Johnny
Mercer's silly-sweet
concoction:
"Cuckoo in the Clock"
chased the sorrow
from my heart
and gave me
a fresh start.

Benny had learned classical clarinet playing at Alice Adam's charitable settlement house in the South Chicago slum where he was born, and he imbibed the jazz spirit by listening in on other people's fun.

At fifteen, to help support his extremely hard-pressed family, Benny started undertaking protracted jazz gigs at private parties.

When a high school teacher asked why he kept falling asleep in class, Benny confessed his moonlighting activity.

"What does it bring?" the teacher asked.

"Five bucks a night, minimum."

"Well," the teacher told him, "you're making more money than me. Why not quit school altogether, and get some well-earned rest!"

The kid happily complied, except that he was always disinclined to rest.

When Benny first played the Ritz Roof in Boston, I had to be there. The crowd mostly consisted of teenagers, like myself. Jasmine-laden May breezes flowing up across Arlington Street from Boston Garden fluttered the Ritz's striped awnings and billowed the girls' dirndl skirts.

Between sets, while the band retired for half an hour, Benny's newly formed, daringly "mixed" quartet came on. Its dark-skinned members were Teddy Wilson and Lionel Hampton. Gene Krupa and Benny himself completed the ensemble.

They swung into "Lady Be Good," with its baroque niceties of counterpoint.

We kids instinctively knew this was a historic occasion. Within minutes, we'd formed a semi-circle and sat right down on the dance floor to listen.

Years later, when we'd become good friends, I told Benny this tale. He in turn confided to me that Alice Hammond, his wonderful bride-to-be, had invited him to her room for the first time on that very night!

During the 1950's, as the Big Band era faded out, Benny reluctantly withdrew to the cushy, boring existence of a millionaire squire in Stamford, Connecticut.

He'd always felt drawn by the majestic reassurance of such works as Mozart's *Clarinet Concerto in A-major,* so now Benny determined to re-invent himself as a classical performer, and hired the reigning classical clarinetist, Reginald Kell, as coach.

Under Kell's irking direction he drastically modified his fingering and lipping technique, which produced fresh calluses.

At that point I eagerly persuaded my bosses at *Time* magazine to let me go and originate a thousand-word "Personality Piece" on him.

My piece inspired a successful Hollywood epic called "The Benny Goodman Story." Benny expressed gratitude. We drew close, and after that we used to meet as often as possible in various parts of the world.

Alice, and their sparkling daughter Benjie, also became dear to me.

Remembering how I had jumped, gyrated and jived to the sweet beat and beautiful blowing of Benny's big bands, I once asked this implacably stoic joy-giver whether he himself had ever actually jumped for joy.

"Just once," Benny told me—

"Benjie was flying down to visit us here in Saint Maarten. Arriving at the airport to pick her up, we were informed that her plane had crashed into the sea! Well, you know Alice. She set herself to comfort the folks wailing and moaning around us. But I just died...

"An hour later, here came Benjie! She'd taken a different flight. That's the one and only time I totally left the ground."

Benny's bravura percussionist Gene Krupa was among the very best. But one night, at an Atlantic City resort, Benny transfixed him with a sternly disapproving public glare, the notorious "Goodman Ray."

Krupa arose from his instruments and stalked off the set, never to return.

I once inquired of Benny what had been the trouble between him and Gene.

He smiled: "I think it had to do with timing."

"I shouldn't have asked," I said.

"That's okay. Arturo Toscanini once tore the face off his number one clarinet for mucking up a Mozart concerto rehearsal. 'Itsa no Motz!' the Maestro screamed. 'Itsa no me! Itsa YOU'!"

Gene soon formed a fine band on his own. But then he happened to be incarcerated for the less than heinous crime of possessing marijuana in Hollywood.

Benny made a special trip to visit Krupa in stir, and told him—

"You got a lousy rap. I'd love to have you back in my band when you get out."

Sadly, Gene never took him up on that.

Crossing a city street one night, I happened to catch a glimpse of Krupa off the bandstand. Misery streaked his wild look as he brushed past. What was he after, a quick fix? That doesn't matter, does it.

To envy genius would be irrational. The great have ups and downs like the rest of us, only more so.

I recall noting Frank Sinatra's despair, one evening in a Chicago hotel elevator, back when he was beginning to sing under Tommy Dorsey's dictatorial command.

I also remember catching the fiery radical song writer and singer Harry Belafonte in what he thought was a private moment of utter discouragement.

One day, while strolling to work through Central Park, I saw the novelist William Faulkner come toward me with a cold-sober, scared-stiff look on his face!

That alcoholic genius just happened to have stopped in New York on his way to receive a richly deserved Nobel Prize...

When I asked Benny if he had any secret desires, he confided that he'd love to hold down a steady job in Boston's Symphony Orchestra! He enjoyed excellent relations with its conductor, Serge Koussevitsky, but the "King of Swing" could hardly hide out in Symphony Hall.

Who was Benny's own favorite jazz musician? When I asked, he responded immediately: "Ella Fitzgerald!" I wasn't a bit surprised to hear it.

AT THE RAINBOW ROOM

When Ella grooved, well gone in song
and Benny blew sweet licks along
they cast a sylvan silence on
our late-night, sky-high Babylon.

Like those four-winged cherubim in Byzantine art, Ella sported one pair of wings for flying plus another for warmly enfolding one. How she could improvise!

But "improvisation" (from the Latin: "to come upon") sounds flat today. We need an Ella-vating expression for the central dynamic of every art.

Instead of trying to make up one's mind, one can experiment with personal thought-processes and passing emotions themselves.

For instance, while composing a poem I listen inwardly to associations, memories, echoes, rhythms, rhymes and tangents, whose syncopated interplay determines the outcome. In jazz, the same applies.

Fletcher Henderson's orchestrations had been the making of Benny's best big band work. One night at a party Benny gave in Henderson's honor, someone said—

"Things don't change, do they?"

Benny nodded soberly, but I sat stunned. For one thing, Mr. Henderson was terminally ill by then.

For another, Jazz itself has everything to do with freshly discovered sounds. In fact it was rapidly changing at the time, fraying out and turning "cool" thanks to Dizzy Gillespie, Miles Davis, and Charlie ("Bird") Parker, who was partly native Indian.

Lots of Americans have native blood, by the way, far more than you might expect.

Looking at photos and paintings for my book called *Abraham Lincoln: a Life in Pictures,* I became convinced that our "Great Emancipator" must have possessed a partly Tennessee tribal ancestry.

Just recently I made friends with a wonderful lady named Rachel, who informed me that her grandfather was a Lakota Sioux.

He could conceivably have connected with my own Grandpa: the young Unitarian missionary Samuel Atkins Eliot. Yes, and he might even have offered "many horses" for a night with the reverend's lovely bride!

Truth and change can't very well dance together; they dance to differing tunes. Yet I suspect that truth is actually change, like the once almighty American dollar.

Parmenides of Elia maintained that under the aspect of eternity no changes can ever occur! William Blake cut through the classic paradox or semantic problem by beautifully observing—

"Eternity is in love with the products of time."

"I've got three friends," Benny once remarked, "and that's enough for me!"

"Fellow musicians?" I asked.

"Not likely. First comes my doctor Arthur Localio, whom you know. Second, someone I'd rather not name. Third, yourself! Don't ask me why."

Benny once turned up at a cocktail party which I gave to honor the Australian war correspondent and novelist Geoffrey Blunden, plus his Parisian partner Marie, who had served as an underground gun-runner throughout the German occupation of the City of Light.

Marie's closest call, she told me, came one evening when S.S. troops abruptly blocked off the street down which she strolled, with handguns for delivery hidden in her purse.

Stepping sideways, she'd looked deep into the eyes of the teenage trooper at the end of the line confronting her. With a wordless nod, he'd let her slip through.

"The lad must have been human," she said.

When Benny arrived, Marie's sad brown eyes opened wide, and she rushed over—

"*Maitre,* I want you to know something. We in our country who survived the German Occupation have strong love for you."

"Why?" he asked.

"We freedom fighters used to hide in cellars with no lights and no talk, listening to your jazz recordings."

"Such as?"

"*Blue Skies, Goody Goody, There's a Small Hotel, Goodnight My Love.*"

"Yeah. Those were fun to do."

"Your music brought us close. We heard freedom in it!"

"Freedom?"

"Sure. We'd touch hands, hug maybe, and then leave without having spoken or seen each other's faces."

"Why was that?"

"Because we might soon be captured and tortured to make us betray our comrades. We knew the ones with whom we worked directly, but not the others who came to those cellar meetings."

Beaming, Benny took Marie's outstretched hand in both of his, holding on to it for a long moment. Applause he always expected, and received impassively, but such rare tributes as hers spoke to a hungry cavern in his heart.

A comparable incident occurred following a Goodman concert in Kyoto, one drizzly, frigid night. His performance had been wildly cheered, but Benny was unhappy about it. "Nice rehearsal," was his wry comment.

We left the auditorium together. In the stage-door alleyway, a white-bearded Japanese gentleman with an umbrella blocked the passage of our limo.

Stepping around to Benny's side he knocked on the car window. Benny rolled it down. Bowing, the man said—

"Mistah Goodman, I lespect you!"

On that occasion, also, Benny was thrilled. "Gee, thanks!" he cried: "You've made my night!"

It so happened that Allan Arbus obsessively practiced clarinet. A Goodman worshipper, he even taught himself to mime certain of Benny's best recorded riffs with extreme precision.

When I mentioned that to Benny, he said he'd like to meet such an assiduous admirer.

So I phoned Allan and told him: "I've got someone here whom you really ought to know."

"Bring whomever right over," Allan said. "We just finished dinner."

Our evening festivities went fairly well, I thought, with Diane in a joyful mood, and Benny cordially noodling away on Allan's instrument.

But the next morning Allan phoned to icily inform me that he would never—ever—forgive my springing Benny on him as a surprise!

An hour later came a call from Benny to thank me for bringing him together with "the charming Arbus's."

I told him about Allan's anger.

"Oh, that explains it then. I was wondering why the heck I tossed my cookies when I reached home."

BLUES FOR BENNY

When we examine this or that
who knows where which is at
or why they won't stand pat
as factual matters should.
If only they just would.

4. Soothing Laughter

Yesterday two dear friends, the poet Richard Beban and his partner the novelist Kaaren Kitchell, dropped by for tea and conversation. Here are just three lines from Richard's voluminous work:

> *Sometimes the wind is poem enough,*
> *the way a mountain hunches, the play*
> *of sun across ocean in the space of a day.*

Kaaren's an acute student of classical mythology, which she interprets in her own highly positive fashion. She'd come with a question: Which lost masterpiece of art would I most like to visit?

After some thought, I chose the "chryselephantine" (gold and ivory enhanced) marble statue representing the Greek father-god Zeus enthroned, which Phidias carved at Olympia.

This was long regarded as first of all among the "Seven Wonders" of the classical world, whose gods enjoyed bodily form and whose people often achieved godly grace.

Plotinus wrote—

"*Phidias did not sculpt this image by copying any visible thing. No, but as the sky-god himself would appear, if he actually showed himself to us.*"

Contemporary critics complained that if the masterpiece came to life and stood erect, Zeus would burst out through the temple roof! That's long-gone, of course, together with the statue.

Byzantine Christian looters doubtless dismantled the work, which lives on thanks to human imagination alone. Now it can reach us from places past its first, firmly ensconced silence.

FATHER GOD

He stipples the sheen of the shimmering bay
with lightning-blink and thunder-bray
plinks the drinks on our cocktail tray
soaks the greensward, halts croquet
shoos our guests indoors to play
cloaks the oaks a ghostly gray
polishes holly, flattens hay
and claps a purple beret
upon golden day.

Power, Authority, Energy, and Lust, characterize Zeus. Not Goodness, nor Compassion. He was and remains wonderful, but by no means lovable.

I picture Zeus's mountainous figure returned to the dimness of its original temple home. Blades of sunlight slice between the surrounding columns, angle over the marble floor, and reflect up onto the ivory bas-relief illustrations of Olympian legend which panel the god's golden throne.

His mother was the Titan Rhea, daughter of Gaea and Uranus, or Earth and Sky. His father was Rhea's brother and husband, Cronus the time god.

Cronus had cruelly castrated his own stardust father Uranus. Not to take the old man's place in Rhea's bed, as Dr. Freud insisted, but rather to rescue his mother from rough, painfully impregnating cosmic storm.

Cronus gave Gaea the rest she required to peacefully ornament herself with clouds, swirling ocean, waving grass, and forest foliage.

Like one's wrist-watch, "Time the Devourer" cuts the daily round to pieces and swallows them. Soon after Rhea gave birth to baby Zeus, her brother arrived to swallow his infant son as well.

She slipped Cronus a small boulder instead.

Zeus's dear old dad was ravenous enough to pop that pill. Taken in by the earth goddess, the time god himself took in the intractably solid, whereupon the whole world became three-dimensional.

I'm reminded of a South Pacific legend according to which an archetypal tree deity managed to stand on his head and heartily kick paternal Sky well away from maternal Earth.

The widely separated Greek and Maori accounts alike suggest that human consciousness may long ago have held a dream-like recollection of Earth's physical evolution!

That may seem an extreme fantasy, but I could cite a hundred and one myths which support it...

The Hellenistic wanderer Pausanius, who seems to have invented travel journalism, wrote—

"The measurements of the Zeus at Olympia fall far short of the impression which the statue projects.

"When it was completed, Phidias prayed for a sign that his creation pleased the god's mind. So Zeus hurled down a thunderbolt, close by, into the ground. A bronze urn set to mark the spot where it struck was still there in my time."

Zeus once decided to set up an "omphalos" or navel stone at the exact center of the universe. First, he sent eagles flying in four directions to Earth's furthest horizon.

Returning, the birds converged at Delphi, so the navel stone was duly erected on that spot, which later became the shrine of the sun god Apollo.

Earth's physical center lies deep inside, yes, but our electromagnetic center is Apollo's solar sphere. The Sun comprises a fiery pivot around which mother Earth twirls her diurnally spinning self at sixty-seven thousand miles per hour (!) in the course of a year.

A priest named Epimenides, from rival Phaestus in Crete, once inquired of Apollo's Oracle whether the omphalos really and truly stood at Mother Earth's precise mid-point.

Receiving a typically ambiguous response, the Cretan scoffed—

"Either there is no true navel stone, or, if so, it's Apollo's own secret."

Plutarch's comment on that exchange reflects the ambiguous Delphic tradition to which he himself, as a priest of Delphi, belonged—

"No doubt the god was endeavoring to discourage Epimenides from tampering with an ancient myth; as if it were a painting the reality of which the questioner was trying to test by means of touch."

Phoebus Apollo established his personal shrine at Delphi, on Mount Parnassus, in order to greet and enlighten suppliants, who flocked there from as far west as Gibralter's "Pillars of Hercules" and as far east as Phasis on the Black Sea's eastern shore. In other words, the whole zone covered by pagan shipping. This went on for at least a thousand years.

Archaeologists tell us the female "Oracles" who presided at Delphi transmitted Apollo's advice while in states of trance, perhaps induced by inhaling fumes from a fissure in the rock. Or perhaps not.

Intercourse with the divine requires searchingly deep roots and sweeping upward reach. So physical factors cannot have mattered half so much as the Oracles' own oak tree qualities.

Apollo's Delphic oracular priestesses were far from being maddened, cold, or vague. Instead, they proved attentive and sharp to the point of paradox.

Take the story of the island prince who was nicknamed "Battus" for his terrible stammer. One day Battus appeared at Delphi and struggled mightily to blurt out a question for the Oracle. Impatiently she cried—

"You came for a speech-cure, but Apollo sends you to conquer Libya, rich in flocks!"

While shouting urgent orders in the stress of ensuing battles, Battus got rid of his stammer forever.

I empathize with Battus, for I, too, once had a stammer, reflecting my father's far more serious one. This often forced me to pause in mid-sentence and select some alternative word which I could manage to articulate.

Strangers didn't know I stammered; they thought me slow-witted. My affliction gradually diminished, and during my twenties it passed off altogether.

But what I call affliction may well have been a blessing in disguise. Didn't this pressure me, time after time, to review the varied potentials my native tongue has to offer?

By the way, my earliest nightmares often started with a friendly visit from a boy like myself, a reckless twin. Although I knew better than to follow his lead, I did so anyhow. At the last moment he would vanish every time, leaving me to face the consequences.

He and I would sometimes climb a forbidding cliff, to reach a cavernous picture gallery in the sky. The paintings I dreamt about were deep-framed. I put my head inside and they came alive with motion! The rivers flowed, the clouds sailed, and the leaves of the trees shimmered. How could that be?

Since this was a recurrent dream, I half expected the disaster in store, and now an apron-clad ogress, ten times my own size, busily brandishing her huge broom of bound twigs, emerged from the cavern depths. I was not supposed to be there, not yet, she shrilled, whisking me out and away, over the sill of space/time...

Arriving at Delphi after a difficult sea-voyage, the early Greek philosopher Parmeniscus confronted Apollo's Oracle in silence. Weighed down by what he felt to be his own dreadful absence of understanding, Parmeniscus was instantly understood. Through the Oracle's human throat, palate, tongue, teeth and lips, Apollo told the suppliant—

"You ask for soothing laughter, O, inconsolable one! Mother at home will give it to you. Pay her special honor."

Accordingly, Parmeniscus hurried home to his mother at Metapontum in Magna Graecia (southern Italy), but found nothing to laugh at there. His depression steadily worsened.

After his mother's death he felt that he himself had no further use in life. So Parmeniscus decided to die on ancestral soil. Namely, the Aegean island of Mykonos, from which his grandparents had emigrated. He sold off his house and library, said goodbye to his friends, and once more departed for Greece.

The small, volcanic island called Delos, which happens to occupy the geometrical center-point of the Aegean Sea, lies within sight of Mykonos, a short boat-ride away.

Not long after his arrival, Parmeniscus sailed over there to take a look around. He found a Doric temple dedicated to Apollo the sun god, and an Ionic one honoring Apollo's twin sister, the moon-goddess Artemis.

With their tall, fluted columns and beautiful marble statues, both temples struck his jaundiced eye as pretentious. Sitting down on a stone bench in the sunshine, halfway between the two, Parmeniscus rehearsed in his mind the myth of the divine twins.

Their mother was a dark-skinned Titan called Leto, whom Zeus the cloud-gatherer secretly impregnated. When Leto's condition became apparent, Zeus's wife Hera fell into a jealous fury. Leto was therefore banished from the home of the gods, and Hera maliciously commanded—

"Let no land under the sun provide a birthing-place for this wicked, lascivious creature!"

So, the belly-swollen Titan wandered heavily over land and sea, unable to rest anywhere, until at last little Delos island spontaneously arose from beneath the sheltering waves and offered herself for Leto's lying-in.

Thanks to bravely arisen Delos, steaming and shedding her sea-water gown, Leto at last brought forth the twin children of Zeus...

Standing up again, Parmeniscus noticed a low gate situated behind the temples. Beyond the gate, a dirt pathway curved out of sight up along a hillside blanketed with daisies, buttercups, and poppies.

Intrigued, he climbed the path, which brought him to a cave-temple with huge, upright boulders for doorposts. Its horizontal rocks were cantilevered together, forming a stepped archway.

Such a temple as this, Parmeniscus realized, must date back to Titan times. Bowing his bald head, he entered the Cyclopean structure.

Its dimly cavernous interior was clean and bare except for a single crudely carved, hand polished driftwood idol. Leto, the dark Titan herself, stood glimmering in the dimness. This was no pious portrayal of feminine virtue and gentleness.

Instead, the sculpture appeared to have emerged in a forthright, jolting, jolly mood, with volcanic force, from incomprehensible depths. In Leto's hour of desperate need, Delos island had done the same. One thing led to another, and presently a new generation of divinities had sprung into being!

Parmeniscus laughed. That was the special honor which he paid to Apollo's "Mother at home." Happy at last, he expired on the spot.

Telling this story, I intend no irony. As our premier poet Walt Whitman affirms—

All goes onward and outward, nothing collapses
And to die is different from what anyone supposes, and luckier.

5. The Origin of Deities

While writing my survey of world mythology, which was first published by McGraw-Hill International back in 1976, and translated into six or seven languages, I coined the word "mythosphere" in order to encapsulate my chosen subject.

That word turned out to be a portmanteau expression for something much bigger than I myself had realized.

As everyone's aware, the atmosphere embraces, protects and enhances our planet. I myself believe the mythosphere operates in similar mothering, nurturing and protective style, for each and every human psyche.

Three modern thinkers cry out for quotation here. First comes Ralph Waldo Emerson —

"We lie in the lap of immense INTELLIGENCE, which makes us receivers of its activity. When we discern justice and truth, we do nothing of ourselves, but allow a passage to its beams."

The pioneering pragmatic psychologist William James appended a footnote to his Harvard lecture *"On Human Immortality"* (1897), which states that each and every human mind—

"Must necessarily derive from SOMETHING MENTAL that pre-exists and is larger than themselves."

Finally, half a century ago, the pivotal quantum physicist Erwin Schrödinger concluded his Cambridge lecture on "Science and Religion" with this assertion —

"Physical theory strongly suggests the indestructibility of MIND by Time."

"Immense Intelligence," "Something Mental," and "Mind," constitute a trio of expressions for the self-evident reality that I myself presume to label "mythosphere." What it's called, scarcely matters; what it does is offer saving grace.

My grandson Eliot Stier, aged fourteen, and his elder sister Samantha, spend their summer vacation months with us. El has a playful disposition, but he could be seething, steaming, and crying on the inside, like myself in adolescence.

While the others went swimming yesterday, El stayed home nursing a mild summer cold. To my surprise, he popped into my study and inquired—

"Do you believe in miracles?"

"It's not about belief," I said. "They happen all the time."

"They do?"

"Yes, if one takes the trouble to ask people whether they've experienced miraculous moments in their own lives, nine out of ten respond in a positive vein."

"Positive vein?"

"It's a matter of believing what one already knows."

"I *don't* know. That's why Mum said to ask you. What exactly *is* a miracle anyhow?"

I shrugged: "Defining the word wouldn't help."

"Then, could you give me an example, at least?"

"Sure... Let me think of one."

"No hurry, Granddad." He sat down on the chair beside my desk.

"I've got it!" I said. "The biosphere is a miracle of nature and the mythosphere is a miracle of *human* nature."

"Wait. You're way ahead of me. What's the biosphere?"

"It mostly consists of air and water. Thanks to our biosphere, sunshine does not come through to us as blasting light and heat but rather as a life-giving force of growth."

He nodded: "Now tell about the mythosphere."

"By that I mean the life of the mind, soul, and spirit, which bathes our tiny individual wits in warm connection with all things."

"Excuse my asking, but what makes you so sure?"

"Personal experience of an emotional kind."

"Can you trust your own emotions?"

"Maybe not, but they're the main thing I've got, and emotional life matters most. 'Think!' people tell you. But logic ties one down, ideology can be toxic, and the factual world is a masked ball."

"I'm hearing you now."

"In my own case, at least, the mythosphere offers immaterial sustenance, lends meaning to memories, and makes the human adventure possible."

"Wow! Can I get there?"

"You never left."

"You mean the mythosphere is *here*, around us now?"

"It's everywhere at once. For you, the mythospheric middle is right where you're sitting now."

El nodded thoughtfully. Getting up, he said: "Thanks, Granddad."

He'd grasped the truth in my heart, which I'm usually at a loss to express. Now, that's another miracle, right there...

All animals possess intelligence plus communication skills. So, what makes humans "different" from the rest? Neither logic nor language, evidently.

We're the most puzzled, inventive, compulsively creative species,—awed and fascinated by things we cannot physically perceive.

Genetic research has ascertained that every living person harks back to an African "Eve" who lived about 200,000 years ago. She was more delicate and "gracile" than her Neanderthal cousins.

In scientific lingo, a rhinoceros is robust whereas a gnu is gracile.

My friend the poet Richard Wilbur offers food for thought on this matter. Each time a pignut falls and splits in two, he muses, we get a brand new gnu!

What if our African Eve was not only gracile but also intuitively grateful? Unburdened by presumed knowledge, she would have been well suited to achieve subjective rapport with mother Nature's multitudinous forms, thankfully addressing the forces that live and move within physical beings.

I'm proposing that the original Mother of us all was genetically blessed with emotional empathy.

In other words, Eve possessed inborn capacity to step outside herself and sense the spiritual existences of sun, moon, stars, flowers, trees, hills, clouds, and fellow animals.

What first sparked human evolution was appreciative concern for invisible dynamics of a spiritual sort. My word "spiritual" connotes actualities, including consciousness itself, which human consciousness can't register directly.

Our progenitors proceeded to welcome, sing about, ritually embody, supply with sacrificial offerings, give fresh guises, dance, and celebrate in fireside stories, the spiritual world. Thus our extended mutual consciousness became a distinct entity, which it remains to this day.

Minus individual experience of a spiritually insightful sort, "*homo sapiens*" might well have become extinct. Our Neanderthal cousins did indeed die out, having enjoyed 250,000 years of practically speechless hunting, gathering, feasting, grunting, humming, dreaming, drumming, and ecstatic dance.

Neanderthals were a good deal larger than ourselves, but they had limited manual facility between thumb and fingers. Their crudely chipped hand-axes lacked a keen cutting edge, which put the physically majestic species at a fatal disadvantage in the Age of Flint. Our Bible says—

> *There were Giants*
> *on the Earth in those days,*
> *but the waters covered them.*
> *The waters covered them,*
> *and none escaped.*

Between 60,000 and 50,000 years ago, our species spread out of Africa and around the world.

It now appears that the first people to emigrate interbred with Neanderthals. Hence all of us except for a few totally indigenous Africans possess about four percent Neanderthal genes.

Along our way around the globe, we developed innumerable mother languages, plus the ability to build fires, sculpt small figures for hand-held worship or magic, and paint devotional images on cliffs and cave walls.

Thus, deities flourished, and kept on changing. Some grew glorious, and increasingly interacted with people, making psychological waves behind the scenes...

All figures of legend, are human inventions, obviously, but let's not be so irrational as to dismiss them on that account. Language, law, notation, trade, money, politics, the stock market, electric light, skyscraper cities, computers, and the Internet, also are human inventions.

To deny their actuality would be eccentric. The same goes for denying the spiritual beings in one's own experience.

Don't certain figures encountered in the books you've perused appear more "real" than the majority of folks who cross your path in life? If such characters, whether historic or fictional, with their comparatively brief and flimsy credentials, can profoundly imbue one's consciousness, then the same goes for deities...

Humanity's most crucial invention to date was the alphabet. This appeared about three and a half thousand years ago, in the eastern Mediterranean region which is still called the Holy Land.

What brought it about? I guess that some anonymous shaman, witch-doctor, prophet, or poet, found it hard to recall his—or her—own sayings!

This led whomever to invent a notation for each of the twenty or more sounds one can articulate. By grouping such notations into words in ink on papyrus, the father, or mother, of world literature produced humanity's first portable, easily reproducible, memory and communication device.

Thanks to that historic creation, you and I are in touch at the present—timeless—moment.

Originally conceived through imaginative human awareness, our gods and goddesses gained relatively vast power. To doubt their continued presences in our own lives, or dismiss them as dead on arrival, seems arrogant.

It's equally inappropriate, however, to regard deities as "supernatural." Nature is the mother of us all; there's no getting past her. Far from being "above" Nature, the divine remains intrinsic to her very existence.

According to the Noonucal people of Minjerribah, Australia, a "Dream-time" great-granddad shines through the stars of the Southern Cross.

ADAM DOWN UNDER

Come nightfall
in the present tense
First Man beams
benevolence.

A croaking pair
of cockatoos
acquaints him
with the latest news.

This Aboriginal perspective on the firmament finds a frosty echo in the myth of the Norse deity Odin (or Wotan) whose cold kingdom of drifting mists, wistful giants, busy gnomes and monster-haunted seas lay right around the globe from Australia.

Worshipped as the All-Father, Odin sacrificed his own right eye, and then hung himself in a tree for three days and nights of agony, to earn understanding.

Gazing down into the round recess of an old-time well, I glimpse a glimmer of daylight afloat in the darkness below, like a pale eye dropped by the sun.

Or Odin's eye?

Forever after his ordeal, Odin had two ravens who counseled him. One would return from exploratory flights to perch on Odin's left shoulder. The other stayed put on his right.

The Cockatoos of the Aboriginal First Man, followed by Odin's Ravens, have long since metamorphosed into Reason and Memory,—twin sources of human progress.

China's Kwan-Yin ("Kwannon" in Japan) is worshipped both as "Merciful Mother Goddess," and as Avolokitesvara, the "Lord who Looks down in Pity."

Navajos ritually invoke Etsanatlehi, the double-sexed "Yellow Changer," glazed by slanting rain.

Forked lightning is downright male in the Navaho tongue, whereas the distantly pulsing sort comes across as female.

The bi-sexual mystery-deity called A'wonawil'ona underlies Earth Mother, Sun Father, Moon Mother, and Corn Maiden—all four—in Zuni Pueblo theology.

She, or He if you prefer, is the true source.

Every earthly creature dies into the resounding, roundly chiming space/time continuum, but the actual here and now does not expire. We feel the permanence of the present in our very bones.

The past is not merely history; it's everybody's story, which continues on...

Some six thousand years have passed since our species began its long fall away from the previously firm ground of what anthropologists patronizingly label "Pan-psychism" or "Savage animism."

I mean, the instinctive understanding that mother Nature is all one thing, which imbues entire space/time, and is itself imbued with conscious feeling.

When the reassurance of that instinctive wisdom evaporated, tribal shamans lost their ways and whole peoples suffered abandonment. Primitive feeling/thought required replacement, but with what?

Accordingly, a few gifted women, children, and men, set themselves to work in patient, puzzled, spider fashion, projecting translucent threads from their own brains to create Astronomy, Agriculture, Engineering, Ethics, Law, Logic, Medicine, Mathematics, etcetera.

Each person alive presents a palimpsest of body, mind, bubbling emotion, partial recollection, and uncertain reflection. In short, the sheaths of abiding spirit.

Nordic bards described the spiritual world as a tree called "Yggdrasil."

California's Chomash Indians sensed looming divinity in redwood trees.

Middle Eastern folk associated this with date-bearing palms.

The Japanese have a worshipful feeling for mountain pines, and so do I.

In boyhood, I used to stand for hours watching my Eliot grandfather chop down and burn pine trees which "obscured the view" from the veranda on his and Grandma's Mount Desert Island property.

Half a century later, in Japan, I reverently witnessed Shinto Mountain priests building and tending ritual pinewood fires.

Hence, I myself picture the mythosphere as a towering oak in winter, with very deep roots. High aloft, amid its bare black branches the waning and waxing moon appears.

We're all invisibly swathed in biologically generated electromagnetic swaddling clothes. We grow up infused with multiple force-fields, immune systems, ballooning beliefs, personality patterns and imploding passions, plus everything we've seen, heard, or read...

Everyone's start in life recapitulates human evolution. Hence, the crucial moments in children's existences prove to be proto-sexual, proto-religious and proto-scientific. There's no division, as yet, between such impulses.

I recall one occasion when a terrific thunderstorm shook our creaky, leaky old house. Gusting rain rattled the roof shingles and silvered the windowpanes with sinuous brush strokes.

Soon after the tempest passed, I slipped out front to investigate. Serenity reigned, but the oak tree beside our walk had shed small sections of leafy twigs. Picking up a twig, I squatted and thrust it into a rain puddle. The underwater section of the twig slanted off at an angle to the part in my hand. Astonished, I carefully pulled the twig from the water, whereupon it stood straight as before!

PERIPHERAL VISION

Rain angels whose labors lay
dimly gleaming, silver-gray
at angles to our dripping tree
smiled kindly down on me.

6. Purposeful Portraiture

Charles Hopkinson was a fairly famed portraitist in his day, privileged to portray a pickled peck of politicians, a clucking clutch of ecclesiastics, a bookish rack of crack academics, and a quiver of absolute ladies.

Hoping that I'd follow in his footsteps, my lean, spry, hairy-eared great-uncle (Grandma Frances Hopkinson Eliot's brother) did his best to help me try.

Uncle Charlie made the oil sketch of my four-year-old self that hangs in my studio today. Having been ordered to sit still, I did my best whilst he peeked out from behind his easel; perhaps for an hour, but it seemed forever.

When at last he pronounced me free again, I leaped off my chair to dash madly about the room, returning to my motion-body. After I'd calmed down, Charlie kindly invited me to look at his picture.

The wet, white smear across one shoulder of the image's blue sailor jacket intrigued me. Pointing, I asked: "What's *that*?"

"Why, that's a streak of light from the window!"

I glanced at the window and back again. How had the streak crossed over, and what made it stick? I yearned to ask this, but words failed me. So I simply waved my arms about, to his evident amusement.

TECHNIQUE

Had Charlie said he'd caught the light
in a slick flourish of zinc white
might I have got the matter right?
Why no, not by a long sight.

Charlie did not actually intend the streak to look as if it were on the jacket. In fact it stands well in front, like a random gleam across window-glass. My image gazes innocently out and across the gleam. By means of that light-streak he conveyed a haunting sense of timelessness permanently fixed in space.

Timelessness is tricky, however. Minus time, it could not very well exist.

NIGHT WATCH

Grandpa Eliot used to let me stop
on my way up to bed and rewind
the grandfather clock standing
on the landing of his staircase
with a key that he handed me.

Through the vertical window
below the clock's moon face
I saw its brass pendulum
softly swing, repeating
"Tick-tock, tick-tock."

Do we give time
enough credit?
Maybe not.
Take a minute
and think about it.

Charlie always signed his notes to me "Affly," short for Affectionately. Yet my "idle and disgusting" cigarette habit must have grated on the good old man.

He was instinctively egalitarian, but very strong on moral matters. "Any *gentleman*," he once remarked to me in his innocent way, "is of course a *communist!*"

After pausing for consideration, he added: "Tolstoy was a gentleman, but Stalin may be something else again. What most interests me as a painter, is the *finer things* that one perceives in a person's character."

At the time, that struck me as hopelessly virtuous. But such old masters as Titian, Rembrandt, and Velasquez took precisely the same exalted approach.

In youth I assumed that portraiture was a somewhat secondary thing, a way for artists to make a living. But I've since come to understand that creating likenesses stands at the very heart of art in general.

Recalling my teen-age conversations with your tentative old self, Uncle Charlie, I wish that we could carry on. Here I sit, a failed painter who disappointed you, since you died before my writing career got underway.

What most interests me as a writer? "The finer things," of course.

While portraying Calvin Coolidge for the White House, Uncle Charlie desired to capture a far-seeing look in the eyes. It just wasn't there, so finally he said: "Mr. President, I have a question to ask, if you don't mind."

"Shoot."

"When Mr. Harding died, and you became President overnight, what was your first thought?"

After pondering for a few indrawn minutes, "Silent Cal" (as he was known), offered six short words—

"I thought I could swing it!"

Coolidge had begun his political career as Mayor of my home town, which remained his preferred place of residence. In boyhood, I once dared to walk along behind him, spoofing his deliberate, head-down pace. He gave no sign of noticing, naturally.

I've often been impertinent, although not by any means immune to fear. At a reception held at the American embassy in Athens for Lyndon Johnson when he was America's vice president, I failed to return his strong "press the flesh" handshake with proper appreciation.

The tetchy Texan, who's still a scary figure in my book, glared with sudden rage straight into my eyes. I staggered, shuddering, as if Johnson had actually blurted—

"When a pipsqueak like you presumes to piss on MA parade, ah have ma Secret Service CONFISCATE his Yankee pecker!"

Just now, I'm looking at a vertical portrait of Supreme Court Justice Oliver Wendell Holmes Jr., standing tall in his commanding manner at a very advanced age.

This also was painted by Uncle Charlie, who admired Holmes for his dissenting opinion in a 1919 Supreme Court case that made legal history. I'll quote the key passage—

"When men have realized that time has upset many fighting faiths, they may come to believe, even more than they believe the very foundations of their own conduct, that the ultimate good desired is better reached by free trade in ideas. That the best test of truth is the power of the thought to get itself accepted in the competition of the market. That, at any rate, is the theory of our Constitution."

Amen, say I, to Holmes's timely dissent. No matter how abusive it sometimes gets, free speech remains our best bulwark against Ignorance, Complacency, Corruption, and Oppression,—the Four Horsemen of Apocalypse. Besides, "free trade" allows breathing room, which enlivens ideas themselves.

Late in the 19th century, Uncle Charlie created a poignant portrait of the Cambridge, Massachusetts kid who was to become the poet Edward Estlin Cummings.

His father, the reverend Doctor Cummings ordered that his child: "Must not be told distracting and inaccurate fairy-tales whilst posing."

Charlie disobeyed because, as he reminisced to me—

"The boy craved nourishment for daydreams."

I once presumed to phone the poet, who was old enough to be my father, at his Patchen Place residence in Greenwich Village.

"I'm the incumbent art critic at Time magazine," I said, "and I've just been to see your gallery exhibition of paintings. Well, I'm crazy about your books and I've memorized dozens of your poems. But the pictures don't grab me. So I wonder… "

"Wondering is okay," he told me gently.

"Thank you."

"Composing poems is really difficult. I make them look easy; that's an illusion. The fact is, I paint pictures mainly to relax. They're not nearly so poised as my poems."

"I see!"

"Right now, I've got my eye on an unopened bottle of White Horse. Would you care to split this with me, drink for drink?"

"I'd be delighted! When?"

"Why wait? Hurry on down."

Our conversation went on for a couple of hours, until his willowy wife stepped in to amiably dispose of the empty bottle and my well-filled self.

She was Marion Morehouse, a former fashion model whom he'd married in 1932. They stayed close until his sudden death by cerebral hemorrhage thirty years later. The following lyric must have been for Marion—

(i do not know what it is about you that closes
and opens; only something in me understands
the voice of your eyes is deeper than all roses)
nobody, not even the rain, has such small hands

Setting its goofy punctuation aside, that's quite some quatrain! Cummings conveyed what he felt in his heart. They can't take that away from him…

Painting remains a traditionally lonely pursuit. The brief connection between Vincent van Gogh and Paul Gauguin, however, offers a dramatic and arresting example of mutual experiment in art.

Fluent in French and English alongside his native Dutch, Vincent van Gogh adored Charles Dickens' novels and relished the latest developments in science.

The man had madness in his bones, however, plus a load of socially unwelcome characteristics.

At Arles, a thriving market town not far from the French Riviera, van Gogh came into his own creatively. The windswept contours of the surrounding countryside, plus the few natives willing to put up with his weird ways, and even sit for their portraits, enchanted him.

He pictured everything with an eye to the might of colored light and the energy of rhythm. In a letter to his brother (a large-hearted, small-time art dealer named Theo), Vincent enthused—

"To express the love of two lovers by a marriage of two complementary colors, their mingling and their opposition. The mysterious vibrations of different tones."

Gauguin had written something similar, as follows:

"Color, which is a matter of vibration, like music, can express that which is the most creative and at the same time the least definable thing in nature. Its inner force."

Part French and part Peruvian, Gauguin lived hard and painted soft. His best works are girl-gentle, sarong-cool, and nourishing as a cup of coconut milk. But the man himself was prickly, willful, and difficult in the extreme.

Geniuses seldom recognize each other as such, but those two lonely, love-starved, fully obsessed painters did so. Urged on and financed by Theo van Gogh, Gauguin agreed to spend some time with his fellow-artist at Arles.

BEFORE THE STORM

Said van Gogh to Paul Gauguin:
"Tell me how you're feeling, man?"
Gauguin replied: "I just don't know!
What goes on with you, van Gogh?"
"Who, me? Let's see. I'm out of hand
but how these colors glow! It's grand.
The yellow STRIDES into the blue.
Besides, I've found a friend in you!"

Theirs was never a tranquil association. The tragic finale occurred just before Christmas in 1888, following nine weeks of tormented togetherness. Gauguin's eloquent, posthumously published and still unappreciated journal called *"Before & After"* remains the only reliable source for what actually occurred at Arles, so I'll excerpt it—

"How long did we stay together? I couldn't say; I have entirely forgotten. In spite of the swiftness with which the catastrophe approached, in spite of the fever of work that had seized me, it seemed like a century. The public had no suspicion of the fact, but we two were performing a colossal work that was useful to us both. Perhaps to others?

"During the latter days of my stay, Vincent would become excessively rough and noisy, and then silent. Some nights I sensed him getting up and coming over to my bed. To what can I attribute my waking up at just that moment? Anyhow, it was enough for me to say quite sternly: 'Vincent, what's the matter with you?' He'd return to his bed without a word, and fall into heavy slumber."

Gauguin goes on to report that one night at the local cafe, van Gogh hurled an absinthe glass at his head. The following evening—

"I felt I must go out alone and take the air along some paths that were bordered by flowering laurel. I had almost crossed the

Place Victor Hugo when I heard behind me a well-known step. Short, quick, irregular.

"I turned about on the instant as Vincent rushed toward me, an open razor in his hand. My look at that moment must have had great power in it. He stopped, lowered his head, and set off running for home."

Gauguin checked into a hotel, and took the next day's train to Paris. Van Gogh had meanwhile sliced off most of his own right ear. Or was it the left? Touch your right ear; in the mirror it's your left, right?

Trotting along to a house of ill-repute, he'd humbly presented his bloody rag of cut flesh to an inmate. She wasn't interested.

The most poignantly poetic and representative artist of modern times created "Self-portrait with Bandages" while wounded, still hung-over, yet absolutely "there," a day or two after his crisis.

Resolute before the mirror, he portrayed himself in free-fall as it were, thoroughly bandaged and bundled up, while smoking a pipe. His face glows with cold. Or is he chilled through from having lost so much blood?

Mirrors show what they see, or do they? Are mirrors realistic? Samuel Butler opined that we should feel grateful to them for presenting appearances only, and never revealing our true selves.

Victor Hugo, whose square at Arles was the scene of Gauguin's final encounter with van Gogh, once made the following comment—

"Drama requires a mirror which, instead of weakening, concentrates and condenses the colored rays. A mirror which creates of a mere gleam, a light, and of a light, a flame."

One might expect van Gogh's self-portrait to depict a latter-day Icarus, staring from some sun-seared abyss of bafflement. But in this picture his madness of one night's accident is no more.

Now he's the hero, or anti-hero, of a drama that is all in the wings. This barely rational vessel of sheer, thunderbolt spirit is falling, yes, but minus fear, suspended in the mythosphere.

My great-uncle Charlie viewed both van Gogh and Gauguin with alarm, whereas he revered and emulated the portraitist John Singer Sargent.

I took the opposite position. For me, the two innovators were "real," whereas Sargent looked "fussy."

Following a full discussion of the matter, Charlie generously bowed to my obstinacy. "The boy's so young and ignorant!" That's what he doubtless decided.

The splendid, scowling, American-born sculptor Jacob Epstein, who made his home in London, used to be reviled for his radically "African" figure sculptures, and much admired for his traditional portrait busts of such celebrities as Paul Robeson and Winston Churchill.

In my opinion, the wistfully leaning, backward gazing "Lazarus" of Epstein's old age stands among the world's most awesome self-portraits. Epstein once told me—

"When I want to see a great artist, I have to look in the mirror!"

When I look in the mirror, I see an old man shaving. Yet many notable painters have seen fit to mirror me. No two artists ever did so the same way.

I've always admired Ad Reinhardt's abstractions, most of which feature a black cross barely distinguishable from its blue-black field. But he was no admirer of my reviews. Hence, in 1946 or '47, Ad created a full-page cartoon for a New York newspaper called "PM," depicting me as a repulsive three-toed sloth!

Ad's implication being that I was obviously too damn lazy to climb down and take a good long look at his stuff.

A decade later, the Italian surrealist Domenico Gnoli tossed off a cruel sketch of me, resembling Britain's brutally murderous King Henry the Eighth. Gnoli did the drawing at a dinner party which I threw to honor his twenty-first birthday.

Savo Radulovic set a flattering stoic gloss upon my volatile self. But Savo was the stoic, not me. He'd bravely fought the Nazis up and down his native Yugoslavia. The only sigh that I ever heard him utter was when he found that burglars had filched a ham from his fridge.

"They took *none* of my paintings!" Savo complained.

When the Ecuadorian firebrand Oswaldo Guayasamin and I first met in Venezuela, I suggested that he travel widely to nourish his clear genius. Taking my advice, he followed the course of empire west to China, where Chairman Mao welcomed him for an extended stay.

Years afterward, meeting on a street in Rome, we became good friends. Oswaldo perceived me as a fellow anarchist of the conflicted, non-violent kind. His portrait conveys that emotional aspect via Chinese Zen brushwork.

The Three Ages of Man might be described as "Promising," "Prime-of-Life," and "Looking Good."

Recently the rising painter Gregg Chadwick chose to portray my white-bearded, thoroughly furrowed face from memory. He deliberately blurred things, leaving one crystal-clear eye to see, appreciate, and speak for me.

I regard this "Looking Good" picture as my most poetic likeness...

William King and I first met while we were both on Guggenheim Fellowships in Greece.

When we happened to encounter each other at Athens' Archeological Museum, Bill ruefully confessed that the classic Greek sculptors left him half dead of envy and sheer discouragement.

GODLINESS

Hellenic sculptors
beyond praise
captured Heracles'
calm gaze

The balance of
Athena's head
and Poseidon's
tidal tread.

"I know how you feel," I said. "Ralph Waldo Emerson complained that all his best thoughts had already been stolen by the ancients!"

Bill was not amused.

We went outside for an ouzo and olives in the garden café, after which he gave me a tour of the museum's best sculptures. Although I can't recall a word of what he said, certain things he pointed out remain with me to this day.

During the next month or so, King sculpted a bust of me in Homeric warrior guise.

He used the notably "long" or self-adhesive clay peculiar to an Athenian suburb called Keramicus, from which our word "ceramics" derives.

Bill had extremely keen visual memory. He brought the finished product to my house as a surprise. It's got archaic monumentality plus ironic observation.

One could guess the subject's age and weight, but what goes on behind the baked-clay brow of Bill King's epic creation? It now stands on my front balcony, overlooking the lane.

Bust's concentrate on character, whereas nudes feature human form and function. John Donne who was Dean of Saint Paul's in

London, once offered the following Pagan/Christian outburst, as I recall it —

> *Full nakedness!*
> *All joys are due to thee.*
> *As souls unbodied,*
> *bodies unclothed must be*
> *to taste whole joys.*

Josephine Baker was born to chaotic poverty at St. Louis, Missouri, in 1906. At eleven she witnessed local race riots that left over two hundred colored people dead. At thirteen she was doing street dances for pennies.

At nineteen she slipped away to Paris, where Negroes were not despised and routinely clobbered, but welcomed as an entertaining novelty.

At *La Revue Negre* and *Les Follies-Bergere,* accompanied and inspired by such Afro-American musicians as Sidney Bechet, she enchanted Continental café society with nude jazz dance improvisations.

Since I wasn't present, it's not for me to dilate upon her syncopating charms, said to give all Paris a hard-on.

She philosophically remarked in her memoir—

"I wasn't really naked, just not wearing clothes."

In 1936, La Baker briefly returned to star in a ""Ziegfeld Follies" Broadway musical alongside Bob Hope and Fanny Brice.

Then, retiring to the south of France, the personally infertile performer adopted and raised a dozen orphans of many different races in order to enjoy their company, and demonstrate that the human family can in fact behave as such.

What an admirable second act! Could the profoundly compassionate character necessary for that final triumph ever be conveyed in a painting?

No, not unless a second Rembrandt were to set his heart on the project...

If I had to choose a single favorite portrait from my whole experience, which one would it be? That's not so difficult a question as you might expect.

Almost immediately, Gorgione's "La Vecchia" ("The Old Woman") at Venice's Academia, springs to mind

While first contemplating that picture ages ago, I gradually became aware that Father Time's tenderly wrinkling fingers and thumbs had rendered extreme youthful loveliness more true than ever before.

Gorgione succeeded in visualizing the space/time dimension of human life-passage there, a heroic, and totally original, achievement.

7. The Reciprocity Tightrope

Here's a tale that Plutarch got from the grammarian Epitherses. It happened on a voyage from Alexandria to Italy, in a ship whose passengers included the narrator.

Off the west coast of Greece one evening, the wind dropped away. The voyagers were still awake, sipping their after dinner wine, when a voice cried —

"Thamus! Thamus! Thamus!"

The vessel's Egyptian pilot was in fact named Thamus. After the third cry, he answered—

"Here I am!"

Then the voice commanded—

"When you near Palodes island, proclaim that great Pan is dead."

Amazed, the passengers and sailors alike debated what ought to be done. Should the strange request be obeyed, or not?

Half an hour later, the becalmed ship drifted opposite Palodes. So Thamus stood up on the stern, cupped his mouth with his hands, and shouted his message.

Thereupon, a protracted moan of astonishment and sorrow arose from not one but a multitude of voices, audible to everyone aboard.

The Roman Emperor Tiberius ordered an investigation of this event. Certain witnesses asserted that a Jewish boy, residing in Nazareth, had told the god to quit the sunlit scene and go down into the underworld.

LAMENT

Brahma's throbbing drum struck dumb
Thor's thunder thinned, a distant hum
Kwannon rendered cold and numb
dark Ygddrasil's roots displaced
Red Ra's countenance defaced
the wind god Aeolus outraced
Wakanda wounded, forlorn
sacred Cord Maiden shorn
Isis out of her veiled head
Tibet's Green Tara dead
Zeus pulverized to dust
Aphrodite become a bust
Spirit-guide Hermes retired
and Pan himself at last expired?

The ancient Roman poet Ovid tells of violent changes charged against divinity. That's the theme of his immortal *Metamorphoses*.

When a nymph named Daphne prayed for help to ward off the sun-god Apollo's urgently lustful advances, Ovid tells us, ironic powers-that-be transformed her into a shady laurel tree.

Metaphorically speaking, Daphne became a bio-divine being who protects one from the heat of the sun, the very thing to which she'd turned in her distress!

Ovid also relates that the mighty tracker and hunter Acteon once happened upon Apollo's sister, the tart, shy, disdainful moon goddess Diana (Latin for Artemis), bathing, naked in a forest pool.

Transfixed, Acteon paused to peek, and she naturally knew at once. Feeling captured and insulted by his sharply glittering gaze, the Virgin Huntress changed him into a stag. Thereupon his own pack of stag hounds gleefully destroyed and devoured their former master.

The Renaissance magus Giordiano Bruno gave his own transcendental twist to Ovid's tale. Acteon had not expired, he proclaimed, but been elevated to godhood!

Bruno dared to call himself a latter-day Acteon, who gazed upon Nature bare, thus achieving divinity in his own right. This mad proto-scientist dared found a "Diana, the Virgin Huntress" cult, which seemed to honor Britain's anti-Catholic "Virgin Queen" Elizabeth.

Outraged Vatican authorities burned Bruno at the stake in Rome's flower market.

Under the aegis of a "Merciful God," Christian churches have done dreadful things. In paganism, however, it was not the disorganized, broadly independent priesthood, but deities themselves who behaved outrageously.

They committed incest, tortured and chained each other up, raped right and left, fostered wars, devastated cities, led innocent folks astray, and occasionally turned them into trees, stags, spiders, birds, or fish.

Still, the pagan gods' crimes were not so monstrous as they were human through and through. As Friedrich Nietzsche famously observed—

"The Greek gods justified human life by living it."

In *La Citta Divina* the Florentine magus Matteo Palmieri dared suggest that the founders of our species were actually angels! This religion-fiction attracted the Catholic Inquisition's murderous eye. With the painter Botticelli's assistance, however, Palmieri defended his epic as pure metaphor, and escaped burning at the stake.

CHILDREN OF LIGHT

Astounded by the battle-sound
rattling around their starry ground
Sons of Heaven hurtled down
to consort with merry, brown
Daughters of dear Mother Earth.
Force & Form, Hope & Dread
kept on grappling overhead.

Angelic angst plus mortal mirth
brought the human race to birth.

The universe is now "known" to encompass about a hundred billion galaxies, each of which sparkles with some hundred billion stars! Meanwhile, the snows of yesteryear may conceivably keep falling in separate snow-globes all their own. "Parallel universes" possibly exist. Such ideas thrill some people, but for me they conjure up a limitless white nightmare.

Plutarch addressed the "multiple-worlds" theory as follows —

"The Zeus of Homer turned his gaze as far as Troyland, Thrace and the nomad peoples around the Danube. But the true Zeus has a worthy variety of sights in many worlds.

"The early theologians and poets used to say: 'Zeus, the beginning, Zeus midway, and everything comes from Zeus.'

"The men who came after them, called atomists, have turned away from the beautiful and divine cause, to see everything in terms of the behaviors, movements, collisions and combinations of bodies.

"The reasoning of both eras is deficient, since the former ignores the question 'From what and through what?' while the latter ignores the question 'Through whom and by whom'?"

Plutarch's summary sounds precisely right to me. Our philosophical dilemma hasn't changed a bit since his day.

I have a question concerning this matter. If "persons are things," as they say, then why can't things be persons? Might every "What" somehow constitute a "Who"?

That sounds like sheer semantic absurdity. In Chinese however, it would not appear so at all. That gives the Chinese poets a considerable advantage over ours, by the way.

I myself maintain, on the basis of experience, that when things are fully recognized they do indeed begin to manifest personhood…

Like mortals, the old gods seldom got along. Every mythology features an anti-authoritarian deity, and Zeus's opposite number was Prometheus, a Titan of Form, whose name means "Forethought."

Prometheus earnestly preached human individuation, plus careful dominance of natural forces via conscious effort. Secretly, the sly Titan presented Fire ("concealed in a fennel stalk") to the Greeks.

He taught folks to light their own domestic fires, cherish them for warmth, use them for scaring off bears, wolves and lions of the night, cook on them, and burn beef or mutton bones wrapped in fat as aromatic offerings to the gods.

"Keep the meat for dinner," he advised. "Gods need not eat. Smell suffices them."

Infuriated, Zeus crucified Prometheus, nailing him to an icy Caucasian peak where he suffered torments that I don't care to think about.

Yet, no matter what his agony, the Titan continued to defy overweening superpower. He invariably favored liberality toward humankind, and formative outreach in our direction.

Zeus relented at last. The penitent Father-god permitted his best-beloved human-born son Heracles ("Hercules" in Latin) to journey out and rescue Prometheus!

That myth puts Heracles in the same saving role as Jesus, and makes Zeus a pagan predecessor of the supreme Judeo-Christian deity.

As the Old Testament abundantly relates. Jehovah packed implacable power plus jealous attention to detail. He also confronted a forward looking opponent, however.

Didn't the much maligned fallen angel called Lucifer ("Light-bringer") persuade Eve to bite an apple from the Tree of Knowledge?

Thus Eve experienced reality directly, in a personally refreshing and clarifying way, instead of humbly believing what she was told.

From the New Testament, we learn that God sent Jesus Christ, his own beloved son and second member of the Holy Trinity, to join humanity, and save our turbulent world...

Gods and goddesses have always played crucial educational roles in human development. That's been true around the world, for good and evil alike, as history demonstrates. But classical Greece offers the fullest example.

DIVINITY SCHOOL

Hephaestus imparted artful metallurgy
Athena instilled strategy and shipbuilding
Ceres inculcated mothering and agriculture
Apollo stood for poetry, medicine and music
Artemis demonstrated wilderness hunting skills
Hermes suggested measurement and thieving
Poseidon coached seafaring and horse riding
Aphrodite enabled women to enchant men
Dionysus did drama and drunken rapture
Pan played his pipes behind the scenes

Any fresh concept is partly a criticism of one's previous assumptions. In my case, they were psychoanalytical. I'd enthusiastically swallowed half a dozen seminal books by two exalted "head-shrinkers."

Sigmund Freud and Carl Gustave Jung saw themselves as revolutionary scientists, and both are still revered as such, to a surprising degree.

Like surgery however, which also depends upon the miracle of healing, psychiatry is no science but a very difficult art.

Freud described the psyche as a three-layered pyramid in effect. Everyman's "Super-ego," said he, is the C.E.O. at its apex. Below that lies the "Ego," a tight white middle class collar.

Finally comes what Freud famously dubbed the "Id." It's a mental/emotional mass, darkly steaming and rocking with inchoate sex.

Such a picture may not apply precisely to women (that's for them to say) but Freud brought something highly important to modern society's attention.

It was not unknown to neoclassical philosophers, by the way. Iamblichus of Syria, for one, coolly noted—

"The amatory mania underlies all the rest."

Carl Gustave Jung also made a crucial contribution to modern thought, by placing psychology in symbiotic relation to mythology.

"Clamp a lid on Freud's Id," Jung argued in effect. "Substitute my Collective Unconscious. This consists in mythic Archetypes whom I myself have finally identified. Ignore them at your peril. They demand obedience!"

Presumptuous? For sure.

But nothing prevents us from turning Jung's Faustian "Collective Unconscious" concept inside-out. This need not be conceived as a musty, scary old sorcerer's den. Viewed instead as a sparkling, inviting night sky, it would begin to resemble happy experience.

The Bull of Zurich and Vienna's big cheese were both raging megalomaniacs. Ambition badly skewed Jung's judgment, and Freud's as well.

My own judgment is wobbly at best, and silly at worst, by the way, as I'm aware. Hence I try and suppress it. I've always ducked authority and the limelight's glare.

Both shrinks preached that introspection is the best therapy. But is that really so? Dwelling upon one's own psychic pain while obsessively rehearsing its putative first causes, could actually exacerbate the wound.

This reminds me of the pagan demigod Narcissus. Hopelessly infatuated with his own reflection in a forest pool, he pined away and drowned, becoming a water lotus, to the nymph Echo's silent sorrow.

Neither Freud nor Jung recognized the equality and reciprocity of the sexes. Sad but so.

Thanks to the pervasive Feminist movement which has been growing amongst us for the past century and a half, millions of folks finally understand that female/male reciprocity promotes mental and emotional health.

According to widely accepted myth, God fashioned Eve from one of Adam's ribs. He's built into her, and vice-versa.

> *In the image of God*
> *created he him.*
> *Male and female*
> *created he them.*

Despite the divisive idiocies we're passing through as I write, America still pioneers in the reciprocity department. Most of us already favor women's and children's rights, minority rights, homosexual rights, total cross-cultural intercourse and finally full-scale sexual equality, by which I mean equality of joy.

Dreams are mainly wish fulfillments, or so Freud firmly asserted. I don't believe it, but I admit to having recently dreamt that I was the conquering Holy Roman Emperor Frederick

Barbarossa! Furthermore, the film star Paulette Goddard had sympathetic advice for me—

PAULETTE PROPOSES

Killing's wicked
pillage sick.
Revenge follows
fairly quick.

So lay down
thy bloody sword
and that severely
dented shield
amid forgiving
lilies of the field.

You're not so bad
a fellow, Fred.
Feel free to mount
this royal bed.

Shaft my aft
if that's the word.
Begetting life
beats making dead.
Besides, it pleases
me to yield.

It's obvious that everyone on Earth participates in Nature's creating, destroying, and re-creating process. One's tiny physical form coalesces, is born, grows, matures, ages, dies, and returns to the elements.
"*In the midst of life, we are in death!*"

One still hears that spoken, especially at funerals. But the opposite is true as well. In the midst of death, we are in life! So why shouldn't we commit ourselves to Stop, Look, and Listen for the poetry of being here at all?

THE UNAVOIDABLE

Despair, my smiling elders taught,
is weak, impractical, and inappropriate.
Yet when unlucky accidents, total defeat
or insupportable deterioration occur
no one around here can persevere.
Like embers flying ever higher
over the family campfire
we'll drift slowly
out of sight.

My daughter May married Fred Paddock, a radical Catholic and longtime mainstay of America's Rudolf Steiner Library, who began his career as a Methodist minister.

Fred abandoned the ministry because overcome by metaphysical doubts.

He's always been a dear, challenging companion and correspondent of mine. I recently received two "Notes" of his in the post.

The first one reads as follows—

"*All human beings ground their lives in certain beliefs. Whether one's belief is in science and technology, reason, secular humanism, atheism, or a good and all-powerful God, one will find times and places where one's beliefs seem contradicted by experience.*

"*How does one handle this? A clue to how the Psalmists handled it is to be seen in their discovery that deeper than 'belief' is 'trust'. Trust in spite of! There is always going to be tension between belief and experience. Trust in spite of is built directly on this tension.*"

Fred nails our basic situation there. Everyone gets by thanks to "Trust in spite of," which is a far more felicitous phrase than "Wishful thinking," "Savage superstition," "Willful ignorance," or "Stupidity, by George."

It is written that King David the Psalmist "danced for joy" before the Ark of the Covenant. Could "Trust in spite of" have endowed the legendary father of the psalms with such intense emotion, syncopating the King's cakewalk? That's my question for Fred.

David was a ready battler, an innovative ruler, and possibly a poet who harked back to a long line of Hebrew psalmists and incorporated their best efforts into his own set of psalms.

He was also a sometime scoundrel, who fell prey to his own passions and suffered insupportable grief. In short, an archetype of the human condition, packed with paradox, like the psalms themselves.

Fred's second "Note" makes a decisive breakthrough. Forgetting that I can't read Hebrew, he inked relevant Old Testament words into the following—

"Psalm 23 asserts that even if we lack nothing we must go some distance. The poem leads us into the desert valley of total darkness, because we do not lack that which is essentially human. It's no lack to be aware of the darkness surrounding us. Darkness is the very world where poetry is most at home,—an enigmatic and ambiguous phenomenon whose abiding mystery points to the hidden source of things, and their deep-down freshness."

Physicists who concern themselves with the energy/matter, space/time continuum confess that they now understand no more than "four percent" of the whole story. All the rest is "Dark Stuff," beyond the reach of current science. This remains fancy-free territory for poetry, however, as Fred suggests.

His notes remind me that when my family and I were eking out a frugal existence on what was then the unspoiled Greek island of Corfu, our seemingly tough situation proved amazingly positive.

SOURCE MUSIC

Safe in bed, almost asleep
I listened to nightingales
concealed in glistening
olive trees overhead
rehearse ancient stories
told via rhyming verse
for customers at hostelries
that angels in moonlight
aprons used to keep.

Book Five: The Blessing Way

My Joys and Desires

Deuce of Hearts

The Dali News

Free at Last

Sistine Chapel Story

1. Deuce of Hearts

Having reached what seemed the advanced age of thirty, and having interviewed many of the world's leading artists, I teetered at the top of my chosen profession.

Being a richly rewarded witness to the art world's wonders, I entertained millions of "Time" readers while giving welcome recognition to hundreds of painters, sculptors and architects.

Yet I felt subject, even so, to the ubiquitous ailment that Henry David Thoreau called "Quiet Desperation." Why? Because I'd ceased to be much use at all to my own wife and daughter,—or myself either!

Walking to work in the morning, I used to stop in at the White Rose Bar for a 25-cent bourbon shot. Why? Seeking courage to continue. What had gone so terribly wrong?

It was like an illness whose symptoms are not apparent, yet intensely felt. Meanwhile, my hard work & hard liquor regimen took its toll. Weary, dissipated, sad, and dull, was this poor devil.

One gloomy off-day, I entered a beautiful church on lower Broadway, to taste its almost empty peace. While I sat there feeling sorry for myself, two priests or deacons brought a ladder out from behind one side of the altar. I wondered what they intended to do with a ladder of such length. Dust the stained glass windows, perhaps?

They wrestled the unwieldy thing laterally around the front of the altar, kept on going, turned once more, and carried it back away from me, out of sight behind the altar's other side!

An inner voice told me that I'd been given a silent demonstration of something, but I couldn't imagine what it might be. Not until the following childhood dream floated back again—

INITIATON

Once upon a time, an angel came
stepping down her long ladder of light.
Bending over my crib, she picked me up
and carried me outside, along a terrace
shaded by huge marble sculptures
of ancient gods and goddesses.
The angel then presented me
to each particular deity.
They nodded and kindly smiled
acknowledging this wide-eyed child.

Nobody knows how and why wonderful things happen to such ephemeral and unworthy little dreamers as ourselves, but they do. So I presume to fantasize the following scene—

One fine morning in 1950, the sun god Phoebus Apollo, his father Zeus, and his ravishing aunt Aphrodite, sat down to a three-handed card game on Mount Olympus.

They'd barely begun when Apollo remarked,

"I've got my eye on a young fellow below. He's a boozy art critic, based in New York, who'll never accomplish much of anything, but he intrigues me. Unbeknownst to himself, that particular mortal has one real potential."

"What for?" Aphrodite asked.

"*Accurate afterthought.*"

Zeus raised his bushy eyebrows: "*Hmm.* I don't see much earthly use in afterthought. Prophecy, yes..."

"Listen, Dad. These days, the world spins much faster than in olden times."

"I know THAT much, my boy. Why harp on the obvious?"

Aphrodite intervened: "It's also true that bygone days never quite go by."

"They do, and then again they don't," Apollo agreed. "There's an elliptically intermittent rhythm and rhyme process at work."

Zeus chuckled: "Come now. Don't try and befuddle your old Dad with poetic diction. What's the *story*?"

"Well," Apollo replied, "no sooner does some prophet open his hairy mouth to note 'the Shock of the New,' or 'the Necessity of Change,' then things have shockingly changed, and it's too late."

Aphrodite laughed.

"What's so funny?" Apollo asked.

"I was thinking that I've got just the right girl for your poor, besotted journalist. She'd give him a whole life-raft of memories to mull over!"

"Good!" Apollo said. They both looked at Zeus, who smiled and nodded approvingly.

So the love goddess leaned intently forward, stretching out her left hand. A droplet of divine perspiration slowly trickled from Aphrodite's downy armpit. Now she flipped a deuce of hearts out of thin air, face-up...

This brings me back to historic events. It wasn't long before a new girl entered my office at Time magazine.

Wearily, I rose to greet the stranger. Attempting to cut a proper figure, I sucked in my stomach and stuck out my chest. Hoping to comport myself in friendly fashion, I gazed directly into her morning-glory blue eyes.

Thereupon I tumbled flat across my desk!

Some irresistible force had drained the strength from my limbs and even blacked out my brain for a few seconds. It was not just her extreme beauty but also our mutual destiny that laid me low.

I knew we had to go on together, for always.

Raised in Spain, Italy, and Canada, Jane Winslow Knapp had labored on a quiz show called "Stump the Experts" at CBS. Now, at age twenty-three, she'd moved down Sixth Avenue to join *Time* as a quadri-lingual Foreign News researcher.

My own researcher, Ruth Brine, had brought her in to give us the gist of a Spanish text on ancient Iberian bronzes.

Listening to the primal music in Jane's voice, while contemplating her proud yet open countenance, her slim, athletic figure and the chestnut-colored hair that rippled down to the level of her hips, I failed to register a single word.

The offices of Sports Editor Marshal Smith and Music Editor Chandler Thomas flanked mine. Hence those good buddies had heard me fall, along with the consternation and relieved laughter that followed.

As soon as I was alone again they piled in to ask what had happened.

"Gentlemen," I said, "I'm in love!"

"This is awful," Marsh told me.

"Yes," Chan agreed. "You must pull yourself together and SCREW the—"

"Not like that," I interrupted. "How can I explain? The whole thing's no use!"

"Well, if stick-work won't cut it," Marsh philosophically observed, "we'll have to think of something else."

"I know," Chan said. "Let's go out and get loaded!"

By dint of discreet inquiry I soon learned that Jane lived with her mother, sister, and brother, in a duplex apartment on Madison Avenue at Sixty-Eighth Street. So she was single!

Anne and May were on Boston's North Shore for the summer, so nothing prevented my making advances to Jane. Perversely, however, shyness set in. What if she were in love with someone else? That would be only natural. Besides, if I got in too deep there might be hell to pay.

When I confided this to my old pal Harry Maynard one mild April evening, he told me—

"There's only so much you can do for Anne. Don't let personal obligations dictate your entire life. Call this girl up RIGHT NOW!"

So I summoned sufficient courage, and phoned.

"Listen. This is Alex Eliot..."

"Yes, I'm aware of it." Jane said at once. Amazingly, she added: "I've been expecting your call."

"Could we possibly meet tonight?"

"Sure."

Our whole first night together was spent in Central Park. We strolled about, sat down on a bench and gazed around, got up and wandered as before, a hundred times or more.

The leaf-misted trees whispered as we passed beneath, and in the dark open spaces starry constellations were playing darts. There was so much to tell each other, and the sooner the better. One striking thing she said was that thought is even faster than light.

I asked how she knew, and Jane responded with a Mother Goose verse—

> *How many miles to Banbury Cross?*
> *Four-score miles and ten.*
> *Can I get there by candle-light?*
> *Yes, and back again!*

At sunrise we emerged unwearied but very hungry from our Garden of Eden. We had breakfast at the original Reubens 24-hour Deli on Fifty-Ninth Street. That's gone, I guess, but we're still here, with the weather between us as spring-like as ever.

Jane is both angel and ladder to me.

She was born in Worcester, Massachusetts, where her father Samuel Knapp owned and managed a bus line to and from Boston. While she and her siblings were still small, Jane's mother "Gigi" persuaded Sam to sell out and move the family to Spain.

The financial exchange rate would be very much in their favor, so they could enjoy a business-free, glamorous life, while giving their kids a Continental background.

After a few years of that, Spain's mid-1930's civil war drove the family to England, where Jane's dad died in an auto crash. She was nine at the time.

Gigi soon took the children to Florence, Italy, where she met and married the Canadian Consul General: John Putnam.

During adolescence, Jane got a thorough Renaissance background from Mademoiselle Juju, the family governess, who inspired her to compose a history of European art in French, illustrated with postcard reproductions.

(Gigi had the manuscript bound in Florentine leather, and we possess it still, so Jane was one book ahead of me in the art-writing department.)

Benito Mussolini's alliance with Hitler finally impelled the family to slip away. They took a train through southern "Vichy" France, and Fascist Spain to Lisbon, Portugal, and caught the last ship out from there.

In Canada, Gigi and John Putnam drifted apart.

Jane meanwhile attended a Canadian finishing school, followed by a year at Rollins College in Florida, but learned hardly anything new except that she was athletically gifted, and hated sports. She yearned to encourage people, not beat them. Competition of any kind repulsed her.

Speaking of competition, I'll excerpt Rainer Maria Rilke's *"Letter to a Young Poet,"* dated 1903—

"Woman, in whom life more immediately abides, must indeed have become more human than Man, who lacks the weight of bodily fruit pulling him down below life's surface, and undervalues what he claims to love.

"Carried to term in pain and humility, this humanity of Woman will become evident once she has shed the conventions of the merely feminine.

"And those men who cannot feel this coming today will be taken by surprise, and vanquished!"

Jane had experienced only two intense connections with men before my turn came.

The first, with a World War Two Canadian fighter pilot called Andy, was romantic. The second, with a Manhattan doctor named Eric, was physical.

Her diary for 1947, three years before we met, describes them as follows—

"Dear Andy, I loved him so, still love him. It is a friendship so deep, more beautiful than what I now feel for Eric... it had an ethereal quality, a spiritual beauty that I shall not find again.

"Eric, for whom my body aches and my mind stands still. Polar opposite to my beloved Andy. Maybe some day there will be a composition of the two.

"But let me tell of Eric—a conceited, good-looking, adorable person who will make love to me over the breakfast table but knows better than to give me anything but a coke, and drives me home with no anger."

What an inherently innocent manner of stating the not so nice!

It took me a few minutes to decipher the unflattering facts of the case. Namely that Eric laid her out across the table in his breakfast niche for male domination purposes, took care to keep her sober, and didn't mind a bit her loyalty to family. The conclusion of Jane's 1947 diary strikes me as prophetic indeed—

"Tonight, drawing close to my 21st birthday, this is the thought I wish to make part of my blood and bones. To seek for good, to do good, to be honest, to be unafraid at all times. An island fortress blending into the light of being true to myself."

Jane's courage had genetic precedents. Her mother Gigi had saved hundreds of lives by going behind John Putnam's diplomatically turned bureaucratic back to surreptitiously stamp *"Approved"* on Jewish applications for refugee visas.

Moreover, Jane's grandmother "Bam" (Ada Davenport Kendall) had helped lead a 1919 "March on Washington" to demand voting rights for women.

Denied any hearing whatsoever, the whole petticoat brigade was arrested and clapped into Washington's most disgusting slammer for a month, under cruel-on-purpose, "Damn the brazen bitches" conditions.

Released with the rest at last, "Bam" reported the whole ghastly and yet glorious story in her husband's Buffalo N.Y. newspaper, to which she regularly contributed a column called: *"As I was Going Home Last Night."*

Gigi told me that Bam always kept her kitchen door unlocked and the icebox well stocked, for hungry prowlers who frequently dropped in. Some lady!

Jane and I enjoyed exploring New York together, seeing it through fresh eyes. One of our first excursions was a walk across George Washington Bridge. At the middle, we stopped to take in the stupendous view. That's when I confessed to feeling somewhat scared.

"Why?" she asked.

"Because I have a weird fear of falling hopelessly down and down into the Hudson River! They call it agoraphobia. The trouble stems from something I experienced at the Grand Canyon."

"Stand closer to the edge," Jane said at once.

"Okay."

"Shove your thoughts downward, into your shoes. Bend your knees. Rock back and forth a bit."

"Like this?"

"Yes. Now look straight down at that barge passing underneath."

"Uh-oh! The fear—"

"That's not fear. It's the power of your greatest gift: a vivid imagination. Your mind follows the trajectory of your eyesight, but your body does not."

"I believe you."

"Not good enough! Instead, try and *feel* what I'm saying."

"Tell me more."

"Now you're gazing around and down from a perfectly balanced bipedal position that's got spring in it."

"I'm with you."

"That's true, and you're happy to be right where you are at this very minute."

"I understand!"

"You do?"

"Yes. I'm fine now."

She'd performed a crucial cure, one which would eventually enable me to reach a hermit's high, precipitous ledge, and enter his hand-crafted Chapel of the Black Virgin.

Also, to enjoy a hundred hours stretched out on my back beside Jane atop a sixty-foot-high, aluminum-pipe tower, within touching distance of Michelangelo's Sistine Ceiling.

On Labor Day, when Anne returned, I acquainted her with the changed situation.

That was a heart-wrenching experience. May suffered most of all, I suspect, although she showed it least, letting a single teardrop fall as she sat on my knee.

We contacted our friend and neighbor David Hoffman, who happened to be a lawyer as well as a chess master. At our request, he wrote a "Separation Agreement" giving Anne custody of May, and our apartment, plus full financial support and a prompt divorce on grounds of "Desertion."

The human psyche has various means of insuring its own health, efficiency and continuity; methods which differ widely from person to person. Memory and Forgetfulness are two such devices.

For me, visual, verbal, emotional, and spiritual events tend to remain vivid. On the other hand I find that hard facts, personal mistakes, precise dates, and terrible disasters, never die. Instead, like old soldiers, they—

"Just fade away."

Anne attempted suicide via a fatal overdose of sleeping pills. Luckily, I noticed the empty bottle, and got her to a hospital in time for emergency pumping out.

She was said to remain in imminent danger of repeating her suicide effort. So I somehow managed to find her a reasonably pleasant "Mental Health" asylum in Pennsylvania's Pocono Mountains.

Its director kindly informed me that Anne seemed—
"Well worth saving."
"She's worth a ton of you, that's true," I yelled in his face. "You're the crazy one, not she!"

Removing his horn-rimmed spectacles, the doctor employed a pocket handkerchief to wipe them clean of my spittle.

We stared at each other, equally helpless.

May recalls that Anne's incarceration lasted about a year. During that motherless stretch, she stayed with Jane and me, or Diane and Allan Arbus, or Gigi, or my parents, depending on our shifting capabilities as time went by.

Feeling that none of us really wanted her, May suffered courageously through what must have been a ghastly time. The truth is that all of us adored May and relished her company.

About a year before we met, Jane had naturally wearied of manipulative Eric. That handsome doctor accordingly departed to pursue his merrily cherry-picking career in Hollywood's greener pastures.

At that point, Jane felt starved for spiritual exercise. Fortunately, friends among Rudolf Steiner's American and refugee European supporters at Threefold Farm in Spring Valley N.Y., welcomed her to their week-end group activity sessions.

Steiner (1861-1925) was an Austrian clairvoyant whose "Anthroposophical Society" sponsored radical innovations in education, agriculture, and medicine.

Today's anthroposophists constitute a cultural community which supports at least a thousand Waldorf schools and another thousand biodynamic farms, plus hundreds of health clinics and homes for the disadvantaged, around the globe. Consider these passages from Steiner's voluminous work—

"The object of knowledge is not to repeat, in conceptual form, something that already exists. Instead, it is to create a totally new sphere which—combined with the world of the senses—constitutes reality.

"Truth is not, as normally assumed, an ideal reflection of something real. It's a product of the human spirit, brought about by free spiritual activity."

Steiner's key books in translation nourished Jane's intellect and reinforced her ideals. She laid them before me, naturally, opening fresh vistas. Inspired, I soon composed an essay called *"The Sense of Truth."*

Surprisingly enough, the Saturday Evening Post accepted and published my piece in its prestigious *Adventures of the Mind* series.

To publicize my essay, the magazine hung an enormously overblown photo of myself aloft in Grand Central Station!

Certain commuting Time Inc grandees were naturally irritated by their publishing rival's ploy. While admitting that they would never have printed such a "think-piece" themselves, my bosses issued a stern reprimand. In future, they commanded, I must confine myself to Time-writing.

"Fat chance!" I said, but not aloud.

Jane and I had to be frugal, so we rented rooms in a brownstone house on a Sixth Avenue corner. (It's now called "Avenue of the Americas," and of course the house itself is long gone.) Our secret haven stood conveniently across the street from Rockefeller Center. We could get to work at *Time* in ten minutes flat.

A wise old French lady named Dora, who had been mistress to a Rockefeller, owned, occupied, and ran the place. Dora reserved the second floor for herself, and kept a black housekeeper named

Lincoln, who used to bustle about with a feather duster stuck upright in his hip pocket, stooping here and there like a flustered ostrich.

The other two roomers were a bravely gay Broadway actor, and a struggling painter from Paris. We all got along fine, forming an impromptu family.

May tells me she remembers that at night the neon light sign, "Radio City Music Hall," reddened our windowpanes.

Here's a valentine I composed for Jane while we were living at Dora's—

MONDAY MORNING

Ochre sunshine sluices through
our green window-shutters' glow
Meanwhile, along Sixth Avenue
buses wheeze and groan below.
We undress-rehearse our new
Manhattan Rhapsody for Two.
I'm playing attentive beau
to your mellow native cello
adagio, si, *ma non troppo*.

I loved "living in sin," especially after Anne's eventual release from hospital care, but Jane gently reminded me that we should formalize our union.

"We could get a Municipal Court Judge to perform the ceremony," she suggested. "Let's keep it small, and please ask my brother Sam to be your best man. He needs a boost, and will do fine at organizing things."

"Okay. What's the guest-list?"

"We'll have Mum, Sam's Phyllis de Morenshield, Pat with her suitor Konrad Kellen, Diane and Allan Arbus, and little May, naturally. She's terribly important to me."

"Right," I said. "But not my parents. They're extremely fond of Anne, and still think I'm the one who lost his mind."

"I know," Jane said. "Afterward, why not celebrate by boarding the sleeper from Grand Central to Niagara Falls for a two-day honeymoon?"

"Let me think that one over," I told her.

BRIEF LIVES

At Niagara Falls, the newly wedded pair
do nothing rash and yet their bed
goes barging out between the red
plush window drapes, to splash
down upon the swift Eerie stream.
The hissing of a terrible swift sword
shakes the night air close up ahead
where grapes of wrath are stored.

"I knew it!" groans the groom.
His bride heaves a brave sigh—
*"Enjoy the downside zoom
before we up and die!"*

On second thought, I approached my bosses with a pretty presumptuous proposition.

"To enhance *Time's* Art Section," I suggested, "how's about sending Jane Knapp and me on a working tour of Europe? She has fine Continental contacts, as you know. We could collect dozens of Art stories while taking in a ton of background information."

"Hmmmm."

"And, by the way, this project would double as our honeymoon."

"OKAY. You've got a deal. But first, give us sufficient copy to fill the Art section while you're gone."

Reaching Paris in chestnut blossom season, we purchased a Peugeot convertible and swung south along the Loire. The Paleolithic painted caverns on our itinerary were still open to the public, and we were especially eager to see them.

The anti-matter "positrons," whose existence Paul Dirac predicted in the 1920's, occasionally act as if they were electrons going backward in time! Basque region cave paintings of animals produce a comparable impression, as Jane and I were now to discover.

ART FOR SEEING'S SAKE

In Altamira's cool basalt cavern
forty-three thousand years ago
tundra-pounding, ten-ton bison
let their shaggy over-soul
be made visible, via charcoal
contours and red ochre smears
applied by our fierce forbears.

The beasts' frequently overlapping sacred images bear off-again, on-again, relations to convexities and concavities in the surrounding rock face. So they doubtless coalesced from raking torchlight and tallow-lamp shadows cast along the cavern walls and ceilings.

Whole communities must have brought those creatures to birth, via drumming, dance, and ecstatic song, all three interleaved with shamanic sketching of whatever loomed through the flickering, intermittently illuminated rock.

The amazing accuracy achieved cannot have been technical, let alone intellectual. Instead, it was devotional and visionary...

During the course of our trip, we visited a number of Jane's old haunts. The revered art connoisseur Bernard Berenson (ritually addressed as "B.B") was a childhood acquaintance of hers whom we stopped in to see.

Pale and frail at about ninety, B.B. quavered—

"*So you're from* Time? *Now tell me, please, what is* Time?"

"Well," I said, "it's rather like *Newsweek*, which I noticed on your hall table."

"Oh? And what do *you* do?"

"I'm a journalist."

"Thank God. I was afraid you might be a *critic!*"

I laughed out loud, whereupon B.B. dropped his mask of helplessly inquiring second-childhood.

"When I was at Harvard," he said, "Charles W. Eliot ran the place as president. His son Sam, who must have been your grandfather, befriended me. Now, I was nothing but a poor Hebrew boy on scholarship, so why do you suppose we two bonded?"

B.B. paused expectantly. I couldn't think what to reply.

"True quality!" he explained, with a triumphant glitter in his eyes. "Quality, you understand, has some indefinable way of recognizing *itself*."

Turning to Jane, he went on: "I recognized you the moment you came in!"

"I knew," Jane told him, with her blue, flashing glance.

"At age eleven or twelve you played about my garden with your brother and sister. Once, when it rained, the three of you retreated to my art library. You in particular thumbed eagerly through the larger volumes, searching out reproductions of paintings you'd never before seen."

"I remember," Jane said.

"Good. I have especially fond recollections of Sydney Knapp Putnam, your dear mother. Is she well? I'm glad. Would you convey my very warmest regards to her?"

"Of course."

"Sydney and I were in emotional concert. She once told me that everybody needs an audience."

"Yes, she still says it."

"Well, masterpieces also require full attention from someone. That's what I give them."

"You do!" I offered.

"Only the great ones. To authenticate something from an old master's hand, I must live with the picture until my senses become attuned to it. Especially the sense of touch. Not physical touch of course, but something similar. That's what tells me if the painting is true to itself."

"Are you suggesting," I asked, "that intimate personal experience beats art-historical expertise?"

He chuckled: "Between ourselves, my boy, expertise is *bunk*."

"I'm relieved to hear it," I said, "since all I've got is a somewhat shaky sensibility."

"That makes a good start."

"Thank you."

"I'm regarded as the leading expert on Italian Renaissance art. For practical reasons, I play the part. But the Flemish Primitives please me even better than my specialty, and ancient Chinese bronzes give me the greatest thrill of all. They're so tactile, don't you know..."

B.B. sat silent for a minute. Then, in a surprisingly tentative tone, he added—

"My passions, if you'll excuse that rather hackneyed expression, are not understood."

"Help *us* to understand," Jane said.

With a tired sigh, B.B. shut his eyes, and explained—

"Scholars, connoisseurs, and scientists examine matters analytically, which is better than paying no attention whatever. But great artists regard the world differently. They experience everything in the *round*. Well, I follow in those artists' footsteps, as best I can."

"Me, too!" I told him.

"Just what do you mean? I thought journalists were paid to get things *straight*, rather than round."

"Both together would be best. It's my policy not to strain after conclusions, but let them appear in due course. I pay sympathetic attention, meanwhile, like yourself."

The fragile old fellow was noticeably tiring, so we got up to leave.

B.B. sat hunched, small, and weak, unable to rise. He blew a heartfelt kiss Jane's way. Then he glanced over at me with an air of inquiry, and blew a second kiss to me!

I felt like bending to kiss his wrinkled brow in return, and should have done so, but didn't dare...

Arriving at Venice, we were greeted by Count Ottavio Zazio, who served as *Time's* "stringer" or part-time reporter and facilitator.

Ottavio arranged our stay at the Gritti Palace Hotel on the Grand Canal, close by Harry's Bar and Piazza San Marco's loitering-space, with its bubbly Byzantine basilica, clock tower, campanile, strollers, pigeons, musicians, and cafe tables.

I was particularly struck by certain Venetian old masters. Titziano of the Brassiere family, and Bellini the Weenie King, plus the big *panetone* Giorgione, were three who gave me quite a wallop. (Just kidding, of course.)

Our new friend had sometimes gone duck hunting with Ernest Hemingway.

"Hem talked a good hunt," the burly Count confided, "but he couldn't shoot worth a damn."

"Why not?" I asked.

"Bad eyesight. Well, never mind. It was fun to drink with him, and I loved watching him at work. When he wrote *Across the River and Into the Trees* out at our Torcello hide-away, Hem used to get so quiet, round-eyed, like a small boy struggling with arithmetic."

On a speedboat taxi ride home from the glass-blowing islet of Murano, Jane pretended not to be aware that the Count was surreptitiously fondling the windblown luxuriance of her long hair.

I also tried to ignore the matter, but Ottavio must have sensed our nervousness.

He got up, said goodbye, and valiantly vaulted up out of the boat onto the first Venetian bridge beneath which we chugged!

SOFT TOUCH

Jane's crowning glory, as they say
has since turned moonlight gray.
When I tousle its radiant glow
these lucky fingers tingle so!

Over cocktails on the Gritti terrace that evening, while Jane was dressing for dinner, Ottavio told me with tears in his eyes: "I fear that I have humpered you."

"You mean 'hampered'," I said. "Listen. Ottavio, the opposite is true. You personally have opened up a whole wonderful new world for Jane and me."

"That's a relief. And what a lucky man you are! Jane will be down on her knees on the rug, playing with your children. But you must never call her 'Mother'!"

"I won't," I promised.

"Americans do it. Of course you wouldn't."

"Thanks, Ottavio."

"Alex, I want you and Jane to come and meet my mother, and my aunt. We've got a shabby apartment. It overlooks a narrow canal that doesn't always smell right."

"What an honor—"

"I never invited old Hem. It's my damn pride! You'll be the only Americans ever to enter my home."

Wending our wine-weary way back to Manhattan, we settled into a wide-windowed, book-walled penthouse off upper Fifth Avenue. It commanded a bird's eye view of midtown, which was growing taller all the time.

The swing era was said to be over, but we still collected jazz records and danced to them at parties that happened almost every night.

Being human involves emotional neediness. There's nothing in the least shameful about that. As Adam needed Eve and vice-versa, we all need each other. So, if two or more join together for the purpose, that's better still.

"We've had enough parties, don't you agree?" Jane finally told me. "What I really want is children."

"Me, too!" I said. "Let's fuck around the clock until they manifest!"

"I'm game," she replied, decisively unzipping my fly to finger-fish the required instrument forth. Raising her right hand, she cupped my testicles with her left, and solemnly swore—

"My heart cries out for a son and daughter!"

It wasn't long before our kids, first Jefferson and then Winslow, came to Jane and me. In the physical sense, Jeff and Wyd had separated out from us. In every other sense, they'd joined with us, forever.

May resided with her mother, naturally, but we were able to see a lot of her, and she sometimes stopped with us overnight. May was always part of the family.

Given Jane's motherly genius and my own relatively clumsy paternal efforts, but mostly thanks to all three children's noble and adaptable natures, home happened.

That was—and still remains—the most rewarding occurrence in my entire life.

Jane and I had meanwhile passed beyond the forest primeval of "I surrender, dear!" infatuation, and begun experiencing normal differences between ourselves. We got less attached, yet more together, as time went by, like opposite poles of the same flowing energy.

Charity, by which Saint Paul meant spontaneous forgiveness, begins at home. That pulled us through occasional dust-ups...

Living two blocks south of Manhattan's Metropolitan Museum, Jane and I often went there. We especially enjoyed the Asiatic section, with its superb installations and absence of visitors, plus the low-voltage lighting.

I admired Alan Priest, the Met's Curator of Asiatic Art, both for his beautiful displays and for his genial essays in the museum's Bulletin. We'd been thrown together on various occasions, yet never really conversed.

Then one day when Jane and I arrived, the guards turned up the lights, full blast. I protested, naturally, whereupon they told me they were following Doctor Priest's explicit instructions!

Angrily, I barged into his office. Priest greeted me with a grin. "I wondered when you'd come," he said. "The best stuff isn't out there. I keep it hidden in my desk."

Opening a drawer, he pulled out a Chinese bronze and passed it over. I called Jane in. We handled and eyed the precious piece while Priest eloquently expatiated upon its history, mythic associations, and significance.

Alan accompanied us home for dinner, and stayed past midnight. Our new-found friend could drink like a fish and perform like a wizard. At one point he put lighted cigarettes in both his nostrils, to mime a Chinese dragon!

A few weeks after that, Alan invited us to enjoy a Sunday outing with him at the Bronx Zoo.

My only recollection of the zoo is that Jane knelt down and put her nose against the wire cage-front behind which a superb leopard sorrowed in utter solitude.

Her heartfelt sympathy attracted the beast, who'd probably been captured as a cub. Hunching close, he pressed his bewhiskered snout to Jane's face through the wire. My heart went out to both parties.

Primitive tribes around the world relish myths of human intercourse with fellow animals. There's a Tlingit Alaskan myth of the Girl who married a Bear, and a Chukchee Siberian myth of the Girl who married a Whale.

Other marriages involved beavers, seals, buffalo, caribou, and swans. The partners taught each other their languages, plus many a magic trick. Then, as a rule, they parted, with tragic results.

The myth survives, of course, in fairytales and poems, including one by Denise Levertov, which I'll excerpt for its evocation of otherness.

> *Rose Red's cheeks are burning,*
> *sign of her ardent, joyful*
> *compassionate heart.*
> *Rose White is pale,*
> *turning away when she hears*
> *the bear's paw on the latch.*
>
> *When he enters, there is*
> *frost on his fur.*
> *He draws near to the fire*
> *giving off sparks.*
>
> *Together Rose Red and Rose White*
> *sing to the bear;*
> *it is a cradle song, a loom song,*
> *a song about marriage, about*
> *a pilgrimage to the mountains*
> *long ago.*
>
> *Raised on an elbow,*
> *the bear, stretched on the hearth*
> *nods and hums; soon he sighs*
> *and puts down his head.*

He sleeps; the Roses
bank the fire.
Sunk in the clouds of their feather bed
They prepare to dream.

Rose Red in a cave that smells of honey,
dreams she is combing the fur of her cubs
with a golden comb.
Rose White is lying awake.

Rose White shall marry the bear's brother.
Shall he too
when the time is ripe,
step from the bear's hide?
Is that other, the bridegroom,
here in the room?

Later that same Sunday, Alan Priest served us green tea, in lovely old Chinese cups, at his elegantly austere East Eighty-Fourth street bachelor apartment.

This reminded me of a book I'd read concerning the Zen Buddhist Tea Ceremony.

So I asked: "What is Zen?"

"I can't tell you in words," Alan replied, "but I myself was lucky enough to endure a six months' apprenticeship in the Gobi desert, learning the tradition of the Sixth Patriarch, who got knocked down five times, and jumped up six times."

"Talk about higher mathematics!" I said. "How did he manage?"

"You'll find out."

"I will?"

"Yes. My teacher transmitted enlightenment to me by means of a quick tap on the knee. Then he instructed me to pass on what I'd earned, at the right moment, to ONE person only. Well, I've been looking and looking…"

Alan leaned over and tapped my knee! Bewildered, I thanked him, adding: "But I don't feel any different."

Priest smiled indulgently.

His knee-tap triggered a result, although not for some time. Twenty years later, as Jane and I stood by Alan's grave in Kyoto, Japan, all this came back again...

Time's Sports Editor Marshal Smith sometimes invited me to attend athletic events with him. I recall a sweltering fight night at Madison Square Garden, when the semi-final bout brought us both to our feet.

Pointing toward the victor, Marsh said—

"We've just seen the world's next Heavyweight Champion in action!"

Marsh was right, as usual. The Rock could be bloodied and bruised like the rest of us, but never, ever flattened. Marciano fought the finest Heavies in prizefighting's golden days, and never lost a professional bout, retiring with a *"50 & 0"* record.

MR. KNOCKOUT

He'd plop down on one knee
cross himself confidently
and then arise to mortify
the befuddled other guy.

When the champ was preparing for his historic Philadelphia punch-up with Jersey Joe Walcott, I eagerly talked my bosses into letting me go chat Rocky up at his training-camp in the Catskills. Purpose: to concoct a thousand-word "Personality" piece on him.

Having zero interest in prizefighting, Jane arranged to spend the day with Diane Arbus, while I drove upstate with her husband Allan.

Near Marciano's camp we pulled alongside a mild looking jogger on the road to ask directions.

"I'm Rocky," he said. "Please follow me."

Rocky's father, his trainer Charlie Goldstein, and I, sat under a tree, shooting the breeze with the fighter while he "cooled out" from his jog, and Allan photographed him.

At an extremely compact hundred and ninety pounds ("built like a brick shithouse," as the saying was) Rocky didn't look all that powerful. Yet there was something Herculean about his calm, scarred face and easy manner.

"Champ," I asked, "tell me, what's the best thing about your work?"

"The *money*!" Rocky replied in his soft tenor voice.

"Really?"

He nodded: "Fighting pays a hunnert times more than the Army, where I learned how."

"What about the glory?"

"That's good, too, I guess. To tell da troot, what I most enjoy is hitting a guy's sweet spot."

"What's that like?"

"I feel da trill up me arm."

"And the other fellow?"

"Falls down like a sack of Purina!"

"Well, what do you enjoy next best?"

"Dunno. Getting hit maybe."

"You must be kidding."

"Nah. Wakes me up to fight. It don't hurt, see?"

"The hell it *don't*!" Charlie Goldstein put in.

Surprised, Rocky stared at his trainer, who glared back.

I guess concentration on the job at hand immunized the Rock from pain in the prize-ring, whereas faithful Charley Goldstein must have been agonized with concern each time his man took a solid hit.

"My boy is strong," Rocky's Dad remarked. "Yeah, but I'm stronger still. Comes of work at the Brockton Shoe plant."

The Champion smiled, with filial respect.

Like prizefighters, writers also tend to be intensely competitive. Quite a few used to dream of creating "The Great American Novel."

"Great" is an elastic word, frequently employed where "mediocre" would suffice. Hence I've never aspired to greatness. Instead, I try and celebrate a host of better people than myself. Those "larger than life," so to speak.

The 19th century was the novel's apex, I believe, featuring Trollope & Dickens in England, Flaubert & Stendhal in France, Tolstoy & Dostoevsky in Russia, and Herman Melville & Mark Twain in America.

Twain was a keen-eyed Mississippi riverboat skipper, who left that position to become a free-lancing newsman, whereas Melville had been an ocean spanning Yankee seaman.

Melville's albino whale and Twain's "Nigger Jim" translate our nation's historic essence into black & white, for people not yet born to peruse and wonder over.

Cleo the Muse of History meanwhile composes her own invisible volumes concerning American efforts at liberation from our racial, religious, class-war, gender-bending and generational hang-ups.

We, the multi-racial people of this nation keep leading the way, in our admittedly stumbling, bumbling fashion, toward full human decency. That's one thing to write home about...

Way back during the 1930's, sex had been regarded as off-limits, unmentionable in polite company. Yet Henry Miller, a Bronx-bred, Ur-male master of the raspberry, dared clang a bright brass Liberty Bell for sexual license.

His staunchly raunchy autobiographical novels, *The Tropic of Cancer* and *The Tropic of Capricorn*, were first published in Paris by Olympia Press, with great success. Jean Cocteau, Blaise Cendrars, Ezra Pound, T.S. Eliot, and Aldous Huxley all praised them to the skies.

Both books were banned in America, naturally (until 1964) but we'd bought them on our honeymoon, and much enjoyed the two.

So we soon made a point of tracking Miller down to his West Coast retreat at Big Sur, California.

His proudly erect frame and bald, sunburned head, piercing pale, beady eyes, projected phallic dignity. I could easily imagine Henry Millering about in the slender white arms and Grand Central hospitality of Anais Nin.

Who was she? Miller's discoverer, passionate lover, and a second sex writer, if I may so describe her.

We found Miller proud and vain, condescending to us but disgusted with America. U.F.O.'s, or "Unidentified Flying Objects," were a hot topic, and he had a theory concerning them.

"It's obvious," Miller informed us, "that aliens from Mars or wherever are checking us out to see whether we should be allowed to fester any fucking further. They'll let us have it any day now."

A color-blind painter named Emile White, who lived nearby and kept a kindly eye on the old man, informed us that Miller's young wife had recently left him cold, taken their infant daughter and gone home to her mother.

Miller's abandoned fate reminded me of a lament by the ancient Chinese classic Po Chu'i, which I knew from Arthur Waley's translation. So, instead of reporting on our fairly barren interview, I chose to recast Waley's labor in free-wheeling style, as follows—

PO'S PLAINT

When my princess departed
she forgot her bronze mirror
like reflective pond, minus lotus.
Long time not to see her dear face.
Why not pry open mirror case?

Holy Confucius! What is this?
My withered visage, of course.
Etched upon mirror's reverse
a cumulous cloud-dragon pair
copulates, and I feel worse.

The novel called *Go!*, by button-nosed John Clellon Holmes, well documents the Manhattan clam chowder in which we aspiring young writers simmered and seethed.

Holmes and his girl inhabited a Lexington Avenue walk-up of the dark, narrow sort then called a "railroad apartment." One night they threw a small party there to celebrate Jack Kerouac's having found a publisher for *On The Road*.

Like Jackson Pollock in painting, and Charlie Parker in music, Jack had achieved unprecedented freedom in prose. How? By scrolling one end of a tracing-paper roll (120 feet long) into his typewriter, and ad-libbing ahead for three weeks with no interior dither or second thoughts, while his typescript curled, un-edited, like a left-behind highway on the rug.

Rolling up his achievement, Jack took it down to Union Square offices of Farrar, Strauss & Company. He triumphantly unscrolled his creation across editor Robert Giroux' carpet, only to be told—

"Get that thing outta here!"

Feeling furious and unstoppable, Jack had then offered the work to Malcolm Cowley at Viking, who demanded a host of revisions. Jack objected—

"This was dictated by the Holy Ghost!"

Then, on second thought, he obediently re-wrote and assiduously revised his typescript, which was finally about to see the light of day.

The phonograph was playing "That Old Black Magic," as I recall, and I was dancing with Luba "The Tuba" Petrova, whose powerful figure threatened to split her satin dress.

Luba's paramour, my old friend Alan Harrington, leaned against a wall meanwhile, disagreeing with Jane about something.

Muscular and very handsome, Kerouac sat relaxed in his barebulb circle of light, palm-patting an up-ended steel waste-basket for bongo-drum.

Kerouac had attended Columbia on an athletic scholarship, to play for the noted football coach Lou Holz. The game did not appeal to Jack's gentle and undisciplined nature, so after some time he quit cold, explaining to sportswriters that he felt "beat" by it all.

Thus he breathed the first self-pitying sigh of what would come to be called "The Beat Generation."

Pious justifications of the term, such as "Beat" for "Beatific," were manufactured later.

The footloose, pilgrimage-prone 'Sixties, and the Flower Child cloudburst, were still on the horizon, no larger at that point than the back of Jack's hand. Yet, during one of those silent spells which occur at parties, he looked around and announced—

"I represent a *different breed* from you guys! You slave at stupid jobs, sit around in your blue serge suits, and fuck somebody come Sunday, while my kind is smoking pot, stealing cars, and driving top-speed away to dig the fabulous U.S. of A!"

"Sounds irresponsible to me," Harrington wistfully observed.

The women present did not regard themselves as rivals to the men. That's how it was back then, but Jane would finally become a really swell author and a "different breed" for sure. To tell the truth, she's a better writer than me.

Witness her memoir called *"Around the World by Mistake."* This concerns a months-long freighter voyage upon which we fecklessly embarked with little Jefferson and Winslow, back in the 1960's. Jane plumbs the truth of that fabulous family adventure, as I can testify.

Our Kerouac party concluded very late, at Minton's jazz hangout up in Harlem. Jane gladly danced with members of the black clientele who dropped by our table. We white boys didn't dare approach the black girls, however because those were savage, razor-blade times, which would gradually get worse yet...

Journalists like me were envied and pitied, both at once, for having sold out to the enemy. "You can't write a novel and work for Time," friends warned, but they were wrong.

Our editorial working hours ran from around ten or ten-thirty in the morning to six or seven at night, with a long boozy lunch out. I made a practice of getting in at eight-thirty to work on my first novel.

Composing my twenty-four-hour tale cost me no less than seven years of piecemeal effort.

The plot, such as it was, concerned a teen-age brother and sister. During summer vacation at their family retreat on the Maine coast, the siblings find themselves sexually drawn to one another.

Jane provided moral support plus editorial advice, and typed out the final version. We pasted up the prize-winning dust jacket together. Diane and Allan Arbus shot me looking like a tough guy for the jacket's back cover. I remember Diane giggling as she lit the Marlborough cigarette between my lips.

I called my virgin effort *"Proud Youth and the Priest."* Its publisher, Roger Strauss, cut that down to *"Proud Youth"* for fear of offending ecclesiastics.

The hardcover edition did poorly but got encouraging reviews, and the two "mass paperback" 25-cent editions that followed sold half a million copies altogether.

Sadly for me, however, *"Proud Youth"* left most of my friends and relations cold.

The austere designer Ward Bennett, a pal with whom I generally saw eye to eye, urged me to: "Put this forlorn effort behind you, and tell the story of your love for Jane!"

Diane's brother Howard said he liked what I was "trying to do."

My former wife Anne Dick offered a typically generous and yet acute comment, noting that the work possessed: "A peculiar yet poignant hand-made quality."

Grandma Frances Hopkinson Eliot let me down gently, writing that she herself preferred Anthony Trollope.

Huntington Cairns, the lawyer/sage at Washington's National Gallery, noted that I had picked a subject of which I knew: "Little or nothing." Meaning incest.

The truth is that I'd long regarded my old-time yen for Diane Arbus as incestuous. Guilty confusion used to tear at my heart because, after all, Diane's husband Allan and her brother Howard were both like brothers to me!

Since I couldn't explain or justify my behavior, I transposed and fully fictionalized it, for the double purpose of entertaining gentle readers while easing my own troubled psyche. That's a novelist's privilege.

Proud Youth is concealed autobiography, crammed with crucial moments in my personal existence, plus a few early verses.

The story climaxes with its protagonist attempting to commit suicide by wrecking his sailboat on an Atlantic reef. His formerly estranged parents barely manage to motorboat out there and rescue him in the nick of time. Afterward, the siblings get together, yes, but on a firmly platonic level, and start understanding each other...

My friend Arthur Lubow is hard at work on what may be the definitive story of Diane's art and life. He recently phoned with news about a just-published psychobiography, so-called, of Diane.

"Psychobiography" appears to be a fiercely growing fashion today. I myself can't condone it, because I don't suppose that the defenseless dead enjoy being patronized as badly conflicted, emotionally pitiable, and mentally unstable out-patients.

Besides, such truly touching and indeed great artists as Diane deserve special consideration, don't they?

The author of the volume in question had dug deep into the Arbus archives. They reveal that Diane maintained a lifelong, incestuous entanglement with Howard!

Apparently, Diane's first biographer, Patty Bosworth, knew all about the stunning facts of the case, but chose to suppress them for Howard's sake. (The only decent course under the circumstances.)

Arthur's news reminds me that ages ago, one day at the Cummington summer school, where Diane and I met as teen-agers, a lone mosquito approached her bare, scarcely developed bosom.

She smiled in welcome.

Alighting, the thirsty creature stuck his stinger well down into the purplish aureole of Diane's left-side, puckered pink nipple.

Having serenely siphoned a nutritious drop or two of good red blood from Diane's adolescent, richly pulsating heart region, he lifted off again in tumescent condition, and gratefully whined away.

I don't suppose Diane ever turned anybody down!

2. The Dali News

The Persistence of Memory, Salvador Dali's signature image, hangs at Manhattan's Museum of Modern Art. Painted in exquisite Flemish Primitive style, this features a half-melted watch dangling from the outstretched arm of a dead tree.

Done in 1931, that picture eerily foreshadowed the horrors of the Spanish Civil War, followed by World War Two. Hiroshima and Nagasaki were great cities until American atom bomb attacks melted and tossed whole multitudes of Japanese urbanites in mid-thought and their wristwatches in mid-tick.

The limp watch that Dali depicted still ticks, tocks, and knocks upon public consciousness. This never would have happened, were it not for the input of an intellectually intense and sexually insatiable Russian woman, nicknamed Gala. (Her given name was Elena Diakonova.)

She had begun her courtesan career by persuading the surrealist artist Max Ernst to believe in the Importance of Being Ernst. Thereupon, he did indeed catapult to the glittering apex of the art scene for a brief spell.

Next, Gala attempted to convince gentle, sad, sex-mad Paul Eluard that he was every bit as poignant a French poet as he was a trenchant lover in the clutch.

Eluard couldn't quite bring himself to take her word on the matter, so Gala began looking around for some new man to whom she might devote her brilliance and vaunting ambition.

She first met Dali at Cadaques, a beach resort on Spain's Costa Brava, near the French border. Gala and Eluard had come down there on holiday. Young Dali was a summer regular, along with his bourgeois father and patient sister.

At that point in the 1920's, Dali's sanity and sexual orientation were both uncertain. The poet Frederico Garcia Lorca, who had been a fellow student at Madrid's Academy of Art, strongly attracted him, along with feminine garments and what he called "stinking perfumes."

Terribly afraid of grasshoppers, Dali also suffered homicidal mania. He even dreamed of hurling Eluard's scantily clad, inaccessible sacred cow to her death from the rocks behind Cadaques!

Being highly intuitive, Gala soon guessed what was on his mind. So, one sultry afternoon, she made a show of sashaying ahead of him, to the brink of a high cliff. As Dali approached, she lifted her gaze from the deathly abyss and turned, keeping her hands at her sides, to confront him—

"Croak me!"

Gala was asking for it. With a simple quick push, Dali could have crushed those hard-boiled breasts, shattered those slim hips, and wiped the thin, jungle-red grin from her tanned face.

But while his antics may have fractured some, Dali never killed anyone. His fine, fantastically embroidered book called *"The Secret Life of Salvador Dali"* tells what happened next—

"I kissed her on the mouth, inside her mouth. It was the first time I did this. I had not suspected until then that one could kiss in this way. With a single leap, all the Parsifals of my long bridled and tyrannized erotic desires rose, awakened by shocks of the flesh."

"You must cut yourself off," Gala earnestly informed Dali, "from everything except painting and me. You and I together will make a single demand upon the hand of Dali. To illustrate Dali's mind!"

How could the soon-unbuttoned unknown resist so flattering a proposal from so bravely seductive a siren? Eluard obligingly departed for France, and Gala stayed.

The mutually infatuated pair used to get mildly stoned on drugs whilst harkening to castanets and tambourines mingled with the cries of long-barreled Catalan oboes, on Gala's sporty little gramophone.

Then, while Dali pondered and sketched, she read aloud to him from a couple of antique tomes.

Namely (as Gala informed me decades later), the 13th Century Kabbalist classic *"Zohar"* by Moses de Leon, and *"The Book of Marvels"* by the Medieval Majorcan Arabist Ramon Lull.

Almost overnight, Dali blossomed as an artist, and became world-famous. The ideally coupled partners spent months at a time in Paris, New York, and London, for purposes of high society play, plus resultant publicity.

Dali paraded his persona with lavish, dare-devil invention. His waxed, black, upright moustache must have been a nuisance to maintain erect. But it put whatever he might utter in hovering portentous parenthesis.

Dali sometimes strolled the streets with his painting arm in a sling. "No, not an accident," he'd assure sympathizers. "It's asleep!"

Having agreed to lecture at the Sorbonne on the subject of Jan Vermeer's "The Lace Maker, Dali arrived in a white convertible sedan crammed with a thousand cauliflowers.

Outraged by a Bonwit Teller window-display which he had deigned to design and the store's Sales Director had presumed to modify, Dali slid a sofa smashingly straight through the plate-glass and leaped furiously out after it, landing amid astounded pedestrians on the pavement of Manhattan's Fifth Avenue.

The following day, when painfully bitten by a television personality (a chimp named J. Fred Muggs) he responded: *"Enchante!"*

Invited to a cultural conference in London, Dali mounted the platform wearing a deep-sea diver's spherical helmet. He meant to give a lecture in dumb-show, under glass, by means of gesticulations alone.

No one had told him the helmet was air-tight. In a few minutes he was desperately signaling for help. Nobody guessed that he might be suffocating. Amid appreciative laughter, he fell to the floor.

Finally, noticing that Dali lay motionless, a fireman dashed onstage, unfastened the helmet and uncorked the purple-faced painter just this side of death...

Soon afterward, Dali met with Sigmund Freud, and produced a poignant sketch of the old man, giving Freud's cranium a twist to make it resemble an indrawn snail's residence.

Afterward, Freud slyly observed that it's wise to consider the Unconscious in Leonardo, say, but seek out the Conscious in Dali!

Although he was far from crazy, Dali's little gray cells were indeed lucid to the point of hallucination.

I first interviewed him at Manhattan's St. Regis Hotel, where he was finishing his *Leda Atomica*, or *Leda and the Swan*. Gala had posed for it, attired in flesh-tones alone, and seated upon the thinnest of turquoise and silver atmosphere.

"Weel appear clouds dans le sky!"

So Dali assured me, eloquently flicking his fingers across the picture's smooth, moist surface. (The clouds never came, so far as I'm aware.)

Although astonished by the work itself, with its rigidly throbbing, frigidly aspiring swan, I composed a story poking fun at the artist and his sexually charged subject for Time.

ILLUSTRATIONS

In Salvador Dali's Galactic follies
drooping noses require crutches.
Elephants pose on brush touches.
Giraffes go by with necks aflame.

Ladies' breast and belly drawers
get yanked open minus cause.
Raging lions pounce upon
presciently absent game.

Such anomalies offer people
sufficient reason to pause.

Our next encounter occurred in the elevator of an art gallery building on the north side of Fifty-Seventh Street near Fifth Avenue. Jane and I were descending from an exhibition. Two floors down, the doors opened and Dali stepped in. He glanced at me, registered Jane's stunning beauty, and immediately lowered his gaze.

Abashed, feeling guilty about my *Time* piece, I failed to greet him. Unforgivably so.

Mute, intense, Dali concentrated full attention upon his well-polished shoe-tips. Then, as the little elevator rocked and squeaked to the street floor, he set himself for action.

The moment the doors opened, he dashed madly away, out of the building. Alarmed, I followed as fast as I could.

With his fedora clapped tight against his head, and his gray, fur-collared cape flapping like a banner behind him, the artist plunged suicidally straight into Fifty-seventh Street's traffic.

Dodging busses and screechy cabs, ignoring the screams of pedestrians and honking curses of drivers, he zigzagged diagonally across, and kept running full-tilt, south along Fifth Avenue.

By then Jane had joined me on the curb. "What was *that* about?" I asked.

Reassuringly, she said: "He wants an invitation to dinner!"

Trusting Jane's intuition, I phoned the St. Regis and asked for Dali's suite. The painter answered the phone, and, with cheerful alacrity, accepted my invitation for himself and Gala.

Jane enjoyed staging small dinner parties with adequate wines and regional specialties which she generally cooked herself. In Dali's honor she served Catalan *paella* this time, containing all the traditional ingredients except unborn mice.

We'd invited our friend Henry Koerner and the young Italian surrealist Domenico Gnoli to join the fun. Both men conversed in sparkling style, while Dali, sipping ice-water, maintained a silent pose of paternal disinterest.

Hoping to draw the master from his shell, I finally stood up, wine-glass in hand, offering a toast—

"To J.M.W. Turner, the father of Impressionism, the grandfather of Abstract Expressionism, and a human angel of light!"

"*Le* Turner," Dali corrected me, "was a disgusting yellowist!"

With a fatuous smile, I subsided back onto my chair. Shocked silence ensued. Gala had been plainly bored up to that point. Now at last she brightened a bit.

Dali himself sat very straight, with his hands folded upon the silver head of the sword-cane between his knees.

"Paul Cezanne is my god," Koerner put in. "He created apples I can touch!"

Dali stared, with Buster Keaton intensity, and Henry did likewise, right back at him.

"Cezanne," Dali declared, "was a walking skeleton. An apple by Cezanne is only geometrical form. Bite, and you choke!"

Like Harpo Marx with a megaphone, Henry rose to stand over Dali, crowing Cezanne's praises.

Dali's upturned face gleamed pale as a flounder's belly. Raising his sword cane, he pointed it at Koerner's nose.

I prepared to throw myself between the contestants if necessary. But Koerner was just having fun; he soon sat down again.

Turning to me, Dali said—

"Le Turner's murky light lacks all moral justification!"

"Could be," I offered in a peaceable tone. "But what about his refulgent shadows?"

"*Fock* le Turner! My divine Raphael subjects both light and shadow to le tendre embrace. Regardez Saint George weeth le *dragon*."

(He was of course referring to the small, radiant panel by Raphael at Washington's National Gallery, with its sweetly invincible saint on a white charger.)

Dali had absently secreted one of our small silver olive forks in his breast pocket. Snatching it out again, he sprang to his feet, waved the fork about, and speared the air for emphasis as he explained—

"Beyond good and evil, comes good again!"

"That's true," Jane said.

"Aha! *someone* understands me."

"Yes, I do. Please continue."

"Eez very simple, my friend. You may devour le dragon comme un *scampi*, with divine Raphael sauce!"

His assertion was extravagant, even comic if you like, yet struck me as dramatically correct, and I thanked him for it. From that point on, the conversation flourished in amicable fashion.

The next morning, Dali dropped by and presented Jane with a small, ear-shaped shell, which he had picked up on the beach as a boy. The same enigmatic symbol of deep hearing appears and disappears, depending on one's distance, in his *Madonna of the Ear* at Manhattan's Museum of Modern Art.

While Gala and I sat vaguely following their drift, our partners used to communicate mainly in English, mingled with a little Catalan for the optimisms of childhood, Spanish for the mystical edges of ideas, and French for artistic precision. They circled in upon a host of unanswerable questions such as—

"One's larynx is a womb of words, but does it also listen and convey vibrations to one's autonomic system?

"Do the Atlantic and Pacific oceans perform as dampers for our planet's liquidly flappable ears?

"When cicadas friction their violin extremities to shrill the summer meadows, what does that one-note Frittata or omelet express?"

Such questions were left hanging, naturally. Although he was incredibly proud and vain, Dali possessed simple reverence also, like a jester who juggles for a god unknown.

Last night, I dreamt that Dali gave me a riddle—

"What makes a tall man luckier than a short one?"

"That's easy!" I said. "He can peer up through the fragrant, heavy June blossoms, and part them with his hands. As darkness falls, his gaze pierces the whispering leaves. He and he alone is still able to read the cast-iron street signs."

I was badly disappointing my old friend.

Angrily, Dali stamped his feet. Clad in alligator oxfords, they made no sound on the carpet. With a final flutter of his fine pale hands, he disappeared.

This dream reminds me of a trip I once made in order to report on some Native American antiquities unearthed at New Mexico's Chaco Canyon.

While standing alone at one of the open kiva ruins, in a vacant mood, I started singing a pop song from my youth called "Little Sir Echo," and playfully bouncing it off a nearby cliff.

That's when a glittering raven appeared out of the blue, to fly right at my face! Veering off at the last second, she flapped out of sight. To say I was shaken would be an understatement.

I was totally unaware of the fact that my elder sister Torka Eliot O'Brien lay dying at the nearby Albuquerque hospital.

Driving to the airport at day's end, I "inadvertently" turned in at the hospital instead. Getting out of the car, I stood aimlessly looking up at the windows, behind one of which—unbeknownst to me—Torka lay.

Feeling idiotic, I drove on to catch my flight home. When I arrived here, there was no more Torka there.

Decades previously, she had spent a teen-age year in London studying for a career in theater, which was not to be her destiny.

Torka was a very beautiful girl. Wearing bright lipstick, a rose in her titian hair, and a white silk second-skin of an evening gown, she attended a grand theatrical ball one night, and found herself monopolized, or "danced until dawn," by a strange man indeed. His waxed, upright mustache tickled her cheeks.

Salvador Dali performed everything from the waltz down through the tango to the Charleston, perfectly. She had adored showing off with him, Torka told me. No thought of past or future smudged that enchanted night...

Without so much as touching a wingtip to Gala, his "Leda Atomica," Dali managed to fertilize an invisible egg which hatched mirages of glowing devotion. Consider for instance his airborne, crucified *Christ of Saint John of the Cross* at Glasgow, for which the Hollywood stunt-man Ross Saunders painfully posed.

The Sacrament of the Last Supper, at Washington's National Gallery, hums with pentatonic resonance. The abyss of the nucleus opens. A fishing skiff lies moored to the Messiah's heart. The bread of his body breaks and parts. The crimson liquid rises in his simple glass.

The Apostles kneel; their thick fisherman-fingers fold upon the unknowable. The table linen hardens, turns to stone. The Savior signals with his hands, pointing down toward the sacrament, and up toward the huge, partly revealed figure above and behind him. It's *El hombre con pechos.* Literally, "The man with breasts."

In *Finnegan's Wake,* James Joyce mysteriously informs us—

"He had buckgoat paps on him. Soft ones, for orphans."

Being an accomplished calligrapher, Dali once took the trouble to ink-brush a French encomium on parchment and present it to me. Translated, this reads—

"Almost demoniacally, Freud penetrates a work of art. Malraux mingles it with his own anguish. Between these poles of promiscuity, Eliot's moral attitude is original: Chastity. He loves art without violating her. He is intimate without so much as a touch. And just as Gala is in all my work, Eliot's partner is in his."

Friends found Dali's reference to "Chastity" hilarious. They thought he was pulling my leg, so to speak. But in fact he well understood my approach.

An open-hearted, clear-eyed observer can of course appreciate a masterpiece of art. Otherwise, it wouldn't be one.

But nobody can appropriate, let alone explain, such things. Hence, I myself practice what St Nicholas of Cusa called "learned ignorance."

Instead of trying to analyze whatever, I simply wait awhile in welcoming style, relaxed yet fully attentive. It's not unlike watching the sun set, as I often do from the beach near my house.

KISS

When our Day Star
plunges down below
like a crimson discus
or deep sea plow

A single green spark
may swiftly flow
from the horizon
to my crinkled brow—

"Weep not, little fellow.
You'll be all right.
Go sleep tight, now.
Tender is the night."

3. Free at Last

During my early years at *Time* I had nothing but black and white "cuts" of artworks to illustrate my section. But Dana Tasker finally succeeded in establishing a regular "art-color" page, with me choosing the material and writing the copy. Soon afterward, Tack left Time to join *Look* magazine.

At fifty-two issues a year, it wasn't long before *Time* accumulated a color reproduction "electroplate" equity costing millions of dollars.

Then one day in January, 1956, over my customary Long Table lunch at the Century Club, I fell into conversation with a visiting French critic, and happened to mention my enthusiasm for American art.

Exuding Continental courtesy, the critic carved the air with his hands—

"*Mais, oui.* Pre-Columbian sculpture."

"No," I said, "I mean painting."

"*Vous avez raison.* Jackson Pollock!"

"Aren't you aware of any other art on our side of the water?

"*Alors.* Nothing to *pause* over."

I gaped at the genial, highly esteemed Parisian gentleman, thanked him kindly for his honest opinion, arose from my chair, and scurried back to *Time*. There I scrolled a sheet of paper into my typewriter and banged out an urgent memo to my bosses.

Time Inc, I wrote, ought to publish an art book authored by myself and designed to re-cycle over two hundred American paintings in our color-reproduction bank. We could, for the first time, firmly establish American painting on the world map.

This idea appealed to *Time's* new Executive Editor (and my good friend) Edward O. Cerf, as well as our Managing Editor Roy Alexander. They agreed that my proposal might well dovetail with Henry Robinson Luce's passionate promotion of what he had already dubbed "The American Century."

So Roy immediately "took the matter upstairs."

A week later, Mr. Luce invited me to outline my concept for Time Inc's top echelon at an editorial luncheon. Most of the bigwigs present welcomed what I said, and positive suggestions were made. Luce concluded the discussion in his typically brisk manner—

"If State-side painting tops the French, or even threatens to do so, that's our hook. Go ahead, Eliot. Get out of the press-box and in the game. Give us a book!"

With tons of help from Ed Cerf, my dear Researcher Ruth Brine, and Time's cool, kindly Art Director Michael J. Phillips. *Three Hundred Years of American Painting* was produced in fourteen months of furious effort,

At 300,000 expensive copies sold by mail order, our volume was a huge success. Moreover, the U.S. State Department's "Office of Information" distributed our volume abroad, free of charge, to thousands of libraries, colleges, museums, critics, and artists.

Eventually, President John F. Kennedy and his wife Jackie picked up on my book. They ordered a batch of morocco-bound, gilt-edged copies for presentation to visiting dignitaries.

Never again could American art be dismissed.

Time Inc's top executives thought it only fair to reward my money-spinning, prestigious initiative, but how?

I hesitantly suggested a sabbatical year off on full salary for art exploration purposes in Europe.

Why, sure enough, that could be arranged!

So Jane and I, with little Jefferson and Winslow, plus May for the summer months, settled north of Barcelona on Spain's Costa

Brava, at a Mediterranean village called Caldetas (for its hot spring bathing facility) where Jane had lived in childhood.

Leaving our kids in charge of the same Catalan family who'd done superbly for Jane's family a generation earlier, we took flying trips around Europe to check out particular masterpieces.

One day, determined to keep his parents from leaving for a week, little Jeff lay down across the doorsill. As I stepped out over him, how my heart sank!

We had a generally happy, vastly educational year, however. It was the turning point in my career, and I believe the children enjoyed most of it as well...

Time's very long-term Publisher, Jim Linen, adored Greece. He had urged us to make a flying visit to Athens and Delphi, so of course we did.

Around four o'clock in the morning at Delphi, I dreamt of a looming figure who addressed me loudly in a deep, resonant voice—

"What will you do, Alex, what will you do, when there are no more museums?"

The question was spoken with fierce, authoritative urgency from the foot of my bed. Wide awake now, I jumped up, ran toward the space where the Oracle seemed to stand, passed through it, and found myself at the open window.

Putting my hands on the sill, I leaned out and gazed around. A yard or so away, swaying and whispering in the wind, was the pointed tip of a cypress tree.

Our small hotel overlooked the olive-grown gorge that opens out and down from Delphi's hill village towards the port town of Itea on the Corinthian Gulf. The moonlit view held me enthralled, but at the back of my mind was the dream figure's question.

What would I do without museums? Art-writing had been my chief concern. Without a thought, I decided—

"It's time to retire from Time!"

Then came a second inspiration. Why not take my family slowly around the world? We could go and see hundreds of surviving art masterpieces, architectural monuments, and archeological sites, along with sacred centers of legend, for ourselves!

Yes, but how? Getting back into bed, I thought about it. How, indeed? In a minute, I was deep asleep...

Museums were not about to disappear. They've since multiplied ten times over. But the Delphic Oracle worked for me, as it has for so many others, via dark ambiguity.

Apollo's oracles were ambiguous on purpose, yes, but not to hedge the god's bets, as classical scholars generally suppose. Apollo didn't have to guess. Nor did he ever intend to befool anyone.

Instead, the sun deity gave each suppliant a thread of guidance, a single intrinsically true figment to be thought about and followed through, toward some new, personal realization.

That much, I know for certain now. Not intellectually but because—at age forty—it happened to me.

As *Time's* Art Editor I'd been ideally positioned to cover the trans-Atlantic climax of the modern art movement. Also, to attest the vital upwelling and major importance of American painting.

Poised in the wings was a relatively dreary procession of Andy Warhol's "Pop Art," followed by "Op Art," "Conceptual Art," uptight "Minimalism," and so on down to the present obscene art market bubble, powered by plutocrats aesthetically blind as the sole of your shoe.

Cindy Sherman, Damien Hirst, Jeff Koon, and their multi-millionaire ilk can't be denied. But so cold-blooded is the present rancid pantheon, and so anxious to scant the joys of life whilst serving up sour porn and sugared horror.

Art criticism calls for genuine sympathy with the subject at hand. Otherwise, what's the point? In short, the time was ripe for me to move on and avoid a journalistic duty that I never could have handled well...

The next day, while driving down from Delphi to Athens Airport, I said: "This need not be goodbye. Let's come back here to live."

"Let's!" Jane agreed, with such cheerful alacrity that I had to wonder how much she knew.

What means wisdom? Nothing permanent. Daily life is quite beyond rational reach or comprehension, but lightning realizations do occasionally kick in. They reflect both "particle" and "wave"; conjoining the minuscule "near" with the enormous "far" of personal existence.

Time Inc was still a loyalty inspiring institution and no mere money mill. I felt that I owed the company a final year's effort. So things were managed accordingly.

Instead of a "golden handshake," Roy Alexander extended a genial offer. I could return to work whenever, and if ever, I so desired!

Neither of us suspected that Roy's own days were numbered. H.R. Luce's publishing policy was to tap, cosset, richly reward, grindingly masticate, and eventually spew out, his top Time Inc executives.

There was "nothing personal" about the process. Not for him, anyhow. One might better call it his enormously successful business model.

Luce soon replaced Roy with tall, genial Otto "Hot Air" Fuerbringer. No nice guy, he.

Otto would in turn be replaced by regal "Henry the G." Grunwald. Luckily for Henry, Mr. Luce died before getting around to booting him...

Sabbatical experience of El Greco, Velasquez, Goya, Bosch, Brueghel, Vermeer, Rembrandt, and others inspired me to write a book which pointed to the latent spiritual content of their masterpieces. Jane's insights were such that I should have named her as co-author, but that wasn't done back then. Instead, I dedicated it to her.

When I showed my final draft of *Sight & Insight* to the Metropolitan Museum's Director James Rorimer, he told me that he himself had once written the same sort of guff. On consideration, Jim had burned it, and his kindly meant advice to me was—

"Don't even dream of publishing!"

Museum directors have good reason to be discreet. For authors, however, discretion is the kiss of death. (That is, unless you happen to be Henry James.)

I did publish, with mixed results. The hardcover edition soon sank, but the Dutton paperback sold well for a decade, and the book has recently been reissued in a better format, with a self-portrait sketch of mine on its cover.

Our savings were zero, so how could we possibly travel? At that point I was offered a confidential U.S. Naval Intelligence Reserve captaincy. Purpose: Cold War spying on the side.

Thousands of journalists worldwide have been tickled pink to receive such assignments. But the spy racket all too often requires making—and later betraying—friends.

That's morally indefensible.

Having discreetly declined Naval Intelligence service, I managed to scare up half a dozen deals with magazines, such as "Roving Editor" for Art in America. Then kindly Henry Simon of Simon & Schuster gave me a book contract.

Thanks to a dear new friend, the philanthropist and painter Jimmy Rosenberg, I also received a small stipend from the America/Israel Cultural Foundation. Finally came the kicker: A full year's Solomon Guggenheim Fellowship, granted—

"For Studies of Greece and the Middle East as Cradles of the Western World."

The consensus among my peers was that I'd lost my marbles. No sane man would trade success in New York, with its cocktail circuit, theatres, concert halls, classy private schools, and excellent hospitals, for some feckless Gypsy existence abroad. How could I wish such a thing on my wife and kids?

"If you're looking for foreign atmosphere," Sports Editor Marshal Smith suggested, "take Jane to an Italian restaurant!"

Music Editor Chandler Thomas chimed in: "The way to a woman's heart is through the stomach, so ply her with English muffins and French wines!"

My younger sister Patience impatiently warned—

"You can't ever run away from yourself!"

"No doubt," I responded. It would have been rude to add that I had other plans.

I booked passage for us and our car on a Greek freighter bound from Brooklyn to the Athenian port of Piraeus.

May was doing very well at school, and her mother naturally wished to keep her near. So, to our sorrow, she would not be coming.

The great day dawned gray with drizzling spring rain. We packed the Peugeot. Friends arrived, champagne popped, and good-byes followed.

In mid-afternoon we drove off, down to Brooklyn Bridge, on across, and then along the dockside until we found our ship at last.

She was rather a rust-bucket.

After meeting the Captain, greeting our half-dozen fellow passengers, and watching our car swing tippily aboard, we went below. Our double cabin looked cramped but at least it had portholes.

Dinner was served in the "saloon," prior to departure. I recall that it featured *spanakopita* (spinach pie), because the dish tasted delicious and its name was new to me.

The ship would not sail until midnight, we were told. The kids wanted to stay up, and we favored that, but they couldn't keep their eyes open. So Jane tucked Jeff and Wyd into their births and began a bedtime story. Minutes later they were off on tangential voyages of their own.

Soon we sensed a new movement through the soles of our shoes. Lamp lit buildings glided slowly past the portholes to swing slantwise away. Jane and I hurried up on deck.

Clear, starry weather. A cluster of officers on the ship's bridge overhead, quietly gazing about. No one else in sight. The breeze came fresh and clean off the Atlantic.

Awed but joyful, too, we stepped onto the platform covering the forward hold. There we danced slowly together, in time to the ship's engines.

The deep-throated diesel sound welling up from below counterpointed the beating of our hearts, as the "Athene" churned past electrically prickling downtown Manhattan, Staten Island, and the shadowy Statue of Liberty.

Later on, with my arms around Jane, I dreamt of a—

PAGAN PASSAGE

The sea-god
Poseidon's
blue-black
silhouette
tugged us
eastward
through
the wet
wine-dark
starry night.

Arrived at Athens, we checked into the Hotel Grande Bretagne, diagonally across from the Parliament Building on Syntagma ("Constitution") Square.

Our suite had a balcony, and so, after putting the kids to bed, Jane and I enjoyed a celebratory nightcap out there.

Some political protest demonstration was going on, as usual in Athens, and presently a large crowd assembled below our perch, screaming—

"U.S.A. Down
down, down!

U.S.A. Down
down, down!

U.S.A. Down
down, down!

"It's so unfair," Jane remarked, "to make Greece to a pawn in the Cold War. The country suffered quite enough under the Nazis."

I arose and bowed to the crowd in my comradely way. Then, with glass in hand, I saluted, whereupon, a cheer went up! Might I have been mistaken for some visiting Russian dignitary?

Greek daylight was crystalline back then, a brilliance through which our family meandered like molecules on the loose. We based ourselves at Ekali, north of Athens, on a shady shoulder of Mount Pendeli, as ancient Pantelakos is called today.

When dawn greeted our village, a fly would also arrive, to alight on my nose. I thought this a nuisance at first. In classic lore, however, the first fly of morning is "Apollo's Messenger," sent on purpose to awaken one.

I would not have wanted to miss those rosy fingers of Aura, the dawn goddess, raying up and out across our mountaintop.

The American runaway sailor and deathless author Herman Melville stopped off at Athens for a few days late in life, during which he noted with typically poetic precision—

"Pantelakos gazing fondly down upon her rosy little daughter, the Parthenon."

The Parthenon's marble was indeed quarried on Mount Pendeli, and has a reddish hue.

My beloved hound, friend, and companion, entered our family as a puppy. He looked Dalmatian, and of course Dalmatia lies just up the Adriatic coast from Greece.

But I maintain that Spoti was a native, descended from the marble hound in the Acropolis Museum, and the indefatigable bitch of a hunter "Lycas," whom Simonides immortalized.

Here I find that I must stop a moment, catch my breath, and reach down with one hand, in imagination of course, to stroke Spoti's silky ears.

When I was writing *Earth, Air, Fire & Water,* Spoti kept me company, asleep by the hearth.

One winter morning a minor earthquake shook our house. Spoti came awake, raised his fine head and looked over at me with my trembling arms locked around the typewriter. Our eyes met in the middle of the room, and his framed an urgent question—

"HOW did you do THAT?"

I had to laugh. With a severely disapproving shrug, Spoti put his head back down on the rug and dozed off again into dog-dream-land.

Every morning we'd go out together, up from our house, past the shepherd's hut and on along the mountain's quartz-covered flank. As I breathed the fragrance of basil and thyme, Spoti would lope ahead to sniff out vipers sunning themselves on the bare ledges.

My protective, keen-nosed guide always scampered back to edge me past their sleepy presences.

GUARDIANS OF THE THRESHOLD

We encountered Orthodox
monks atop the jagged rocks
wearing hats but minus socks.

Spoti barked in cordial style.
I bowed silently meanwhile
like the shadow on a sun-dial.

My dear, patient typist used to drive up from Athens to collect and deliver manuscripts. Once Rita brought her elegant white poodle along to make Spoti's acquaintance. We went out walking together.

"I have to keep Snowball on a leash," Rita told me, "because she runs away. Last time, she was gone for two whole days. I can't imagine how she found her way home at all through the streets of Athens."

"Look how Spoti's ears prick up," I remarked. "He knows what we're talking about."

"You're kidding, of course," she said.

"It's true he can't speak our languages, but he's quite familiar with both English and Greek. Besides, he intuitively penetrates minds."

"I'll believe that, when I *see* it."

Spoti soon took off after some intriguing scent, and Snowball plunged gaily after him. While chatting with me, Rita had relaxed her hold on his leash. It slipped through her fingers. Within seconds, both animals had scampered out of sight.

Rita was in despair, but not for long.

When the dogs returned, Spoti held the leather loop of Snowball's leash between his clenched fangs! Not until we were safe home again, with the gate closed, did he release Snowball.

Spoti himself could clear our gate at a bound, by the way, and often did so for nocturnal adventure purposes...

After a couple of years, with money running short, we moved from Ekali to a peasant cottage in Pyrghi, a seaside hamlet on Corfu island's northeastern coast.

The only school known to the island's peasantry was the school of hard knocks. Angry shouting, screaming, cuffing, and beating were commonplace. Despairing howls arose all around us, which Jane could not bear. So she decreed that nobody was to strike anybody within earshot of our house!

That astonished the natives. "Why not?" they asked.

Diplomatically, Jane explained that her husband wrote for a living. The slightest commotion, she asserted, badly disturbed my work!

"So?" the villagers asked again.

Jane's Greek was already fluent, miles beyond my own. She replied with a hypothetical question—

"Imagine what would happen if something scared the fish away from your fishermen, or shocked your oranges, figs, and olives into inedibility?"

Having thought that over, the neighbors agreed to try to oblige us both. Within days, the village children gravitated to our rented property as a refuge, and took our kids into their gang.

On relatively rare occasions, commotion still occurred. I recall that one child, whom a passing fisherman had crossed the lane to kick, responded by screaming—

"Toe Kyrio na Grahpsie!"

I may not remember that just right, but anyhow: "The Gentleman is Writing!" He could have been crying for me to come clobber his nemesis with my portable Olivetti.

"Paleo!" ("Old!") was the peasant children's constant put-down. It stood for everything despicable...

Once, having drunk too much retsina with lunch, I retreated to the hammock in our garden with J.W. Mackail's *Select Epigrams from the Greek Anthology*.

The dense shadow of our cypress tree fell across me. It's dangerous, Greeks say, to doze in a cypress shadow during the midday. Compared to down-beating sunshine, they explain, such a shadow is tomb-cold.

I had no intention of sleeping, however. Instead, I idly thumbed Mackail's eloquent translations. That is, until the following epigram by Antipater of Sidon brought my thoughts to a halt—

"The herald of the prowess of heroes, and interpreter of the Immortals, a second sun on the life of Greece, Homer, the light of

the Muses, the ageless voice of all the world, lies hidden, stranger, under the sea strand."

My most wistful onset of romantic nihilism occurred at that juncture. Could I myself ever say anything worthwhile to anyone? Or would I die having conveyed "nothing to no one," like a forlorn fart in a hailstorm?

This recollection seems comic to me now. Homer does not lie hidden under some sea strand. He's a living patriarch, surrounded by his offspring. Notably Sappho, Aeschylus, Sophocles, Euripides, Aristophanes, Pindar, Herodotus, Plato, Aristotle, Apollonius, Plutarch, Ptolemy, and Plotinus...

Oh, the fireflies of Corfu! "Lightning bugs," as I knew them in childhood, or "lucioles," as my friend James Laughton called them.

First one or two, then nine, or ninety of those visible/invisible insects might appear. The next night there'd be many hundreds, rising, blinking, presumably dropping in on each other and pairing up.

On the third or fourth night we were greeted by thousands, and whole bands of them were beginning to blink in ragged unison.

Within a week, they had learned to light up and go dark again simultaneously, first here, then there, like a silent symphony orchestra, in wavering, quavering tides of sparkle.

We, used to go out after dinner and stroll part way up the mountain behind our beach to get an extended view of the firefly concert, as Jane called it. Like little golden chariots, the insects flowed around us while we walked, but not a single bug brushed against us.

Finally, as far as the eye could see, the entire lot lit up and went dark together!

Then came an astounding, down-pouring, climactic thunderstorm, whereupon their host of tiny fires vanished away until next year...

Thanks to my dear Hellenic-American pal Connie Soloyanis, a Greek shipping magnate once invited Jane and me to participate with an international clutch of classicists on an Aegean yacht trip.

We found two Oxford dons aboard. Regius Professor Hugh Lloyd-Jones overwhelmed us with his loquacious scholarship and surprisingly confessional asides, whereas M.L. West maintained a not unfriendly distance.

Martin remained "silent in nine languages," as Hugh laughingly complained. But one night, when he and I stood quietly on deck gazing at the stars, Martin pointed out the one called Vega, and remarked—

"Our present sector of the heavens will eventually impact that particular speck of light, resulting in a very large-scale crunch. It's inevitable."

"I never knew that," I said. "You take a panoramic view!"

Following a further minute or two of silence, he confided: "I'm attempting a fresh translation of the Iliad's opening section."

"Good for you!" I said. "Might I take a look at your manuscript?"

That was the start of our friendship, under Vega's patient twinkle.

I persuaded Martin to recite his work one evening on shipboard. It was cordially received by his tough audience, and later published by Oxford University Press.

Our cruise included a visit to "windy Troy, rich in horses," as Homer put it. I did notice many horses grazing near the site. Moreover, my hat blew off.

As we were leaving, Jane and I encountered an imposing fellow who said he was the official guide, and offered for sale a highly polished wood chip which he claimed was: "A genuine fragment of the original Trojan Horse!"

Halting, I told him: "Sorry, sir, but we've already got a piece of that particular horse's ass, permanently stashed at home in our cabinet of curiosities."

Drawing himself up to full height, the self-appointed guide assumed a dramatic expression of shock, followed by sorrowful outrage—

"Here of all places, in this holy precinct, how dare you tell such a terrible, outright LIE?"

Smiling, Jane asked: "How much?" His price amounted to less than a dollar. The chip must still be kicking around here somewhere...

Our trip climaxed on the island of Kos, which our kind host regarded as the birthplace of Homer, that "ageless voice of all the world."

While there, we formally dedicated a natural sculpture, a monumental boulder on the seashore, to honor Homer's memory. An onshore breeze caressed our hands and faces. The moon rose, delicate silver, as Hugh Lloyd-Jones recited aloud the Homeric Hymn to Delian Apollo.

In the awed silence afterward, a shooting-star zoomed southwestward over us. Another diamond scratch followed.

Homeric Greek religion was itself meteoric, streaming sudden light. Among the literary fruits of classical paganism were lyric and epic verse, philosophy, history, comedy, and tragedy.

We tend to confuse tragedy with disaster, but in fact it's an art form. Disaster grinds us down, comedy punctures our illusions, and tragedy majestically unveils the inevitable.

What is inevitable? Disaster yes, along with earned wisdom, laughter, and creative response. In short, the human, godlike reaction...

The ancient Greek philosopher Diogenes experienced a family disaster while still in his teens.

His father served as Master of the Mint in the Lydian market-city of Sinope. The old man confiscated false coins and defaced them with a cold chisel, cutting through gold, electrum, or silver surfaces of counterfeit currency to reveal base metals beneath.

Such honest activism offended thieves in high places. They framed him, got him jailed, and had young Diogenes banished for good measure.

Journeying to Delphi, the bitterly disillusioned youth asked Apollo's Oracle what he ought to do in life. Should he become a tragic poet, perhaps?

He received an abrupt answer—

"Deface the currency!"

After considerable agonizing, Diogenes concluded that the Oracle spoke well. He understood Apollo's terse outburst as a command to tread in his fallen father's footsteps. How? By "defacing" and thus exposing, the rank hypocrisy of current culture.

Strolling down from Delphi to Itea, Diogenes boarded a coastal ferry bound for the rich resort city of Corinth. There, he became a deliberate nuisance, an object of laughter and scorn.

He used to stalk the city streets by day, dramatically swinging a lantern in search, as he loudly proclaimed, "of an honest man!"

Not that he hoped to find any. Diogenes' arresting theatrics were calculated to set citizens back on their heels, driving them to think for themselves.

As the afternoon shadows lengthened, Diogenes would retire to his bachelor-quarters in a tipped-over wine-tub outside the city gates, and quietly introspect.

Alexander the Great made a special trip to see him there.

Haloed by the radiance of the sun at his back, the conquering hero looked majestic, but acted deferential. Leaning down across the neck of his white charger, Alexander doffed his golden helmet, and spoke—

"Would Diogenes be so kind as to accept financial help to open a college, perhaps?"

That brought no response.

"A University of Cynicism might actually change the world!"

Still no reaction.

Following a suspenseful minute or two, Alexander added that he himself, the Human God, would be pleased to sponsor such a venture.

Diogenes offered no reply.

So, veiling his irritation, Alexander inquired: "Then, what CAN I do for you?"

"Move on."

"???"

"You're blocking my sunlight."

My old comrade George Foote once composed an essay called "Money & Soul," at my request, when I was guest editor of Parabola magazine. It begins—

"The Greek soul worked several acts of astonishing brilliance: the geometric development of the Doric temple, the breathless beauty of free-standing human sculpture, and the creation of the coin, an impressed metal weight of distinctive form and quality.

"Thus, via transforming imagination, the Greeks infused cash capital with the birth-giving capabilities of cattle and seed."

Jane and I once accompanied George and his lovely bride Sonia Rosenbaum on an auto trip to Delphi, Olympia, Epidaurus, and other sacred places.

I recall a hot, hard drive across Arcadia to Nauplion, where we settled down at a waterfront café. The evening was clear and cool. Leaning precariously back in his chair, George lifted up his brawny arms as if to hug the stars, and joyously remarked—

"Here and now, I feel immortal!"

"It's true," I told him. "The person who feels as you do at this moment will never, ever die."

ON THE SEA FRONT

Weathervane turning
olive trees shimmering
children roller-skating
villagers promenading
tavern lamp glimmering
bouzouki music beginning
church bells chorusing
small waves chuckling
lamb stew simmering
Athena's owl winging
ourselves enjoying

During our third year in Greece, I was invited to Mount Athos for celebrations of its Thousandth Anniversary as a Greek Orthodox religious refuge.

Athos is actually a peninsula with a mountainous headland, jutting south from Thrace into the Aegean sea. Foreign visitors were not admitted in my time, unless they carried visas countersigned by the Bishop of Athens. Musical instruments of any sort were strictly prohibited, and no female folk whatsoever gained entry!

That's probably still true.

The Victorian artist, poet, and humorist Edward Lear was shocked by what he discovered on Mount Athos. Lear suggested that a Light Brigade of British seamstresses, duly armed with long needles, be dispatched to open up the place!

I guessed I would agree with Lear. But, all the same, I could hardly wait to get there and see for myself.

The Greek government chartered a small cruise ship for the occasion and overloaded it with high church dignitaries. Assigned to a deck-chair for the overnight voyage from Piraeus, I slept out under the wheeling stars.

When dawn cracked the horizon and the sun peeked over the edge of the sparkling sea, a pride of bejeweled, bushy-bearded ecclesiastics arose around me to embrace, chant prayers, and sing hymns together, lifting their crosiers in unison. That impromptu performance had a wonderfully warm pagan air.

But my first day ashore on Athos was inauspicious, to say the least.

The frescoes in the church at Karyes are the work of Manuel Panselinos, to whom Domenikos Theotokopoulos (El Greco) was once apprenticed. I gazed at them for hours in surprised delight.

El Greco never signed that name to his stuff, by the way. Instead he used "Kres," for "Cretan."

Strangely, he was long regarded as a minor figure on the art scene. Not until three centuries after his death did Delacroix, Manet, Rilke, Picasso, and Unamuno, between them, "discover" him.

Finally, an aged monk approached and told me to kiss the icons! They, too, were very fine. However, I declined.

Then four younger monks gathered silently around, grabbed me, and booted me out of the church!

I limped back down the mountainside to the dock and our vessel, which served as a convention hotel.

"What am I doing," I wondered, "in this womanless, childless, grimly medieval, anti-pagan, God-forsaken, madly masculine place?"

That night a lean, iron-bearded Monk appeared upon the deck of our ship. I never learned his name, so I capitalize the vocation of this impressive personage. His black robes had gone ragged and warm green with age. His strikingly large hands looked arthritic. Beneath the tall black brimless hat, his craggy face gleamed with severity.

We were dining under the canopy aft of the ship's bar. At the journalists' table were two Greek newspaper editors, a Greek-speaking French correspondent named Pierre, and myself. The Monk came straight over to us.

Sitting down, he readily accepted a glass of wine and asked if we had any questions.

"*Nay*," (Greek for "Yes") said Pierre. "Can you tell us how many monasteries are on Athos?"

"Twenty."

"Quite a lot!" Blinking, Pierre flipped open his notebook.

"A lot or not, it's twenty."

"Could we have their names?" Pierre adjusted his pen.

"What names do you know?"

"Only three." Pierre obligingly rattled them off.

"Go on," the Monk told him. Then, to everyone's astonishment all the remaining names fell from Pierre's lips!

"*I like that man.*"

The Monk had said it, but not aloud, and not in words. Neither Greek nor English, for example. He did not need words. This man was simply thinking, as it were, into my head! So I thought back: "Why?"

"*Because he's young and brave, like Jesus. But I'm interested in you also. Look, now.*"

I saw darkness, like smoke, wreathing the heads of my fellow-journalists. Again, the Monk spoke silently—

"*That's it! Light flows into people; darkness oozes out. I'll try and help you.*"

I felt I ought to tell him I was no pilgrim. Also, that my dedication to free inquiry made me leery of religious dogmas and restrictions. And finally, that I had a family on Corfu, to whom I was totally devoted.

But his piercing, yellowish-gray glance indicated that any confession of mine would be superfluous. So, on second thought, I silently put the question that stood uppermost for me: "Why aren't women allowed on Athos?"

No response. The telepathic thrust of his mind withdrew. I felt an odd despair at having lost contact, until it struck me that the Monk smelled precisely like my father when I was little!

Thereupon he answered silently—

"*If women came here it would bring about, through no fault of theirs, disruptions in our ranks. There would be bitter rivalries between spiritual fathers and sons. The Virgin warned us of this, so we know.*"

I bowed in acknowledgement. The Monk finished his wine and set his glass down on the table, hard. I expected a banging sound, but no. It seemed that I'd been warned to set my own glass down gently, and acquire self-control.

He stood up. I did the same, and stooped to kiss his hand.

"*Okey!*" (Greek for "No") he said aloud, holding his arm rigid, and swept away over the ship's side.

Two days after the Monk's magical appearance in my life, and thanks to him no doubt, I received a special invitation to visit Dionysiou, an out-of-the-way monastery towering high over the water. Its name recalls Dionysus, the pagan Greek god of wine, and the place produces a strong dark wine of its own.

In his cavernous kitchen the resident Cook handed me a raw, unpeeled cucumber by way of nourishment.

A medieval fresco filled with dark mountains and alight with falling flames stretched across the refectory's north wall. I studied it for some time. Finally the Cook came over and inquired—

"*Ti les, paithe-mou?*" ("What say, son?")

The image illustrated an incident in the final book of the New Testament. It also foreshadowed our hellish modern practice of firebombing cities. But what could I myself offer concerning the significance of the fresco?

My response was a wordless, unhappy shrug.

When that reaction was reported upstairs, the Abbot sent word that he wished to speak with me.

Ten minutes later, we sat drinking wine together, knee to knee, on his tiny balcony, high over the plum colored waves. The Abbot's hair and beard were curly black, his round, brown bear-eyes radiated a cherry-warm glow, and his obvious open-heartedness emboldened me to ask—

"Are we mere playthings of the gods?"

What an inappropriate query to pop at that moment! Presumably the Abbot believed in God, no gods at all.

His only answer was a slow, grand, horizontal flourish of his half-full wineglass. Sunlight streaking through the garnet wine illuminated a swirl of sediment or "mother" in it, as his wide black sleeve brushed the horizon.

Now I found myself gazing out upon the wine-dark, sacrificial sea, the tall earth and rock of Mount Athos, and the sky.

The mother and the wine are one!

That's what the Abbot's silent gesture signified.

Words follow from gesture. Since that comes first, we speak and listen with our whole bodies. The English words "horizon" and "horoscope," for example, derive from a serenely circling Egyptian falcon deity called Horus.

The modern Greek greeting *"Oriste"* or "What can I do for you?" has the same root.

Speaking of words, my father's boundless well of them amazed me in childhood. He used "childishness" for spilling soup, "gastronomy" for cooking with gas, and "adultery for adult behavior.

Once when I was still pretty small, Pop and my elder sister Torka tried to tell me what rhyming means. I failed to grasp the concept. But that night as I was drifting off to sleep a sparkly little person appeared on my bedspread, carrying a ladder made of light, like himself.

Leaning the ladder out upon thin air, he mounted to its top, turned, and descended again. He looked at me as if to say: "Now do you understand?"

As he disappeared I spoke aloud: "A man went up a ladder and he came down pitter padder!" My first rhyme had slanted in!

Having heartened my spirit, the Abbot of Dionysiou passed me on to a fisherman monk, who volunteered to run me down the coast and around Athos' southern tip, so that I might consult the oldest and most sacred person on the Holy Mount, namely, "Simon the Anchorite."

The day was windless, the sea calm. The fisherman's little motorboat serenely put-putted for an hour or two past looming cliffs to reach a sheltered inlet called Karoulia, with a tiny dock.

A succession of chains hung suspended, like a thinly glittering cataract, from the high cliff facing us. So did a single slim cable, and that was all.

Gesturing, the fisherman explained the situation: "Here we are. Holy Simon lives up on that ledge where the chains begin."

"What's the cable for?" I asked.

"When Simon's hungry he drops his basket down along the cable. It's not there now, but if it were I'd deposit part of our picnic lunch in it for him to pull up and eat."

"What does he eat from day to day? Even a saint requires nourishment."

"That's your opinion. Once in a great while, some pilgrim like yourself climbs the chains to visit Holy Simon."

"You mean—"

"No easy climb. Good luck, my son."

It was one of those moments in life when one has no choice whatsoever.

Grasping the chain's lowest links and setting my feet against the cliff, I ascended hand-over-hand. Secure footholds and handholds greeted me here and there. Some had been conveniently carved into the rock, but most were natural features of the cliff-face.

They enabled me to rest a little at intervals. But I was a hedonist and no gymnast.

After struggling upward for a quarter of an hour, I saw that I had passed the point of no return, with a considerable distance still to go! My terror was complete, and at that point I almost fell.

The next thing I recall is reaching the hermit's ledge at last and sprawling out upon it like a beached dolphin. I was gasping for breath, and groaning with gratitude to be alive.

A shadow fell across me. I rolled over onto my back. Skeletal and nearly toothless, Holy Simon greeted me with wide open arms and a single word—

"Oriste!"

From that point on, he said nothing aloud.

The oddest thing about being "newborn" is that one does not feel at all like a newcomer. Not me, but Simon himself, together with the yet more ancient sun, rock, and dusty-blue Aegean expanse, had burst into present bloom.

With silent hospitality, the anchorite led me along his ledge to a tiny chapel which he had handcrafted of stone. Its only light slanted in through the door-less entrance.

Upon the altar stood an undistinguished nineteenth century chromolithograph of a dark-skinned Madonna crowned with stars.

Representations of the "Black Virgin," as she's generally known, adorn thousands of chapels and millions of homes around the world.

The "Black Madonna of Czestochawa" (an icon attributed to St. Luke the Evangelist), is Poland's own protector and Queen.

The last book of the New Testament says that she's "A Woman clothed with the sun." What do those words really mean?

I used to picture her backlit by sunshine, in striking silhouette, but it's more likely that John of Patmos referred to the Virgin's black or tan skin.

Indeed, her statuette at Sicilian Tindari carries the Latin inscription: *Negra sum sed formosa* ("I am dark, but comely"), drawn from the Old Testament Song of Songs.

I'd already gone to see her carved image near the crest of Montserrat in Catalonia.

I'd also visited Turkey's *Meryem Ana* ("House of Mary") near Ephesus on *Bulbul Dag* or "Nightingale Mountain."

There I prayed to a bronze Virgin with compassionately extended hands of the spirit,—her metal ones having been broken off and lost.

At Simon's gestured suggestion, we both knelt down before the altar. I guessed I might as well begin with the "penance" which my mother's friend Monsignor Patrick Cummings always gave me to recite in boyhood—

"One Our Father and three Hail Mary's!"

To my surprise and despite my happiness, tears came to my eyes. The Black Virgin was changing, liquefying as it were, smiling to herself, and laughing in a loving way. I wondered what she meant by doing that.

Then, an overpowering realization occurred. I never would have thought such things were possible but, yes, the Black Virgin was remembering my very first rhyme!

I mean the one about a man going up a ladder and coming down pitter-padder.

After the chapel's dusky peace, Simon and I passed farther along the ledge and around a dripping spring in a crack of the cliff. The rock hollow beneath the spring was about ten yards long and filled with good black earth.

The hermit had transformed that sun-warmed section of his balcony-like residence into a vegetable garden glistening with greens and tomatoes. So that was what kept him alive.

His neat little cave-cell contained a cot, a table, two chairs, and a kerosene burner on which he boiled wild *tsai toe vrouno* ("tea of the mountain") for us both.

Drooping now, he resembled a sunflower, and so terribly thin!

He served my tea with a caramel candy. This reminded me of the general practice in pilgrimage, which is to come bearing a token homage of some sort.

I'd completely forgotten that courtesy. Suffused with shame, I concealed his caramel beneath the rim of my saucer.

Finally, weeping with gratitude, I bowed low and departed. Swinging back down the chains was easy; I felt feather-light.

Sweaty, however. Finding the fisherman asleep, I stripped for a quick swim.

I'd been in the water for about a minute when I was startled by a shrill, weird sort of scream. Instinctively, I ducked beneath the boat.

Emerging to silence, I saw Holy Simon's basket at the base of the cable. So that was it. I'd been scared out of my wits by nothing but the basket's abrupt descent.

Climbing out upon the rock platform, I stooped and peered inside. There was my candy!

Standing back to squint upward, I saw Simon perched on his ledge like a capital "A."

Taking the caramel from the basket, I held it up for him to witness, put it on my tongue, and sensed its burnt-sugar elixir right down to my toes.

I stood dripping on the shore of time as Simon waved good-bye from eternity…

I'd been re-baptized, so to speak. Not into some particular religion but rather in the waters of the Aegean, together with an invisible realm of refuge for everyone.

I now believe it all happened because I declined to kiss the icons at Karyes.

I was unaware of the fact that Greek and Russian Orthodox icons are not regarded as portraits. Instead, they're meant to be looked through, and kissed, so that those whom they represent will come to one's aid.

So there was I, an obviously earnest pilgrim who didn't even know he was a pilgrim, let alone how to behave as one.

Hence a telepathically talented Monk was sent down to the ship to examine my case, and all the rest followed.

My instructors employed three different kinds of direct transmission: the Monk's mental telepathy, the Abbot's clarifying gesture, and Simon's radiant "being there."

Not until a Greek Orthodox Monk, the Abbot of Dionysiou, and Holy Simon, sprang to my rescue did I grasp the truth of St. Thomas Aquinas's discovery that one minute of spiritual grace beats decades of study.

Experience of the divine can happen to anyone. Having met the Black Virgin of Karoulia, thanks to Holy Simon and the rest, I now worship a personal divinity.

The Virgin's laughter did not plant "faith" in my heart, however. Instead, she reminded me of my childhood,—and of the child in myself.

GOING HER WAY

When the Black Virgin
kindly laughed at me
I began to imagine
mythic reality.

The loving deity showed me that doubt has a positive side. Normal doubts don't undermine the poetry of life; they tend to surround and defend it.

The most reasonable people are those who understand that reason alone cannot even begin to encompass whole truth. Hence, we have every reason to doubt our own mental capabilities.

Some instinctively doubt the power of death to end our lives forever. We also doubt priestly dogmas concerning "sinful" pleasures of the flesh, plus eternal punishment in Hell. Such doubts are hardly unhealthy.

In youth, at least, most of us question authority, especially when it takes a moral tone. I'm all for youth in that respect.

Why shouldn't we stand back and question the moral authority of our elders, plus religion in general, and whatever happens to be one's ruling State?

No parent, priest, policeman, judge, professor, military officer, scientific sage, or political leader, possesses moral authority.

This will never be convincingly conveyed via sacred texts, legal precedents professorial precepts, or scientific proofs, let alone arbitrary commands,—but only by personal example.

Among the personal examples whom I myself look up to and piously revere, are—

SEVEN SAVIORS

    Chuang Tsu, Chinese teaser
    Moses, Hebrew law-giver
    Gautama, Hindu Buddha
    Socrates, sly questioner
    Jesus Christ, sacrifice
    Mohammed, Prophet
    Rumi, desert poet
    all of whom suggest
    I try human decency
    fly from disaster less
    cogitate independently
    stretch toward divinity
    practice open-heartedness.

When my sister Torka and I were teen-agers, she kept a framed color reproduction of Sandro Botticelli's "The Birth of Venus" over her bed. (The original hangs at the Uffizi Gallery in Florence.)

The slim, self-contained Florentine beauty called Simonetta served as mistress to Lorenzo de Medici's brother, and posed for Botticelli time and again.

With her cool, pensive air, Venus/Simonetta stands apologetically balanced upon a scudding scallop shell. The gray dawn light is loose and clear. The greenish waters behind the goddess-girl pinch up into whitecaps strewn with soon-to-be-swallowed rose blossoms.

Like an elder sister, or divine sacrifice, Venus appears wistfully aware that her salty sheen and rosemary fragrance shall stir sharp turmoil between sea and shore.

Letting her gorgeous long copper-colored hair stream loose and modestly concealing her lower tummy with one hand, she's almost ashore, coming through to us.

What signifies that scudding, skimming, corrugated scallop shell—the mount, if you like—of Venus?

The Spanish conquistadors who seized control of Central America were astonished to encounter scallop symbolism there. The Mayan bride of the rain god Tlaloc was Chalchiuhtlicue, meaning: "She of the Jade Skirt."

Native priests and maidens customarily donned scallop shells and scallop-shaped jade ornaments in her honor.

Scallops possess no visible means of swimming, neither fins nor tails. So, how can they migrate from one region to another with such flying-saucer agility?

By jet propulsion! They quickly suck in seawater and spew it forcefully forth again, spit-devil style, in any chosen direction.

The eyes of these hinged crustaceans diamond the darkly winking slits between their upper and lower shells, perceiving their world from nearly circular perspectives.

Just once in each year, when the moon is at its fullest and the tide at its highest, minuscule billions of infant scallops brim up like luminous foam from the deep.

Our ancestors assumed that the creatures must necessarily be generated by interactions of sea-waves with moon-pull.

True in a sense, but not the whole story.

Being shell-encased, how do scallops in fact reproduce? Until the other day, nobody knew.

But now the prodding thumbs and invasive nozzles of marine biologists have revealed that scallops are hermaphroditic. Each produces young ones from the virginal privacy within itself.

Death suggests dust—including stardust—whereas birth and rebirth are oceanic. "Through the stars to heaven," is an ancient saying, to which I would add:

"And through the seas to earth."

Ages before tourism, Europeans sought forgiveness for their sins by going on pilgrimage. They favored three main destinations: Jerusalem, Rome, and Spain's relatively accessible Santiago de Campostella, or "Saint James of the Starry Field."

James, the reputed brother of Jesus, first brought the holy Word to Spain. During his mission he once plunged, fully armed, on horseback, into the Bay of Biscay.

Why? To rescue a virgin princess from within a water dragon's toothy grin. The swift, spontaneous Apostle speared the monster and snatched the barely scratched young lady safe away.

Curling his long, talons in an empty gesture of despair, the dragon rolled belly-up and sank beneath the waves.

The intrepid, iron-clad saint, however, firmly astride his snorting mount, plus the shivering goose-pimpled object of his compassion, also submerged! They, too, seemed forever doomed.

That is, until thousands of scallops converged to shape a living raft, upon which the Apostle, his steed, and the maiden, all three shot safe ashore.

Medieval pilgrims who had managed to reach Santiago traditionally celebrated by pinning scallop shells to their hats.

Jane occasionally sports a small pewter scallop on a thin chain, which we purchased at the completion of our own blessed Santiago pilgrimage.

Today's the anniversary of our destiny-deciding first encounter in Manhattan's Time/Life Building. So this morning she put the pewter scallop on again...

For eighteen years and more, my family and I lived well, although in hand-to-mouth style, on the always uncertain proceeds of my freelance articles and books.

Residing in Greece, Italy, England, and Japan, we also made side-trips by car, train, plane, freighter again, and ocean liner, all around the globe, pursuing whatever assignments I managed to scare up.

A dozen book deals helped keep us afloat. So did some two hundred articles for American magazines, with Greek, Italian, British and Japanese publications thrown in.

Time Inc turned out to be my best customer.

The company's new *Life International* magazine sponsored a long-extended series dubbed "The Creative Adventure" which called for exploratory trips of ours through Scandinavia, Britain, Ireland, Spain, France, Italy, Turkey, Jordan, and Iran, at a thousand bucks a crack (top-dollar for those days).

Henry Grunwald accepted and very generously rewarded two six-page color-spreads of mine for *Time*, along with cover-length texts. The first was "Pieter Brueghel the Elder" and the second "Blacks in Art."

I also dreamed up and composed "The Playing Fields of Eton" and "Men Like Gods" for *Sports Illustrated*.

Among the other commissions I generated were more than a dozen pieces for Travel & Leisure, a "Gardens of Genius" series for Horticulture, and my second essay in the Saturday Evening Post's "Adventures of the Mind" series, called "The Sense of Joy."

Compared with what many journalists produce, my freelance record is meager. I value labor as I do wine. In moderation, it's fine.

Our vaunted "American Work Ethic" is an outright fraud, by the way, which benefits today's idle rich alone. One must work in order to live, but it's a good idea to save room for living purposes...

During the course of our travels I learned to make requisite, practical and courteous noises in various languages, yet I still remained unequipped to converse spontaneously, except in my native tongue plus French on occasion.

So Jane's linguistic fluency was a huge asset. She'd assimilated such perfect Greek as to be taken for a native, and later on she even managed a smattering of Japanese.

Jane ran things also, in her gentle style, which freed me up to write.

Jefferson and Winslow charmed the natives of every land, "from Egypt, even unto India," as Scripture has it, and from Norway's North Cape down and around to Singapore. Their unfailing adaptability and good nature helped us to gain acceptance everywhere.

One dark and stormy night, while bucketing through the precipitously choppy South China Sea aboard a Yugoslav freighter stuffed with cotton and explosives, I told our kids about Stone Monkey.

That mythical animal was ebulliently bouncy enough to overleap the Great Wall of Confucian mindsets.

Grinning, flinging his knees and elbows about with angular abandon, he outran brigands' darts, priestly slings, and policemen's arrows alike.

Monkey had access to a cloud trapeze which swung along whenever and wherever he desired. So, he once bet the Buddha that he could travel farther than anybody.

"Jump off my hand," Buddha offered, "and try."

Invoking his ethereal swing, Monkey swiftly swooshed away to the outer edge of the universe, where five huge columns loomed. After pissing on one of them he zoomed back again, inflated with elation, to Buddha's hand.

"Having sped to the outermost rim of the cosmos, relieved myself there, and returned, all within a single hour," Monkey announced, "I demand to be crowned Emperor of Heaven!"

Buddha withheld the crown. Instead, he suggested—

"Smell my pinkie!"

On that same voyage, by the way, Jane invented and conveyed a riddling legend called *Santa Claus's Secret Name*, to help Jeff and Wyd through their first Christmas encounter with nagging doubt. It later became a children's book, written by Jane and illustrated by myself.

Once we found ourselves stranded in Japan, with no money and no prospects. Even so, the proprietor of the posh Nara Hotel invited us to be his guests.

"You will not receive a bill," he told me, "until you ask for it!"

Three weeks later, I received an assignment from *Life International* to go and report on a little-known jungle ruin: Angkor Wat.

When I applied for my required visa at the Cambodian Embassy, however, it was withheld. "Prince Sihanouk," the presiding official sneered, "despises American journalists."

Withdrawing, I walked, or staggered, blindly around the block. Was I about to fail my family altogether, plus our incredibly kind host at Nara?

Fuming at my own shame and fear, I turned around, stormed back into the Embassy, and furiously shouted at the official—

"If you know what's good for you, you better cable home right now and ask whether Prince Sihanouk would be pleased to learn that his own Ambassador had failed to invite Alexander Eliot!"

Weirdly enough, that outrageous bluff worked. Within the hour, I received my precious visa.

Mom once wrote that she prayed for me every night.

"Please don't," I responded. "The angels may not be able to distinguish your wishes from your fears, putting me in danger."

At the time, I thought I was being clever. What I think now is that her prayers may have helped a lot.

4. Sistine Ceiling Story

Among Jane's first enthusiasms as a teen-ager in Italy, the Florentine magus Marsilio Ficino stood especially high. In his *De Vita Triplici* (1489) Ficino asserted that Venus the love goddess still rays down upon us,—but now she's in "Three Graces" guise!

Stepping lightly, with their arms entwined, the Graces shape a deathless—

    RONDO

    Joy
    receives
    what
    Beauty
    shows
    and
    Love
    enjoys
    from
    head
    to
    toes.

Ficino's dedicated circle of seekers used to meet in the Medici Garden for free and easy discussion. They included both teen-age Michelangelo and the young theologian Pico della Mirandola.

Since the Catholic Church was beginning to mount guard against Heresy, so called, "Show, but don't tell!" and "Write, but don't publish!" were among the group's axioms. Yet Pico dared to publicly enunciate the blithe new spirit of the Renaissance —

"Man is a little world, in which we may discern a body mingled of earthy elements, ethereal breath, the life of planets, the senses of animals, reason, the intelligence of angels, and a likeness to God."

During our first years in Rome, I wrote my second and last novel: a bawdy philosophical farce intended to expand upon Ficino, which I called *Love Play*.

The metaphysically inclined poet Conrad Aiken was kind enough to write that my book "should become a classic."

Not so. The work sold surprisingly well in paperback, however, plus a German translation.

Then I got restless. But Jane felt we should stay put for a final year. "There's something in the air of this city," she explained. "You know what I mean. Different places make different demands."

"All I know," I said, "is that Rome's churches, columns, and pretentious palaces, plus the Forum, the Coliseum and the catacombs below those, amount to billions of heavy stone. They weigh me down!"

"Right. That's the negative aspect."

"Admittedly, I love the air of Rome with its lofty skies and twilight parcels of swirling starlings, plus friends we've made, the coffee, and the wine."

"Me, too!" she said. "But I'm talking about a secret, or central challenge of the place, some one thing we haven't noticed."

Then, at three o'clock one morning, Rome-time, I received a phone call from a Capital Cities Network producer/director in Manhattan, who asked if I were free to script a documentary film titled *A Visit to the Vatican's Art Collection*. The TV Special would be hosted, he boasted, by none other than Jackie Kennedy.

"Why pick on me?" I asked.

He explained that the legendary journalist Lowell Thomas, who happened to run Cap Cities, recommended me for the job.

Mr. Thomas and his wife had recently lunched with us when passing through Rome, and I must have told them to be sure and go see what the Vatican had to offer.

We ourselves had frequently visited the Sistine Chapel in particular, with guests from England, Greece, and America. Its vast ceiling fresco was still pretty much as Michelangelo painted it, gloriously whole and well, except for superficial cracks in the plaster surface.

Gazing up through a multilingual mist of guides' mutters, racking coughs, and stray dandruff-swirls, plus actual dust churned up by shuffling shoes in their hundreds, was strenuous however.

The public address system kept urging us in half a dozen tongues to: *"Move on, please!"* and the overhead scene stood well above our floor-bound, rudely hustled comprehensions.

Moreover, the prospect of providing stale art-historical pieties for Jackie Kennedy to relate in her breathless high style (as she had about the White House on a television show) was unappealing, so I declined the director's offer.

He kept right on talking, anyhow:

"Mr. Thomas says you've got the stuff, so we want you aboard. We've already obtained full backing from the American Council of Catholic Bishops, and been promised cooperation by the Vatican! So listen. If and when you think up a better way to handle this project, just let me know."

At breakfast I repeated the conversation to Jane.

"Have you thought about it?" she asked. "I think we should do the film. Okay, without Jackie. What an opportunity!"

"You know how I despise art-collection roundups. I wouldn't consider getting involved."

"Not even for my sake?"

"Okay... What if we were to concentrate on just one Vatican holding which has never before been made public?"

"A secret treasure?"

"Right. Hundreds of tourists pass under it every day. But hardly anyone in history has had a *close* look at the greatest painting ever made! Our show could provide just that."

At Jane's urging I flew to New York and made an ardent pitch to the director. The vault of the Sistine Chapel was quite enough, I told him, for a whole one-hour show. We could create a fly-on-the-ceiling documentary like nothing ever seen before.

My first suggestion was to dispense with celebrity hosts and professorial commentators alike. Instead, we ought to let the Prophets and Sibyls depicted around the sides of the vault narrate the Old Testament tales which Michelangelo had set himself to illustrate. It would be easy and natural to bridge those stories with quotes from the artist's own poems, and favorite reading.

I added that Michelangelo's background in Dante, Ficino, Pico, and the Bible, was all familiar territory to my Florence-educated partner. "You'll be getting two for the price of one on this project!"

"Sounds plausible," the director said.

"Before submitting the shooting-script and voice-over text, my partner and I will need six weeks up near the vault itself, on some sort of scaffold."

"Can do!" he decided.

I hadn't even mentioned money, so the director knew he had me cheap. We cordially agreed that I would receive adequate compensation plus creative freedom, and that the company would get my best effort, free and clear. We parted well pleased with each other.

Weeks later, at two o'clock (the afternoon hour when the Chapel closed to the public) Jane eased our freshly washed Mercedes around the columned perimeter of the Piazza San Pietro to approach the Vatican's gilded, open gateway.

A pair of Swiss Guards in resplendent medieval regalia crossed their halberds to block our car, while two more advanced, one on each side, to check us out. This was an especially happy moment. I felt as if an alarm clock had gone off to waken me from an anxious, years-long dream of Rome.

Turning to Jane, I said: "Hey, let's title our film *Everyman's Dream*."

Cap Cities would eventually re-title it *"The Secret of Michelangelo; Every Man's Dream,"* get an industry award for its production, and sell the show to CBS for repeated Christmas and Easter broadcasts.

Driving around the back of Saint Peter's Basilica and through the Vatican gardens on a short, slowly winding road, we threaded history and parked beside the Sistine Chapel. Seeing its tall stone exterior for the first time, I recalled that the whole thing was built in accordance with the legendary proportions of Noah's Ark.

A genial Monsignor ushered us in at the Chapel's side door and introduced us to the Vatican's maintenance and construction crew.

Its dozen members belonged to a fearless, acrobatically gifted family which had fulfilled the same function for generations. The crew had dangerous work to do; they regularly scrambled up to repair seemingly unreachable portions of the Vatican's buildings.

At Capital Cities' request, they had constructed a slender tinker-toy tower of narrow aluminum pipes, resting on rubber-tired wheels.

Looming up through the Chapel's dusty gloom, this flimsy contraption soared no less than sixty feet, to within touching distance of the vault itself.

Secured by four steel cables though it was, the tower did not inspire confidence; not in me, anyhow. So, I thought I'd better begin with a quick look around.

I can still see Michelangelo's hugely sweeping image whole in my mind's eye. Its triple-tiered mid-heaven of many colors arched way over me in the deep silence of the empty chapel.

The lowest tier of ceiling frescoes discloses the genealogy of Jesus. Michelangelo conceived the Savior's ancestors as solid, opaque people of all ages, living the daily, domestic round with their feet on the ground.

Then come the titanic Prophets and Sibylline Oracles enthroned. Each of these awesome figures is supposed to have predicted, in one way or another, the arrival of the Messiah. Their thrones are set in what appear to be marble niches adorned with babies gladly dancing in bas-relief, like swirling protons and electrons.

From Isaiah to Zachariah, and from teen-age Delphica to agelessly drooping Cumaea, the Prophets and Sibylline Oracles have children, some light-skinned and some dark, playing around or peering companionably over their shoulders.

Along the central apex of the vault come nine panels illustrating the Book of Genesis. As one steps backwards from the altar, they occur in the following sequence—

First, the Creation of Light. Second, the Setting in Place of the Sun and Moon. Third, the Separation of Land and Sea. Fourth, the Creation of Adam.

Near the center of the barrel-vault, Adam appears at the moment of becoming. God has not yet removed Eve from him. The Deity looms from a lilac cloud or sky-boat of summer thunderstorm, whilst reaching out to almost touch the outstretched hand of Adam/Eve.

One senses electromagnetic energy crackling between the two figures. Their eyes meet also; a two-way stream of love.

Fifth, comes the Removal of Eve from within Adam. Sixth, the Temptation of Adam and Eve and their Expulsion. Seventh, the Sacrifice of Noah. Eighth, the Deluge. Ninth, the Drunkenness of Noah.

At the corners of some scenes are very large and beautiful nude figures charged with the force of mother Nature herself. Certain art historians refer to these as "homo-erotic decorative motifs," but that's absurd.

Michelangelo was never frivolous.

It's true, as Mark Twain observed, that "naked people have very little influence in society." But these daemonic images of living energy frame the Ceiling's major episodes in a manner that is by no means minor.

Michelangelo's own writings show that he felt intense romantic affection for at least two young men, but given the fiery force of his Roman Catholic convictions it's a fair guess that he remained personally celibate.

I regard his *Ignudi* as pre-incarnate and pre-potent offshoots of the supreme Deity.

Intensely virile and yet virginal, neither all male nor part female, lusty and yet delicate, they're dancing full-out, freely, vitally, churning up Earth, Water, Air, & Fire,—the classical elements essential to life on our planet.

Over the Chapel's altar, Prophet Jonah hovers in fearful ecstasy, eyeing the Creation of Light. The Bible says that Jonah tried to flee his God by sea. Consequently the Prophet suffered sea-burial for three days and nights, bitterly bemoaning in the belly of a whale, until—

"The Lord spake unto the fish, and it vomited out Jonah upon dry land."

As my eyes fixed upon Jonah that first day, I felt caught up in the barrel-vaulted belly of Leviathan, *comme un scampi!* How could such a poor fool as myself dare interrogate the work of divine Michelangelo? Why had I ever wished such an impossible labor upon myself? It was all Jane's fault. She'd put me up to this...

The Crew Chief tapped my shoulder—

"Your wife would like to speak with you."

"Where is she?" I looked around.

He raised a forefinger.

Lifting my face, I saw Jane wave from atop the tower.

Shamed, yet laughing too, I started up. As I climbed like a laborious bear, the tower swayed and trembled in protest. I didn't dare to look down, or up either, until I'd reached a point about twenty feet from the top.

There, having rested awhile and caught my breath, I clenched the pipes convulsively with both fists, and peered down at the inlaid stone floor. To my amazement it had a dirty brown sheen.

Jane noticed me leaning out to gawk over the void, which could be dangerous.

Quickly she called: "Look up!"

The frescoes overhead seemed dewy-fresh! How could that be? Finally, I realized that the pollution which made them appear dirty and brownish from the floor was not on the ceiling's surface but in the air itself.

Five minutes later, I reached the tower's top. Rolling over on my back beside Jane, I gazed aloft. Immersed in the warm radiance of Michelangelo's colors, we held hands like children.

Alight with streaming sunrise cloud figures, the Creation story rolled above and around us. Swimming amid lilac, daffodil yellow and moss green forms, we felt the nearby presence of God.

The artist's "Nudes" combine male with female attributes. So does his Supreme Deity, who plays Father and Mother, both at once. Yes, Michelangelo's God was double-sexed, majestically androgynous!

The Supreme Deity's breasts, the phallus nodding erect under the robe, those broad female hips, and the stupendously impressive rear view of God zooming away, must often have been observed.

And yet, so far as I'm aware at this writing, nobody before myself has dared to put the truth in print.

Why not? "God knows," as they say, but I venture to guess that male vanity in being male must have played a significant role.

"Down with Women!"

That's the monotheist position, as everybody knows.

Girl-enslaving, veil-imposing and adulteress-stoning medieval Islamic tradition is on the militant upswing now. Orthodox Judaism still offers fervent prayers of thanks for not being female. And it's no secret that Roman Catholicism frowns paternally down upon the fair sex.

Not long ago, for example, the Vatican reprimanded America's nuns for even dreaming of admission to the priesthood, and rebuked some of Ireland's priests for presuming to dream of getting married at last.

What if our relatively liberal present Pontiff and his scarlet-gowned, same-sex College of Cardinals were to convene in the Sistine Chapel, gaze aloft, and finally acknowledge God's benevolent bisexuality?

(I too can dream, can't I?)

Michelangelo lifted off the Pope's private chapel roof, in effect, to admit heavenly sun and wind, plus the formerly neglected female factor. He conferred his own humanistic vision upon Italy...

At the end of the day, the Crew Chief put a finger to his lips and unlocked a narrow door to "the Holy Father's Weeping Room." Each newly elected Pope hastens to seclude himself in that red-brocaded hide-away, in order to prepare for the formal rigors of official investiture.

There was a red phone by the couch. To amuse us, the chief picked it up and exulted in Italian—

"Mama, I made it!"

He had a problem, which concerned Jane's working clothes. Women, he explained, were not permitted to wear slacks in the Vatican, but our tinker-toy tower made such wear appropriate.

In Rome, the Chief went on, all rules were made to be broken. Would she therefore be so kind as to come conventionally clothed in future? She could bring her slacks rolled up in a purse, and change in the Weeping Room! So that was done.

During our six weeks of research, Jane and I spent at least a hundred afternoon hours (from closing-time at two o'clock until twilight) atop our tower, under the rainbow exuberance of Michelangelo's fresco.

The wheeled, precarious contraption was re-situated now and then, to bring us within touching distance of every section.

I never got used to perching up there. The tower trembled, and I dissembled, insisting I felt fine.

Over the course of time we invited a few friends to come and climb the tower with us. But only Newsweek's Rome bureau chief, Curtis Bill Pepper, who had been a World War Two paratrooper, made it to the top...

In *Lives of the Artists,* Michelangelo's young friend Giorgio Vasari makes an intriguing comment on the master whom he most adored—

"His imagination was so perfect that he could not realize with his hands his great and sublime conceptions, and so he frequently abandoned his works and spoiled many. I know that before his death he burned a great number of his designs, sketches and cartoons in order that no one should perceive his labors and tentative efforts."

I wonder. Perhaps he destroyed his most personal, spontaneous work in order to frustrate agents of the increasingly active Inquisition, and thus protect particular friends and relations following his death. (Pieter Brueghel the Elder, for one, took that precaution in Roman Catholic Brussels.)

Michelangelo used live models for his figures on the vault, privately sketching them at home. The mid-air earthiness and fine detail that the painted Prophets, Sibyls, and Ancestors of Christ possessed when we were studying them, stemmed from the artist's passion for verisimilitude. As he explained in a sonnet—

> *My soul can find no stair to Heaven,*
> *Unless it be Earth's loveliness.*

The artist's assistants would transfer his drawings to the fresco itself via brown-paper "cartoons," as Vasari calls them. Having filled in a small section with fresh plaster, they used its wetness as a paste-surface on which to stick a particular cartoon.

Hurrying to get the job done, they would punch out or slash along the charcoal contours to leave guiding outlines on the Ceiling itself, and then strip the ripped paper sheets away.

Up close, Jane and I saw the incisions left.

Alight with enthusiasm, divinely inspired as he must have felt, the master would then paint in the transferred figures, using his favorite hand-ground earth-colors, like flowers in a chalk garden.

But technical problems plagued him. Because of its local *pozzolano* ingredient, Roman gesso crystallizes much faster than the Florentine variety familiar to Michelangelo. If you use too much water, salts effloresce and ruin the surface. Use just the right amount, and the surface goes mirror-hard before you've half-completed your *giornata,* or day's painting.

Faced with so quick-drying a medium, Michelangelo despaired of achieving the effects he had in mind. Terribly discouraged, he sent his assistants back to Florence. Later on, he followed them home himself, hoping to be quit of the whole project.

Finally, as Jane first intuited and the evidence demonstrates, a solution occurred to him.

Traditional Florentine fresco technique was predicated on the strong color-absorbency of gesso made from the local clay. One had to get things right the first time, because repeated applications of color would muddy the images. But Roman fresco surfaces were something else again, resembling porcelain.

They absorbed no smidgen of pigment once they had crystallized. Hence, Michelangelo could work them over repeatedly *a secco* ("in the dry"), while keeping his colors pure. Belatedly, he recognized the possibility of creating his final draft without urgency and minus fear.

His wooden scaffold extended half-way down the length of the Chapel, concealing his revolutionary labors from everyone below. The scaffold also permitted him to move back and forth between parts of the work, making improvements here and there. He could complete the whole thing as a never-before-seen manifestation of prismatic transparency.

To paint the Ceiling one *giornata* at a time in the approved Florentine fresco tradition would not have taken the artist more than a few months. But, as we know from Vasari's account, Michelangelo spent all of twenty months on the Ceiling. He firmly resisted repeated attempts to make him hurry it, which infuriated Pope Julius.

His final draft held innumerable precise details, far too delicate to be discerned from the Chapel floor, such as fingernails and blood veins. It also featured dashes and sweeps of shadow which "punched up" and richly rounded the sculptural forms of his figures.

Still not content, Michelangelo piled on translucent color glazes, washing one across another to create freshly ringing vibrancies of tone and hue.

Why did he bother with all that? As Dionysius the Areopagite put the case, in a Greek text that was doubtless known to the artist through Marsilio Ficino's translation—

"The divine cannot appear to us unless it be covered with poetic veils."

On most days in the Chapel my thoughts were torn between present revelation and what I might draw out of that for my shooting script, and voice-over commentary, whereas Jane concentrated wholly.

She approached each image with boundless empathy, almost as if she were determined to give the artist himself one last look at his stormy, world-enhancing labor.

How else but through the fresh blue flash of her physical eyes?

Jane made a habit of walking sideways all around the Chapel's very high, vertiginously narrow window-ledges. Standing straight and tall with her toes overhanging thin air, she calmly contemplated each and every scene, while working out the narrative and compositional relations between them.

The maintenance crew could tell that Jane was a special case. So they invited her to accompany them on an inspection-tour up, around, and over, Michelangelo's other masterwork.

Namely, the dome of Saint Peter's Basilica, that huge sunshine-caressed stone bud, which crowned the artist's old age.

Thoughtfully, the crew left her alone up there, perched atop the slippery slate slope, for one of her happiest hours...

The Sistine Ceiling manifests a Gordian Knot of energies in stormy, serpentine motion.

Consider the central "Tree of Knowledge" panel, where a double-tailed serpent—or is it really two climbing as one?—spirals up into the Tree's foliage.

That image takes one back to the "caduceus" or pagan, peace-imposing herald's staff, sporting twin serpents entwined, which was originally borne by Hermes, the classic Guide of Souls.

It also points toward DNA's life-organizing "double helix."

Here we see muscular Adam lean across Eve's head to bend a branch of the tree down within her reach. She's been sitting with her face at the level of his loins. Now she twists her torso and arms around to reach up and grasp the forbidden fruit.

Adam and Eve are divinely natural here. One senses that he will soon be drawn to impregnate her. But wait. On the far side of the Tree the same pair look heavy, homely, and sick.

Departing Eden with a sword at their backs, they're prodded down toward the dichotomous churn which you and I perforce inhabit.

The Tree of Knowledge is a dimly whispering green shadow-bower, where Satan the tempter and the avenging angel Gabriel intertwine.

From this very Tree, they say, shall come the wood of Christ's cross.

Meanwhile, the tree stands like a May-pole, supporting dozens of inter-related ideas and images. The spandrels at the Ceiling's corners, for example, celebrate two men and two women. Namely, Moses, David, Judith and Esther, four saviors of Israel.

The first spandrel illustrates the legend that Moses healed his snake-bitten people in the Sinai desert, by setting a serpent of brass upon a pole "for them to look upon."

How could mere looking have helped anyone? That question would not have arisen in the classical world.

The glittery, brazen snake which Moses set upon a pole harks back to Mediterranean myths and images which were by no means unrealistic in the context of their time, when arts and sciences still interwove.

Desert serpents sometimes guide lost travelers to water. That's how they saved Alexander the Great, for one, on his expedition to consult the Oracle of Ammon.

What's more, a huge, rainbow-scaled serpent preceded Apollo as the spirit of Delphi. The newly arrived archer shot a sun-shaft into her.

Ovid's Latin "Metamorphoses" relates—

"The place is now called Pytho, and men call the Lord Apollo by another name, Pythian, because on that spot the power of piercing Helios made the monster rot away."

Apollo suffered nine years of banishment for having destroyed the serpent. Centuries later his half human son Asklepius sailed from Greek Epidaurus to Rome in serpent form, to rid the Latin capital of plague.

Ovid tells us—

"As the vessel of Asklepius proceeded up the Tiber river into Rome, he coiled about the mast, raised his massive, metallic length to the crossbar, swung his flat, scaly, bearded head from side to side and flicked his long forked tongue, graciously acknowledging the Hosannas that rose with smoke of incense along both sides of the river.

"Upon reaching the Isola Tiburtina in the city's midst, the demigod glided over the ship's side and swam ashore. At that point, the serpent son of Apollo put on his heavenly form again."

In Jane's and my time, there was still a hospital at the island's tip, plus a trattoria specializing in therapeutic spinach pasta with walnut sauce, where we often lunched.

INTERMEZZO

It's like I'm kicking a tin can
along a country lane in June.
My tricky subject skitter-skates
to a scraping stop, and waits
for me to boot it on.

The Sistine Ceiling's second spandrel shows a suspenseful moment in David's duel with Goliath. The shepherd boy has felled his Philistine foe with nothing but a slingshot and a smooth stone.

Now Goliath sprawls python-like on the bare ground, and little David bestrides him. The fate of Israel hangs upon Goliath's scimitar, which David has snatched from its sheath. Is the boy really up to decapitating him?

One feels for David and the dazed giant, both.

The third spandrel speaks to the bleak legend of Judith and the conquering Assyrian general Holofernes, who trusted his hands to protect his head.

Judith presented herself as a willing traitor to the Israelite cause. Her dark eyes, long curly locks and lissome limbs entranced the proud invader, who thought himself happy as she unlaced, embraced and pleasured him with apparent eagerness.

Afterward, she seized his sword from the foot of the bed and struck off his head as he lay back, "filled with wine."

Here we see Judith departing in her sinuous manner from the general's tent. Her maid bears the booty, the would-be conqueror's head, on a silver salver.

Holofernes' calm, noble profile looks familiar, for this is Michelangelo's own deliberately inserted self-portrait! Might the artist have imagined himself as a second Holofernes, invading sacred territory, paintbrush in hand?

The fourth and final spandrel relates the legend of Esther and the Persian Emperor Cyrus, who reigned over a vast multitude of cities and tribes lying between India's Indus River and Egypt's Nile.

His Vizier Haman once proposed exterminating Jews as a matter of state policy.

The Emperor sat pondering that poisonous notion, until his beloved consort Esther revealed to him that she herself was Jewish—

"Therefore, my Lord, you might as well begin by destroying me!"

Instead, Cyrus had Haman crucified.

Like a human serpent snatched up and nailed to a tree, this legendary anti-Semite writhes before our eyes. Haman hangs pinioned, magnificent in agony. He's a weirdly noble, secular precursor of Jesus the crucified Jew!

The Italian Renaissance was enormously enriched, thanks to a flood of Jews who had been driven from Spain by royal decree. So personal contact with Hebrew sages doubtless deepened Michelangelo's capacious spiritual insight.

The Sistine Ceiling relates to Christ's story in purely prophetic style. Michelangelo capped the Pope's private chapel with a totally "Old Testament" painted epic.

Just as Esther stood up to the Emperor Cyrus, so the artist stood tall before the Pope. Hence the fond yet tense and sometimes explosively strained relations between those titanic men—equals, each in his own domain.

With the Ceiling behind him at last, Michelangelo moved across town from the Vatican. For the rest of his long life he occupied a modest house on the edge of the Giudecca, the Jewish Quarter.

Titian and Rembrandt also chose to reside in Hebrew neighborhoods. It's by no means impossible that all three supreme artists were Christians of partly Jewish blood.

We'll never know, because gentile families had good reason to keep such matters off the record. But consider Rembrandt's immortal *Self-Portrait as Apostle Paul* (1661) plus *The Jewish Bride* (1665), for example.

Modern times brought us Modigliani, Soutine, Chagall, Jacob Epstein, Henry Koerner, Alfred Stieglitz, and Diane Arbus, plus the mid-twentieth century's anti-totalitarian, abstract "No Graven Images" movement.

Yet present scholarship barely touches upon Jewish aspects of art. Unlike the much-discussed classical influence, the Hebrew stream has entered unnoticed.

Last night I discussed this subject with my son Jeff.

"I tend to agree," said he. "After all, Michelangelo's career first got rolling with the Biblical David he carved in marble for the city of Florence!"

Jeff's own first sculpture, made at age six or seven, was a baked-clay approximation of that very statue, which I'd taken him and Winslow to see. It's looking down at me right now, from a shelf in my studio. Jeff is now a brilliant conceptual designer, artist, and writer; and he designed his cozy and yet open-hearted Venice home.

On the night when shooting of our film began, with takes of Jane and myself ascending and descending our tower, we brought Jeff and Winslow along to enjoy that occasion.

The work went on and on, so our children slept in a choir stall, dreaming beneath the floodlit, resplendent ceiling.

Gazing down upon them from sixty feet above, numb with mingled awe and love, I wondered what they might be witnessing in sleep.

When I told Winslow this story the other day, my daughter said she still recalls the choir stall's cushion-less discomfort, and in fact hardly slept a wink!

Winslow's an author, editor, publisher, palm reader, tarot-card interpreter, astrologer, and Waldorf teacher, with an amazingly extended memory-bank.

Here's what the poet Goethe had to say in an ecstatic letter home from Rome—

"Not until you've set your feet on the floor of the Sistine Chapel and gazed up into its painted vault, do you get a clear idea of what the human spirit can accomplish."

The life-changing revelation that Goethe received won't happen for anyone ever again.

Why not? Because, about a decade after the completion of our film, Michelangelo's final draft began being obliterated by long years of "cleaning" and absurd refurbishment on the part of the Vatican's conservation team, bankrolled by a Japanese television firm.

Willfully blind to the miracle before their eyes, the Vatican's curators had jumped at Japan's offer to help brighten up Roman Catholicism's number one tourist attraction.

"Scientific authorities" were brought in for publicity purposes. They performed forensic tests, and solemnly condemned the Ceiling's outer layers as—

"Dirt, soot, glue, and over-painting by unknown hands."

The conservators then set about liquefying, swabbing, and scrubbing Michelangelo's poetic veils forever away. They used commercial chemicals developed by America's "Elmer's Glue" people for washing down stone exteriors,

The artist's first-draft under-painting remains, but it's blurred, sweetened and reduced to a money-spinning, crass, candy-box "tourist destination."

Still, to be fair, we're not faced with total loss. The general scheme of things survives in its original setting, and God's hermaphroditic aspect remains evident...

My lifetime friend, the painter Frank Mason, taught at Manhattan's Art Students' League for over half a century, imparting traditional methods and ideals to a host of devoted students. He was born ebullient, with a baroque artistic sensibility.

(I'm told our word "baroque" stems from the Portuguese for an unsymmetrical, oversize pearl.)

Frank soon persuaded me to take an active role in his quixotic campaign to save the Sistine Ceiling from its "restoration" disaster. I say quixotic, because we might as well have been tilting at windmills.

"You can't buck City Hall," I reminded Frank, "let alone the Vatican!"

"So what?" Mason boomed. "We've got the merest ghost of a chance. But think how awful you'll feel if you don't even try!"

I'm eternally grateful to Frank and his dear partner Anne, for persuading me to set normal caution aside and help them undertake a universally scorned struggle to halt cleaning of the Sistine Ceiling in mid-operation.

The whole affair was onerous, however, with negative impacts on our reputations. I was called "a traitorous son of a bitch," and Frank suffered similar abuse.

Once, when we were invited to show my Sistine Ceiling film at an international museum curators' conference, I was asked—

"How did you fake it?"

"Easy," I said, "since I can paint better on film than Michelangelo did on plaster."

Thereupon, Dr. Mancinelli, the Vatican's highly regarded Chief Art Curator, arose and graciously informed me that he respected my opinion. Smiling, he added that he sincerely hoped I could bring myself to respect his opinion in return.

"You and I don't matter," I replied. "No, but the Holy Father will go down in history as *destroyer* of the world's greatest painting."

The Chief Curator's formerly beaming countenance scrunched up into a silent scream of rage. He whirled around, and rushed off.

A security guard stationed by the exit door managed to fling it open in the nick of time. Otherwise a furious ecclesiastical crash would have occurred.

James Beck, who presided as Columbia University's Professor of Italian Renaissance art, soon threw in with Mason and myself. He'd been alerted, he said, by an article of mine in *Harvard* magazine.

His wife was Florentine, he had first-hand knowledge of the Italian art-cultural scene, and his connoisseurship was legendary, so Beck made a mighty advocate.

Alarmed at last, Vatican officials commissioned a savvy Madison Avenue public-relations outfit to puff their Ceiling scrub-a-dub-dub, while fluffing off Jim Beck, Frank Mason, and myself as a childish trio of publicity-seeking "nut-cases."

They fully accomplished that mission. Mainly by offering private, free, red-carpet, "See for Yourself" junkets to key magazine editors, museum officials, art historians, and critics.

Each junketeering V.I.P. would be escorted up onto the cleaners' comfortable scaffold, shown the elaborate equipment at hand, and unctuously instructed concerning the Church's "Historic, purely scientific, necessary and timely task."

Thomas Hoving, the ostentatiously opinionated Director Emeritus of the Metropolitan Museum, and Editor of *Connoisseur* magazine, was cordially presented with a prepared cloth and invited to wipe away portions of the Ceiling's "accumulated filth" himself!

Thus, Hoving plus a dozen other instant "experts" were made, piously anointed, and forever hooked.

Robert Hughes happened to serve as *Time's* Art Editor back then. I'd written him to beg that he embrace our cause, but he never vouchsafed a reply.

In his final book, Hughes stoutly maintained that getting to examine the "restored" ceiling from very close up and on his back "the way Michelangelo painted it" was indeed—

"A privilege, probably the most vivid one I had in a fifty-year career as an art critic."

Hughes basked in public adulation of his frequently addled critical and art-historical rhetoric. Beck meanwhile endured sneers and snubs from corrupt and/or pusillanimous art-world colleagues.

He soldiered on, however, founding a non-profit society called "Art Watch International," for spotting, and if possible preventing, further desecration of masterpieces.

Soon indicted for "libelous defamation" in Italy, Beck bravely went there to face the music and risk incarceration.

Following his outspoken performance at a trial which turned out to have been rigged from the start, all charges were dismissed.

Then suddenly, to my sorrow, Beck up and died. His beloved Florentine partner expired just five days after he did. I don't know the circumstances, which may or may not have been suspicious.

England's forthright Michael Daly carries on with the Art Watch initiative that Jim Beck founded. In a recent issue of his "U.K. Art Watch Bulletin," Daly reports—

"The Vatican Museum's chief Antonio Paolucci has told the newspaper La Repubblica that between 15,000 and 20,000 people a day, or more than four million a year, visit the Sistine.

"'In this chapel people often invoke the holy spirit. But the people who fill this room every day are not pure spirits,' Paolucci told the newspaper.

"'Such a crowd emanates sweat, breath, carbon dioxide, and all sorts of dust!'"

Dr. Paolucci is not such a ninny as to suggest curtailing the dusty, sweaty, breathing, but high-price ticket-buying pilgrim horde.

Instead, he proposes installing an elaborate air-conditioning system, which will doubtless do more harm than good.

Hardly any of the many suckers in the hushed-up Sistine disaster ever summoned sufficient courage to confess that they were cleverly manipulated out of their minds. Word gets around, however, and the ghastly evidence hovers in plain sight.

Hence, today's professional art community knows perfectly well what horrors occurred in the Sistine.

Some years ago now, Frank Mason suggested that the time was ripe for us to "collaborate on something new."

I complied by posing for Frank to paint, while occupied with a somewhat irritating book called *"Conversation on a Country Lane,"* and improvising a retort in my head—

ON A COUNTRY LANE

A sheep and a goat were
going to the pasture.
Said the sheep:
"Can't you walk faster?"
Goat told her:
"I'd stroll right past yer
did I not prefer
to take it slow."

"Excuse my rudeness,
Goat. I did not know
you hesitate while
trudging through
This pearly, early
morning dew
for reasons
peculiar to you."

Goat cleared his throat:
"Our Gospel states
that all things come
to him who waits.
Just look upon
the rising sun.
That's everybody's
Number One."

Sheep gave Goat
a graceful gambol.
"True," she bleated,
"so let's amble."

My final conversation with Frank occurred when I phoned in order to congratulate him on a fresh honor—

"I'm told that you received a medal."

"True," Frank bellowed into the phone, "but that's not important."

"What is?"

"A chemist comrade and I have rediscovered the amber-based medium Rubens used for those goldy-brown shadows."

"Good for you!"

"Yes, and on top of that, my large *'Crucifixion'* is going better at last.

"How come?"

"Since Anne is sacred to me, I thought she ought to model for the Virgin Mary. But no. The role requires a darker sort of beauty."

"Understood."

"Well, finally I found the right person to pose, and I can hardly wait to start in on her eyes."

"Why her eyes in particular?"

"Because they'll be gazing up, don't you know, at what *we* don't *see*!"

Speaking of what we don't see, Frank himself has since passed away.

Book Six: Coming of Age

As Above, so Below

Rose Covered Cottage

Westward East

Cure for War

Mortal Coil

Negative Capability

1. Rose Covered Cottage

At the crest of Ashdown Lane, in a village called Forest Row, on the northern edge of Ashdown Forest in British East Sussex, stands a rose covered, flint-stone cottage where we lived off and on for a decade.

A winding cow-path connected our place with Kidbrooke Mansion, which housed the historic Michael Hall School, a Waldorf institution which Jefferson and Winslow attended.

Meanwhile both Jane and my daughter May, who had grown up and joined us at last, took Francis Edmund's foundation course in Waldorf Education at Emerson College, a one-mile stroll in the opposite direction.

The Wych Cross residence where A.A. Milne composed the "Winnie the Pooh" books stood within walking distance of our own.

Like the author of Alice in Wonderland, Milne was a brilliant mathematician who turned his head for logic upside down in the interest of literature. He dedicated *The House at Pooh Corner* to his wife, as follows—

> *You gave me Christopher Robin and then*
> *you breathed new life in Pooh.*
> *Whatever of each has left my pen*
> *goes homing back to you.*

Pooh Bear, with his friends Piglet, Eeyore, Rabbit, Owl and Kanga, welcomed us, we felt, to the stretch of heather and ancient woods that lay between us and their creator's longtime lair.

Our family often played "Pooh Sticks" on the wooden bridge across a volubly vocal brook in the forest. First, each of us would select a distinctively shaped twig from the ground for a personal wooden horse. Bending over the railing we would simultaneously drop our sticks into the upstream warbling, and then run across to watch them shoot out from underneath.

The racers bobbed and twirled downstream along the lower-octave water-talk. We would cheer our separate entries on as they swirled out of sight. There was no way to tell which twig might win...

One full-moon night, while we were watching for badgers in a beech grove, Wyd impishly kicked up the phosphorescent leaves into silvery swirls, thus giving us a glimpse of the "Horrible Heffalump" who'd panicked Kanga's baby Roo.

The next day was rainy. So Jeff in his yellow oilskins and red rubber Wellington boots, went off to explore part of the forest which we'd not yet visited. That was when he slushily discovered "Eeyore's Gloomy Place."

Jeff once created a very small rear bumper sticker for our faithful Mercedes, which read:

"What is the use of reading this sign?"

As I observed in my rear-view mirror, Jeff's message fractured some tail-gating lorry drivers.

Our excursions from Forest Row were north to London, south to Brighton, and west to a few cathedral towns. We also visited prehistoric places of legend, lying open to the four winds, such as the White Horse of Uffington, the Giant of Cerne Abbas, Stonehenge, Silbury Hill and especially Avebury.

Each New Year's Eve at midnight, our family circumambulated the massive earthwork that enclosed Avebury's sacred monoliths. Between the tree branches, stars like diamond acorns swung around us.

An old country inn called the "Ashdown Forest Hotel" stood next door to us. We lodged our guests there, and drank with them in the tiny bar. That's where I once entertained American visitors with a tale-out-of-school concerning William Butler Yeats's private life.

In middle-age, the poet proposed marriage to the fiery Irish Nationalist icon Maude Gonne, who had been the primary passion of his youth.

Regretfully rejected by Maude, Yeats then proposed to her lovely, neurasthenic daughter Iseult, who had been deflowered by Ezra Pound. She also declined.

Reeling from the double rebuff, Yeats finally proposed to a young Sussex lady who possessed a psychic streak plus an odd name. Georgie Lees-Hyde jumped at the chance.

For their honeymoon, Yeats engaged a room directly above the bar where we sat. But things did not go swimmingly at first. As Colm Toibin recently surmised—

"She realized now not only that the famous poet did not love her and had married her on a whim but that the idea of the poet... was far removed from the grumpy, sickly, indifferent and miserable man with whom she was now confined in a small space."

After three nights of limp romance and feverish disappointment, Yeats's sweetly resourceful bride said she felt an urge to take dictation from the spiritual world.

In their ensuing séance, spirits conveyed the message that Yeats was better than okay. Moreover, he should feel free and uninhibited in his marital relations with George! The poet happily consummated their union forthwith.

In his obscure volume called *"A Vision,"* Yeats relates—

"On the afternoon of October 24th, 1917, four days after my marriage, my wife surprised me by attempting automatic writing. What came in disjointed sentences was so exciting, sometimes so profound, that I persuaded her to give an hour or two day after day to the unknown writers, and after some half-dozen such hours I offered to spend what remained of life explaining and piecing together those scattered sentences. 'No,' was the answer. 'We have come to give you metaphors for poetry.'"

Repeating this story, I meant no disrespect to Yeats, whose poetic genius I revere.

It's true that he lacked a healthy, saving sense of humor, but that goes with the literary territory. Writing is a lonely profession, conducing to narcissistic gloom. What's more, self-importance haunts the halls of notoriety.

My point is simply that spirits choose to work in mysterious ways, and very often through wonderful women! That's one thing to which I can personally testify.

A year later, in the same hotel bar, my family and I witnessed the historic television broadcast of America's "giant step for mankind" upon the moon.

Thanks to television, our nation's "Moon Walk" hit an unprecedented peak of public interest, delighting millions, worldwide.

Stripped of national borders and manmade features, Earth spun veiled with air, washed with water, and dappled with sunshine. I felt like a little boy at a garden party, who sees a noblewoman step out onto the lawn, and realizes that she's his own mother.

Afterward, I told the kids about Benjamin Franklin capturing a bright thread of lightning with his key-hung kite. The word "scientist" had not yet been coined, so Franklin conducted his experiments as an "electrician."

A British zoologist named Walsh was the first to notice what goes on with electric eels. Back In 1773, Walsh wrote a letter to Franklin which seethes with poetic intensity—

"*He who predicted and showed that electricity wings the bolt of the atmosphere, will hear with attention that in the deep it speeds a humbler bolt, silent and invisible.*

"*He who analyzed the electrical Phial, will hear with pleasure that its laws prevail in animate Phials.*

"*He who by Reason became an electrician, will hear with reverence of an instinctive electrician, gifted in his birth with a wonderful apparatus, and skill to use it.*"

Removed from school at an early age and apprenticed to a physically abusive elder brother in the printing trade, Benjamin Franklin soon "ran away" from Boston to Philadelphia.

Setting up his own print shop there. Ben rose rapidly, becoming an industrious printer, witty writer, charming ladies' man, businessman, anonymous philanthropist, inventor, strikingly honest diplomat in London, wise, benevolent old midwife to the birth of our United States, and superbly successful ambassador to Paris.

Herman Melville opined that Ben was: "Everything except a poet." I hesitate to contradict so eminently poetic a writer. Yet the epitaph which Franklin composed and designed for his own tombstone suggests that he was a poet also—

>   *The Body of*
>   *B. Franklin,*
>   *Printer,*
>   *Like the Cover of an old Book,*
>   *Its Contents torn out,*
>   *And stript of its Lettering and Gilding,*
>   *Lies here, Food for Worms.*
>   *But the Work shall not be wholly lost.*
>   *For it will, as he believ'd, appear once more,*
>   *In a new and more perfect Edition,*
>   *Corrected and amended,*
>   *By the author*

Peregrine Eliot, Earl of St. Germans in Cornwall, was one who helped our family feel at home. He'd sent a letter inviting us to visit him.

The Earl thought we might enjoy seeing the Eliot family chapel, which dated from medieval times, and had once been a cathedral. The extensive grounds, he added, had been designed by the 18th century landscape architect Humphrey Repton, and were still preserved intact.

On our initial visit to Port Eliot, we fell into first-name familiarity over the second round of martinis. Perry proved to be a young, thoughtful and generous "Mod Lord," who wore beads, played silly pranks on guests, and owned a million-pound chunk of the Beatles.

He showed us Humphrey Repton's "Red Book" of designs for the estate. Repton wrote that he had considered demolishing the former cathedral because it overshadowed the mansion. On second thought, he gave it a motherly role, and the mansion a daughterly one—

"By drawing an umbilical curved path from the garden door of the mansion's smoking-room to the church."

The Rembrandt dominating Perry's dining-room lent a warm glow to our discussion there. The Earl informed us that Eliot forbears had helped lead the Norman invasion of Britain back in the year 1066. They filled two ships, in fact.

There's still a village called "Eliot" in Brittany, by the way. I'd once driven through there, but lacked sufficient wit to pull up and take a look around.

Five centuries later, in 1564, the family settled at Port Eliot in what could be Great Britain's longest-occupied house, dating from Romano-Celtic times.

A century after that, it seems, my own "younger son" branch of the family departed from nearby Plymouth for America. This was all news to me. The family history I'd been given went back only so far as the American Revolution.

Where I came from, of course, names meant very little. The American dream did not include notions of genetic nobility. We'd jettisoned those, along with the "Divine Right of Kings."

But it would have been bumptious of me to mention that. Besides, Perry's real virtue was not "nobility" but *"noblesse oblige."* In other words, his guiding sense of responsibility to family, the arts, and British culture.

After dinner we retired to the game-room, where our host unrolled a long scroll out across the snooker table. It was inscribed with the family genealogy. And at the scroll's very end, stood the name *"Alexander Eliot."*

Apparently, I myself was the least, last leaf at the tip of our American branch. In other words, the eldest son of the eldest son, etcetera, dating back to the second son of the incumbent Lord Eliot in 1664.

Normally, second sons of nobility entered the military, and third sons took Holy Orders. My ancestor broke the mold, perhaps because he was a Puritan convert who rejected military service on religious grounds.

That's my wishful theory, anyhow. It's also possible, as I'm aware, that he had committed some heinous crime and therefore felt compelled to flee for his life.

"If it so happens that I and my heirs expire in your lifetime," Perry announced, "then my title and this estate will pass along to you!"

"Not so," I told him.

"Why not?"

"I'm too much of a wild Indian."

"Wouldn't that be shirking?"

"Yep. Call me Shirking Bull."

"Well, but one's family should come first, as I'm sure you'll agree."

"Perhaps, but I could never successfully shoulder so vast a responsibility. The fact is, I'm a dope at practical matters. So here's a toast, Perry, in your own rare port, to your long, happy lordship and that of your children on down."

Having managed to keep Port Eliot private (free from Britain's "National Trust" control) he now utilizes the estate as a summer venue for hugely popular music and literature festivals...

The next notable individual to welcome us was a Scottish doctor named John Raeside.

He'd patched up wounded Brits in the bloody muddle of the Korean War.

John returned from that carnage revolted by warfare, disgusted with stopgap medical practice, and sick unto death.

A German-born nurse named Anneli, who happened to be profoundly versed in "anthroposophic medicine," rescued John from suicidal depression.

He married her, took the same esoteric training, and finally made a name for himself as a diagnostician, becoming homeopathic consultant to England's Queen, for example.

John, with his daffy old witch of a mother, his wife Anneli, and their children Mark, Dominic, Susan, and Nicky, used to come down from London for week-end relaxation.

We enjoyed conversations interwoven with desultory rambles, Frisbee matches on the nearby cricket-pitch, and wildly obscure contests in Ashdown Forest, which had me totally confused,

AMBUSH

"Seen ya climbin, Dominic!"
"Dint neither. I ain't there.
Invisibility's my trick.
Mind yer manners, dear."

"Bang! Bang! Sue, yer shot."
"I am not 'cos ya nae got
a proper gun, ya bittie bum."
"Lookit, finger an thumb!"

On the evening before her thirteenth birthday, Wyd confided to John Raeside that she dreaded not being twelve anymore because she had loved it so much.

"What is good about thirteen?" she asked.

Thereupon, all the Raesides dreamed up twelve good reasons why she would be fine and dandy at that advanced age.

"You see," she cried, "there's not even a thirteenth reason!"

"Oh yes there is," said John: "Jesus and his twelve Apostles add up to that magic number."

On the last of our many wonderful week-ends together, John remarked that he'd been invited to address an important medical convention in Amsterdam.

"But I'm terrified," he told me privately, "of making the plane-hop!"

"Don't be silly," I said. "There's not one chance in a million that your delegation's plane will fall."

The plane did fall, shortly after take-off, and John perished along with everyone else aboard.

Isn't reality non-dual, all of a piece, and timeless in that regard? Yes, but our instinctive sense of this has stumbled, tumbled, and drifted down out of sight below the mist and snow of a Ginnungagap in human consciousness...

One week after my dear friend's memorial service, I went up to London in a teary mood, and visited Foyles' bookshop. There my eyes "just happened" to light upon a tome with an intriguing title: *"The Dramatic Universe."* Opening the book at random, I read the following definition—

Eternity-blindness—the property of human sense perceptions which permits them to experience only actualizations and not potentialities.

Ordinarily, that would have struck me as just one more abstract idea. But, yes, I was "eternity-blind," for sure. How terribly I'd failed John Raeside! His nearly blind mother possessed what she called "second sight." It never occurred to me, however, that John might have it, too. Hence, I'd fatuously cheered him on to doom.

The volume for sale at Foyle's was by John Godolphin Bennett. I purchased it, and eagerly perused the text. Bennett agreed with Shakespeare's Prospero that "All the world's a stage." Meaning, not only the present panorama, but past and future, too, including astral time, geological time, and so on, down to one's own tiny, lightly vibrating string of time.

His book urged that each one of us can do a little something to help wrench the whole Globe Theatre of past, present, and future toward the positive side. Instead of aspiring to permanent existence in heaven, why not devote one's personal moment to strenuously stretching and molding earthly matters for the better?

Profoundly impressed, I sent Bennett a postcard which read—

"You're suggesting that tragedy is the skeletal scaffold of comedy!"

He responded with an invitation to come and see him at Kingston. While driving over there with Jane, I asked her if John Raeside's spirit might possibly be involved in what we were about. She nodded: "He's helping."

A craggy-faced septuagenarian, with merrily glittering eyes, Bennett stood tall by his blazing hearth and greeted us in the upper-crust British manner from what seemed at first to be an aloof distance.

The marble mantelpiece at his back lay bare except for a large chunk of coal. That exhibit stood in stark contrast to the display I'd once noticed at Henry Robinson Luce's Waldorf Astoria suite. There, the mantelpiece boasted a pair of bronze busts, representing my tough old boss beside his ice-cold bride Claire Booth.

NATURAL HISTORY

Bennett's coal chunk could have come
from under a Welsh mountainside
like the side of Christ crucified
when a Roman centurion
made certain that Jesus died
by mercifully spearing the divine one.

Two hours into our first meeting, I asked Bennett what friendship means. "It means working together," he told me firmly. "Let's try that!"

Accordingly, I composed an essay on Pieter Breughel's "Children's Games" for his magazine *Systematics*. I also gave an illustrated lecture on glyphs (delineated by myself) at his "Institute for Comparative Studies." Bennett kindly arranged a small private printing of my illustrations.

Meanwhile, he presented me with his autobiography, a tome called *Witness*. Here I'll excerpt the passage which concerns his almost fatal wounding in World War One—

"*My next memory is of waking up, not inside but outside of my body. I knew that I was not dead. I had no sensation of my own body, yet I was aware that stretcher after stretcher was being brought in and that there was no place for them all.*

"*When my body was taken to the operating room I went with it. I heard a voice saying, 'Fine, please,' and a woman's voice answer: 'There's only coarse left.' Several days later, when I returned to consciousness and the stitches were taken out of my head, the nurse said, 'I wonder why they used coarse hair.' I said, 'They had no fine left.' She seemed surprised. 'How did you know that? You were unconscious!'*"

Although he seemed averse to organized religion, Bennett made discreet retreats at a Benedictine monastery in Normandy. There, he sang for his supper, with the Abbot's enthusiastic support, by offering the monks a crash course in Asiatic "Reincarnation" doctrine.

POSSIBLE PASTS

Did I fall from the tree of night,
alighting here, time after time
like a storm-torn twig that's quite
unaware of whence it came?

Was I a frightened campfire-tender?
Hand-axe maker? Seasick sailor?
Famished hunter of the deer?
Plodding, footsore pioneer?

Could I have been a robber baron?
Brown girl traded down the river?
Absolute hogwash professor?
Seamstress on a lonely shore?

I've got nothing against religion in general, but to me the whole notion of Hell is evil. I've insisted on this point ever since my seventh Christmas, when I passionately attempted to convince my elder sister Torka that *"Noel, Noel!"* really meant: "No hell, no hell!"

At age ten, Torka wasn't having any of that. We little siblings stood gazing at each other in total bewilderment...

Work together with John Bennett soon extended to include family visits back and forth between our Forest Row cottage and the Bennetts' weekend retreat at Glastonbury.

There, one blazing hot Sunday, Bennett led the lot of us, except his young second wife Elizabeth, who knew better, on a strenuous "expedition" designed to gain the crest of a hill where, according to legend, King Arthur's Camelot once stood.

Looking like a veteran Bengal Lancer in his shorts and pith helmet, and actually hallooing with enthusiasm, Bennett led his two children and ours (with Jane and me struggling in the rear) up along a painfully pathless and perfectly pitiless climb of his choosing.

Scrambling down into dry moats whose muggy stillness swarmed with mosquitoes and black flies, we clambered up again over a steep succession of ancient earthwork redoubts bristling with thorn bushes and fallen trees. Panting and sweating we emerged upon a pasture inhabited by a scattering of recumbent cows.

Those animals turned their small-horned heads to view us—as we did them—with surprise. The children had expected to find a ruined castle at the very least. There was a pause, a silence, on all sides.

Finally I suggested that the peacefully gleaming cows around us might be transmigrated Knights of the Round Table, enjoying a respite from their struggles of old.

"How did the cows get up here?" Jeff asked.

Bennett pointed: "By the cow-path on the south side."

"Then, couldn't we have come that way?"

"Ah, yes. But would we be here now?"

"Well," Jeff glanced from Bennett to me, and back again. "Wouldn't we?"

Smiling, Bennett replied: "The cow-path could have conveyed us comfortably to this hilltop, but the direct route has brought us farther up than that."

"I get it," Jeff said happily. "We can circle the pasture and look for arrowheads or whatever. We may even find Excalibur, King Arthur's sword!"

Wyd, and the Bennett children also, caught Jeff's excitement. They all ran off together.

"You're a born teacher," Jane told Bennett, adding with imperative emphasis: "You should start a college!"

The last time I saw him alive was at his new college. He welcomed Jane and me as honored guests, which disturbed my easygoing American-style sensibility.

Later, in faraway Japan, John appeared to my dreaming self. "I built you up for the students' sake, not yours," he explained.

"Gotcha, and I'm so happy to see you again."

"The feeling is mutual, but now I must go at once."

He pressed the long, strong fingers of one hand to his chest. They curled in between his naked ribs as he faded from my sight.

John had dropped in on his way out, sealing our comradeship.

2. Westward East

When May returned to the U.S. to embark on her teaching career and Jefferson and Winslow entered college, Jane and I felt the pangs of separation that parents usually experience. But, thanks to Fred Sontag's recommendation, I received a Japan Foundation Senior Fellowship for—
 "Studies of Zen Buddhism in the Arts."
 That got us back to Japan at long last, for a full year's residence in garden-hearted Kyoto.
 Jane had never learned to play a musical instrument, so now she jumped at the chance to study intensively with the great Koto player Kimiko Hayashi.
 Kneeling opposite her teacher, with their instruments placed parallel between them, she would mirror Kimiko's musicianship in reverse.
 I meanwhile explored Zen traditions, and we both meditated at a temple called Myoshin-Ji, under the direction of the noted Zen-Buddhist Sensei: Masao Abe.
 We sat on thin pillows, with our knees spread, ankles crossed, and hands open in our laps, while remaining as straight-backed and motionless as possible, for what seemed horribly long stretches of group meditation.
 Mainstream zazen practice of the "Soto" school is a matter of firmly resisting the power of gravity to collapse one out of position, while at the same time devoting one's consciousness to deep, steady breathing along with "no comment" observation of one's own passing thoughts.

Like military drill and forced marches, zazen is a comfortless discipline, designed to foster composure by straining the same to the limit.

"*Am I getting there?*"

My hopeful, characteristically American query elicited Masao's courteous, typically Japanese response—

"*Yes, you are playing at not quite!*"

"Right," I told him ruefully, "that's been the story of my life."

"Mine, also," said he, smiling at me. Zen masters tend to be theatrically temperamental, but Masao's humble good humor distinguished him from the rest.

Carried on past comfort and past commonsense as well, zazen pushes one to an altogether different place. It's not impossible to drop both body and mind for a time. Body with its buried memories, and Mind with its multiple concerns.

One does the same in sleep, of course. Achieving this in a waking state proves to be weirdly worthwhile. That's one thing I tried to convey in my book *Zen Edge* (1976).

DISTANCE

>   I gaze from the invisible
>   at the palms of my hands
>   and now I get the risible
>   idea they're foreign lands!

I'd suffered a small sacroiliac problem for decades. Although not painful by day, it regularly awakened me in the night. Zen practice cured me of that annoyance, at least, by firming up the small of my back.

I've always assumed so, anyhow, but just now a second possibility springs to mind. That particular blessing could have come from an expert Japanese masseuse in Kyoto, upon whose services I once splurged. Having loosened me up to a gratifying degree, the little lady asked—

"Permission, prese, walk on you back?"

The slight, wisely distributed pressures of her little feet lightly dancing up and down again along my spinal column may very well have done the trick...

Zazen occasionally enabled me to exchange my sullen blues and callow fears for clarity, symmetry, wholeness, and harmony. This blessed condition naturally passed in the course of things. For me, meditation ended with an involuntary shiver of recognition—

"I'm here!"

Reconciled to the relatively chaotic conditions of existence ahead, with heart and mind alike void of anxiety, I'd arise refreshed and energized. But sometimes one or both of my legs would have gone to sleep without my noticing, in which case I sat down again with a bump.

"Rinzai" Zen is an elaboration of the Soto kind. This calls for intense mental concentration, while sitting, upon a particular conundrum or nonsensical command which defies human reason.

Buddhist literature is packed with such hard-to-crack walnuts. Take the famous query: "What is the sound of one hand clapping?"

No, "Castanets" doesn't cut it. Words won't help. Here's another tough one—

"Stop the ship on the distant sea!"

To seriously ask what might be meant is not, after all, the way. Instead, I imagined a beautiful ship on some far off ocean, sailing along at chest-level, within easy reach. I waited awhile, enjoying my mental picture. Then, without a thought, I extended a forefinger and stopped the ship.

No problem. It's we who create and pile up unnecessary problems for our body/minds. As Robert Burns put it—

But human bodies are sic fools
For a' their colleges and schools,
That when nae real ills perplex them
They make enow themselves to vex 'em.

The 17th century Japanese artist Hakuin vertically deployed his ink brush to set swirling ciphers on rice paper. I'd seen an exhibition of those and been much impressed. So, as a private method of maintaining outward calm, I used to visualize Hakuin's splashy zero marks in contexts drawn from occidental culture.

CIRCUS

Seven splendid horses swing
 swiftly, round a sawdust ring
whilst atop their dappled backs
five acrobats do jumping jacks
making twelve performers, or
exemplars of *esprit de corps*.

Inspired by Hakuin, I decided to paint once again, for the first time in decades.

American "Duco" enamels had been invented for touching-up sports vehicles, using the short brushes attached to the inside of each can lid. I thought it might be fun to brush those enamels onto aluminum pizza plates.

The plates were cheap; the paints pricey. Hence I chose my colors with care, over the course of about an hour, in a neighborhood shop kept by an elderly couple. Finally, I paid a peck of yen, bagged my twelve small cans, and left the premises.

I was halfway across the street, when something told me to look around. The store's proprietors were both kneeling on the pavement and bowing in my direction!

Bowing humbly back, in my awkward Western style, I hurried on, happy to have been recognized as an unusually dedicated colorist.

Masao Abe chose to "exhibit" my abstract efforts at Myoshin-ji one afternoon, by skimming those painted pizza plates at random onto the tatami mats. He thought they might make nice adjuncts to tea ceremony rituals.

Once I heard a small creature come into the zendo. That's how quiet things were. The scratchy sounds it produced on the tatami mats caused me to think of a kitten. I kept my eyes half-shut and nearly crossed, as usual, focused upon the tatami mat in front of me; not moving except to smile at the animal's approach.

It played about for a while. Then it came and sat right in front of me. The kitten soon sensed me looking, turned and gazed wide-eyed into my own eyes. I sat within its field of consciousness, while the kitten sat in mine.

There was an actual merging, which we both felt.

"Enlightenment" and "Mastery" are thought to be the goals of Zazen, but such things are no more attainable in fact than Christian "Salvation" and "Eternal Bliss."

Zennist meditation does, however, foster one's best qualities. Namely, Empathy and Equanimity.

CHINESE CHECKMATE

From a moon bridge across the Ho
Chuang Tsu and Wan Hong Lo
watched a few minnows below.

"How those critters dart and sway,"
Tsu enthused. "Sheer ecstasy!"

"Sentimental mush," grumped Wan.
"Don't say to me that fish have fun.
Impelled by some unfeeling force
they just react, like us, to stress."

Tsu responded: "Beneath our toes
the sacred Ho eddies and flows
while her fish, who relish mirth
display great joy in life on Earth."

Indignantly, Wan muttered: "You
seem to think everything's a Who."

"Well put," said Tsu, "and very true.
Congratulations! I just knew
that you, my friend
would finally come through."

    As I was winding down my year in Kyoto, things went bleak for me personally, thanks to nothing but my own inadequacy.
    We'd been offered a chance to house-sit for friends of friends in Honolulu, during June, July, and August. So Jeff and Winslow would be with us once again! Jane went ahead to set things up, while I stayed out the final month of my Fellowship.

She'd bonded with her koto teacher, who kindly drove her to the airport. As they parted, Kimoko handed her a silken scroll with an ink-brushed Japanese message. Translated, it reads—

"Jane is among my musical daughters, and the only person authorized to teach my Koto method in America."

Left on my own, I felt lonely and deprived. Zazen practice had staggered my psyche in some respects, and the Japanese language left me tongue-tied.

My only pal in Kyoto was a Japan Foundation Senior Fellow like myself, named Walter Gardini, from Buenos Aires.

Intuiting my distress, Walter kindly persuaded me to participate in the renowned philosopher Kejii Nishitani's seminars, which were conducted mainly in English, at Otani University.

Walter and I helped celebrate our revered Sensei's seventy-fifth birthday, with a party propelled by convivial toasts in tiny cupfuls of hot sake.

To cool off afterward, Nishitani led Walter and myself on a brief stroll along the Kamo river front. The balmy night sky shone all awash with silver. It seemed as if some bright full moon might have concealed herself nearby, beneath a bridge, perhaps, casting luminescence upward instead of down.

Nishitani halted, glanced around, scratched his bald head, and asked—

"Does either of you gentlemen see the moon?"

Walter eloquently stirred the refulgent air with a forefinger: "Not I, Sensei."

Our teacher giggled politely, the Japanese way—

"Then, you should study more!"

We three stood swaying slightly, high on sake, smiling at each other with silent delight. Nishitani had been joking, naturally. The moon cannot be studied into existence. Her absences are not actual, however. They're merely apparent,—and the same goes for Jane's!

Walter eventually composed an essay called *"Critical Points of the Buddhist–Christian Dialogue,"* published in Japanese Religions

(1976), which concludes—

"Dialogue must concentrate more on values than on dogmas. Buddhism and Christianity, so different from a dogmatic point of view, agree on such spiritual values as silence, meditation, detachment, self-denial, poverty, the monastic life, wisdom, and the need to transcend this world.

"Both are dynamic phenomena rather than abstract systems, and both are ways of living whose true teaching must be verified by verily taking the path."

"Taking the path" reminds me of a burly Britisher named Hearn, who was born in Liverpool and became a merchant seaman.

Following a murderous brawl on the Korean waterfront, Hearn had been arrested, tried, and convicted of manslaughter.

While serving years of jail time, he'd learned the Korean language, been converted to Zen Buddhism, and taken the name Ryong Song.

When we first met, Ryong spontaneously gave me a Zennist nudge, just as Alan Priest had done many years previously.

And now, although thousands of miles distant, he somehow intuited that I needed help. So he mailed me a postcard whose message read in full—

"Entering water, he does not drown. Entering fire, he does not burn."

Alan Priest, Ryong Song, Abe Masao, Kejii Nishitani, Hawaii University's East/West philosopher Eliot Deutsch, Smith College's Pure Land Buddhist Taitetsu Unno, and Columbia University's Tibetan Buddhist Robert Thurman, all seven helped me get a grip on Zen over the years.

Tai Unno once suborned me to give a seminar course with him on Nishitani's final book: *"Being & Nothingness."*

"Why do you need me?" I asked, and he replied—

"As a prime example of Being!"

When my father approached his physical finish, Bob Thurman arranged for Jane and me to attend a Tibetan Buddhist retreat in upper New York State, for students of death and dying.

RRRRRRRRR mmmmmmmmm went the monks' long, buzzing bass horns. *"Ssssssst! Ssssssst!"* the sand drums replied, while the Rimpoche chanted sonorous invocations of the fierce, obstacle-removing Tibetan deity Green Tara. Then I thought I witnessed—

MISS TIBET

Tara twirled
three times
jangling shrill
ankle chimes
dangling forth
her froth-hung
forked crimson
dragon tongue

I'd witnessed nothing solid, such as a masked dancer performing for the occasion. But neither, from my viewpoint, was she a mere illusion.

When I mentioned that experience to the Dalai Lama, who had ordained Thurman a monk, he registered smiling interest, so I added—

"Green Tara may have taught me more than all my zazen practice put together."

Oh, no, she DIDN'T!" he cried, pointing and giggling with radiantly sympathetic glee…

Eventually, Zen-Buddhist practice endowed me with sufficient calm to gaze through Jane's physical presence and glimpse the guardian angel standing in back of her morning glory eyes. I wish I could put that simply, instead of resorting to allegory, but the best things in life are impossible to describe.

YOU

Hosting a Gypsy family
"travelers" like ourselves
who understood you instantly
at our red rose garden hideaway
down along Ashdown Forest lane.

Being your very own sweet person
like the delightful silver moon
or William Blake's "Flower
in heaven's high bower."

Interchanging silent talk
with a stark white stork
aslant the tawny sky
in the high desert
at Persian Pasagardai.

Revealing those daemons
who ride astride the air.
They inhale, exhale
natural divine power.

3. Cure for War

While we were living in Greece, I visited Jerusalem together with my family. There we happened to meet the Greek Orthodox Patriarch, who welcomed us warmly.

"Just look at me," he said, "right here in the Holy City, addressed in my native tongue by the small children of Americans! This calls to mind Saint John of Patmos."

The Patriarch was referring to the "Revelations Given to John," which concludes the New Testament in Apocalyptic style. The poet prophesied universal disaster, followed by the successful building of a "New Jerusalem"—

> *The Glory of God did lighten it*
> *and the Lamb is the light thereof.*
> *Nations of them that are saved*
> *shall walk in the light of it.*
>
> *Kings of the Earth do bring*
> *their honor and glory into it*
> *And the gates of it*
> *shall not be shut at all*

Historians tell us the author of that astounding text must have been a Hebrew Christian who flourished three generations after Jesus' time.

Many ecclesiastics draw a line around such appallingly reversible dynamics as "Love" or "Goodness," and piously refer to the abstract result as "God."

But the Protestant minister and Pomona College professor Frederick Sontag deplores such super-slick theology. My favorite among his books is called: *God, Why did You do That?*

We first met in Rome, when Fred was guest professor at a renowned Roman Catholic seminary: the *Collegio di Sant' Anselmo.*

I recall sitting with him at an outdoor table on the Piazza Navona, sipping "Americano" cocktails. That was the time he suggested that folks don't question hard enough.

Fred was talking about myself. But instead of rising to his bait, I asked,

"Is that what you tell students here?"

"Sure. Once they've been ordained Catholic priests, they'll have to deal with creeping atheism, not just in their parishes but in their secret hearts as well."

"No doubt," I said.

"When you stop to consider the existing concepts of God, and the difficulties involved in arriving at a satisfactory one, it's not easy to keep God alive."

"I'll bet you're right on that point, as well."

"Yes. We must continue to try. Faith is not enough!"

His sincere enthusiasm finally dawned on me, and I began to develop lasting faith in Fred himself.

Taking "Three Steps Backward" is often practiced in Hebrew prayer. The idea is to allow room for "the Other" to enter one's soul space. This effort lies at the heart of Fred Sontag's thinking. His book called *"American Life"* tackles intractable horrors with gentle care—

"My father entered Ellis Island as just another immigrant Jew, and gave his family the start he wanted for them in a land free of violent pogroms.

All prejudice has not been eliminated, nor is it likely to be, so long as it remains so much easier to judge and to generalize on the basis of external signs rather than struggle to discern the inner life of another.

"There is blatant evil in the world. But in our hearts we could try to understand others only as we discern their interior life. In doing so we might prevent answering prejudice with prejudice, thus perpetuating what we claim to want to eliminate."

TESTAMENT

Once upon a time, in holy Palestine
I sipped a stein of kosher wine
whilst gazing down upon
the silver sea of Galilee
which teemed with fish
for Peter and his crew
until Christ Jesus
invited them
to dine with him
in an upstairs room
at golden Jerusalem
becoming fishers of men
women, and little children.

Our single stupendous modern Hebrew philosopher Martin Buber saw the dangers ahead for his people.

Back in 1921, at a Zionist rally in Karlsbad, he proclaimed—

"As we enter the sphere of world history once more, and again become standard bearers of our own fate, the Jewish people who have been a persecuted minority worldwide for two thousand years, abhor and reject the nationalistic policies under which we've suffered.

"Hence we hardly aspire to return to the land of Israel in order to dominate and suppress any other people."

Two Old Testament injunctions address the present situation. The first is from Exodus (23:9) and the second from Leviticus (24:22):

"You shall not oppress an alien; you know well how it feels to be an alien, since you were once aliens yourselves in the land of Egypt.

"You shall have but one rule for alien and native alike."

Martin Buber and the holy Bible agree perfectly, it's true, yet billions of religious fanatics keep screaming at each other.

Each of the main factions fragmenting the Holy Land at present has good reason to boast of its participants' unconquerable stamina, unquestioning faith, and suicidal loyalty. That having been said, it's un-Jewish, un-Christian, and un-Islamic, to poison the whole region, perpetrating horrors in the name of God.

TRYST

Swathed in gleaming damascene,
an almond-colored southern queen
clambers up the secret staircase carved
inside Mount Mariah's sacred citadel.
Emerging, the Arabian monarch
blows a kiss to the new moon.
Lapped in lilac-hued shadow
below the palace portico
Sheba shrugs off her
soft saffron gown
and slips in between
the King's linen sheets.
as the pair tenderly embrace
she senses Solomon's heart race.

"Hi there, Sol, my shyest love.
Wouldn't it be wise for us
to engender peace?"

Jerusalem's extremely compact, well defined "Old City" is still defensively walled most of the way around, as in ancient times. It centers upon the little citadel called Mount Mariah, which is flanked by the Jewish "Wailing Wall" and capped by the Moslem "Dome of the Rock."

The whole square-mile complex has a population under 30,000. Her four sections are Armenian Christian, Greek Orthodox, Muslim, and Hebrew. Strolling her cobbled lanes, I wondered why that bitterly divided ancient neighborhood isn't recognized as the historic mother of monotheism...

After we moved to Rome, I returned to Jerusalem at Karl Katz's kind invitation, for celebrations connected with the Bezalel Museum which he directed.

They concerned our mutual friend Frederick Keisler's Holocaust Memorial, plus the building of Billy Rose's sculpture garden designed by the superb Japanese-American artist Isamu Noguchi, whom I came to know.

Canaanites, Hittites, Hebrews, Assyrians, Babylonians, Persians, Romans, Byzantines, Arabs, Crusaders, Turks, European powers, Israeli Zionists, and native Palestinians, all have polluted Jerusalem's citadel of divine love, by drenching it in human blood.

If "War is Politics by other Means." as hawks in high places insist, then strangling your wife or poisoning your husband, also is politics by other means.

Hence it's high time for us to re-define both war and politics.

So, when President Jimmy Carter first brought Israelis and Egyptians together at Camp David for peace talks, I wrote an essay called: "What Shall Become of Jerusalem the Golden?"

My piece proposed that the sacred, walled, interior section of Jerusalem be reborn under United Nations sponsorship, as a minuscule city state, like the Vatican.

Let "New Jerusalem" be relieved of external pressures, and endowed with a synod of Jewish, Christian and Islamic clergy which maintains a rotating chairmanship.

Leaders of warring nations could convene there at ease in order to erase racial and religious hatreds. Their summit conferences should feature quiet conversations, interspersed with daily rituals, rotating between a synagogue, a basilica, and a mosque.

Experts will doubtless protest that it's absurd to imagine the spiritual leaders of three world religions cooperating on anything.

But professional expertise isn't helping. "National Intelligence" becomes its own opposite

If what I proposed were done, then pilgrim gold and goodwill would flow to the Holy Land as never since King Solomon's reign...

My old colleague Robert Manning edited the *Atlantic Monthly* magazine. Bob disagreed with my impassioned piece, but purchased it anyhow because he found the "historical material interesting."

I mailed run-off copies of the article to well-positioned politicians, including Jerusalem's liberal mayor Teddy Kollek who had cordially entertained me at his home.

Not one single official cared—or dared—to respond...

Some years ago now, I tried again.

From Palestine to Pakistan, my second essay argued, civilization's cradle keeps contracting in agonies of everyday mass murder.

Although we're not directly to blame, our incredibly clumsy interference helps prolong the present impasse.

This brings me to America's admittedly necessary alliance with Israel. She's our closest, although most quarrelsome, friend, and by far the strongest nation in a boiling witches' cauldron.

Like ourselves, however, she's got an utterly dismal record of racial injustice.

A THREEFOLD WAY

The world knows our ongoing wars
fought far from these native shores
are nothing but revolving doors
with mass graves for their floors.

By our Founding Fathers' mothers
we should pursue peace with others
greeting them as long lost brothers
whom communal trust restores.

Oh, let Islam's crescent Moon
Christ's holy Cross of sacrifice
and the Hebrew Star, be set
on flags flown together from—

Sacred Mount Maria's crest
at the human family's behest!
If that much cannot be done
what earthly use is religion?

Since Bob Manning had retired from the *Atlantic*, I dispatched my follow-up article to an old acquaintance there.

He responded with a curt note deploring my imposition upon his valuable time and unnecessarily adding that he had plunged my "clotted purple rubbish" into his wastebasket.

I replied on a plain postcard—

The formerly friendly gatekeeper
who shot me so shitty a letter
should try to remember
despite his distemper
that courtesy works rather better.

Did the apoplectic old gentleman get a kick out of my limerick? I hope so, but I'll never know, because, within days of receiving it, he expired.

4. Mortal Coil

The modest and obscure American painter Albert Pinkham Ryder means a lot to me. I used to visit his "Toilers of the Sea" at Manhattan's Metropolitan Museum for extended contemplation purposes.

Ryder lovingly labored over that image for a decade or more, not letting go of it until about 1884.

Gazing at his age-darkened little masterpiece, I step aboard an open fishing boat with a blackly straining sail. This narrow vessel plunges down and splashes upward again, like a lost daughter reaching for the halo of her moon mother.

The moon has no atmosphere; therefore no life. If the human psyche had no poetic mythosphere, no numinous embracing and surrounding mystery, wouldn't we be lunatics?

The varnishing and retouching to which the artist subjected the picture made it luminous but chemically unstable, vulnerable to the obscuring passage of years. In *"300 Years of American Painting"* I speculated—

"Perhaps it was not his pictures that really interested Ryder, but the experience of painting.

'Perhaps his reason was not to bring them to a perfect and ephemeral pitch but simply to have the fullest possible experience of them."

My friend Richard L. Miller of Woodlands, Texas, is a physicist, and author of the swell science-fiction novel called *Dreamer*.

One of his letters informed me that he'd purchased a helium balloon for his daughter Tracy—

"It's a valentine heart, 20" in diameter at the top, which I counter-weighted with paper-clips and colored feathers, so that it floats midway between floor and ceiling, and moves about with the air currents. Last night Tracy slept with it guarding her bed.

"This morning I stopped downloading nuclear fallout data from the NCI web site and leaned back to read your recent ruminations.

"Coming to the last page, I felt a presence looking over my left shoulder. It was the balloon, hovering inches behind me, as if reading, too."

I read Rich's letter aloud to Jane. "What do you make of it?" I asked. "Coincidence?"

"Yes," she said. "That is, unless you can imagine your own brain billions of light-years in diameter."

"Describe it."

"Dark yet clear at the same time."

"That sounds like you."

"The quicksilver flickering of its synapses spurts comets and meteors. Can you see what I'm saying? Watch a few odd thoughts as they hurtle from one cloudless quadrant to another. Eventually, both kinds crinkle into algebraic clumps."

"Algebraic?"

"Yes. They zip through and around invisible folds in the dark matter overhead. Some turn around and return. They shape rolling wave-patterns, bubble up as island galaxies, and spiral inward as constellations."

"I'm with you most of the way," I said. "But it all becomes a bit overwhelming."

"Relax, and things slow down a bit. Planet Earth spins into being. A frosty breath is inhaled; a warm one exhaled. Humanity happens."

"Now I get the picture. You're suggesting that it's not far-fetched, or even out of place, to imagine that space/time occurs, life germinates and evolves, we're born and gradually become as we are at present, not only outside, but also inside our own craniums!"

"Right."

"But what's all this got to do with Rich's story of the curious balloon?"

"You asked whether that was just coincidence. Looked at close-up, the answer would be yes. But not when you back far enough away to view the sequence of events from a larger perspective—"

"I see!" I said.

That was an absurd exaggeration. One can't gaze up into the top of one's head; although, for a dazed minute or two, I came near to supposing that I did.

It's no exaggeration to state that I've experienced extreme ups and downs. The ups were all miraculous. As for the downs, they were mostly my own fault.

Plus the pesky Persistence of Misapprehension which plagues us one and all.

The worst stretch in my life so far occurred during the dark Northampton days of Pop's gradual demise. My market had dried up. Scrabbling hard for a bare living, I regarded myself as a has-been.

On top of that, Jane had absconded to her brother's Manhattan flat. Why? Because my kid sister Patience and most of her family treated her with icy contempt.

They stubbornly assumed that she had "stolen" me from Anne Dick, whom they adored. Also, that her present plan was to steal Pop's house from them!

Jane had left her blue velvet hair-ribbon behind.

I remorsefully recall waving it in poor Pop's face and yelling, "This ribbon here contains more REALITY for me than your whole damned house!"

Subsequently, Pop sent Jane a plain postcard: "While I'm dying, my dear boy dies for you. S.A.E."

That drew her swiftly back again.

Jane is a superb writer, koto-player, housekeeper, weaver, and cook, but her main drive is to help others fulfill their own potentialities. That's why she keeps on devising rituals to foster love and courage.

So now Jane got all the neighborhood kids (who held a variety of faiths, including atheism) involved in celebrating the Winter Solstice.

As early darkness gathered, we drank hot cider from Jane's inherited punchbowl, and did some ragged Christmas carol singing.

Then she delegated me to lead the children out onto the snow-covered front yard, each of us carrying a lighted crimson candle.

We spiraled, single-file, in silence, to the center of the yard, where we planted our candles in the snow crust to create a centered effect.

SEASON'S GREETING

With soaked socks, happy hearts
freezing toes, and cheeks aglow
primed to play our separate parts
although mystified by the show
we set our candle-circle deep
inside the exponential sweep
of slantwise-falling, silent snow

Tiny diadems of frosty light kept attaching to our hands and faces as we spiraled out again.

Each snowflake that one thinks about has danced to three big bands. Namely, Nature, Mathematics, and one's own Imagination. People do likewise...

Last night I experienced the following dream—

When green earth cocks her icecap at the sun, mackerel flock through the tops of oaks. Jellyfish glue themselves to cathedral glass. The tide climbs stairs and elevator shafts. Paris, London and

Manhattan drown. Our sadly diminished species takes to ships, and fishing for sustenance. Sperm whales readily mate over Kansas, the breadbasket of ancient Americans. Then, as motherly Ocean subsides again, Himalayan, Alpine, Andean, Rocky Mountain and Adirondack archipelagos emerge. Joyfully disembarking, people get down to earth again, and soon fresh blooms appear.

Waking up this morning, I thought of Diane. It was as if she wished me to round off her story.

Following a productive and generally tender two decades together, the Arbus couple found it necessary to separate.

Allan took an acting course and made himself over as a Hollywood performer, best remembered for his role as the psychiatrist Sidney Freedman in the TV Series called *Mash*.

Strolling into the solitude of her own soul meanwhile, Diane turned herself around and was born at last as a documentary photographer who originated rich and strange picture stories for magazines.

Most photos picture people either looking or not looking, and being looked at, or not. But Diane often showed individuals alone for a split-second while starting to interact with the neutral camera's eye-click.

She often caught people out, half-empty of hope and half-done with despair, in the precarious privacy between performances.

The reborn Diane took tremulous delight in risk, becoming vulnerable on purpose. She once shot the famously cool gossip columnist Leonard Lyons with his eyes bugging out in horror.

It happened after a stand-off luncheon at a Manhattan restaurant. As they emerged onto Fifth Avenue, Diane turned and aimed her camera at him whilst backing away from the curb into traffic.

Leonard later told me he thought she'd be run over for sure.

She'd already created quite a few marvelous photos of May, who was her own beloved God-daughter.

The print that moves me most is an unusually large, story-telling scene, which depicts May, myself, and Jane, skating together on Manhattan's Central Park ice rink in the cold winter dusk. Someone ahead of us has fallen, and we're reacting, in different ways, to that event.

It's like a painting by Pieter Breughel.

As Allan Arbus remarked in a recent letter, Diane's writing was always amazingly "original." Consider, for instance, her successful third application for a Guggenheim Award—

"I want to photograph the considerable ceremonies of our present, because we tend while living here and now to perceive only what is random and barren and formless about it.

"While we regret that the present is not like the past and despair of its ever becoming the future, its innumerable inscrutable habits lie in wait for their meaning.

"I want to gather them, like someone's grandmother putting up preserves, because they will have been so beautiful."

When Harvard's Fogg Art Museum requested a brief statement about photos, her response ran as follows—

"They are the proof that something was there that no longer is. Like a stain. And the stillness of them is boggling. You can turn away but when you come back they'll still be there, looking at you."

In a 1968 letter to a British art director, she noted—

"Somewhere at the very end there is a joke, and even though I forget it there are moments when I have fancied I knew for just a second what the punch line was."

So, why did I never cease to adore Diane? Not for physical or sentimental reasons alone.

Here I must mention a stunning book called *Diane Arbus: Revelations* (Random House, 2003). Her daughter Doon Arbus put the volume together in expansive scrapbook style, for a retrospective exhibition which toured major museums in America and Europe.

That very disturbing and richly definitive show began at Manhattan's Metropolitan Museum. When Doon was helping to hang the exhibition she noticed Patty Bosworth's bio for sale in the museum's bookstore.

Furious, Dune threatened to pull the whole exhibition unless the book was banned from the premises. The museum complied.

Should one person ever own another, whether living or dead? No way, say I. It's very bad for both parties.

I attended the Los Angeles opening of the show with mixed emotions, mostly miserable. As a solitary, fragile, female freelancer in a cut-throat buyer's market, Diane suffered psychological and economic attrition throughout her sunset outpouring of genius.

"I'm accepted as an artist," she moaned, "Yet I can't make a living as a photographer."

Since I had abandoned Manhattan to pursue freelance journalism in Europe, the Atlantic Ocean stood between us. While on assignment abroad, however, Diane visited me and my family for a week-end in Sussex, England.

May and I drove to pick her up at the East Grinstead railroad station. Arriving late, we saw no sign of Diane. Then, suddenly, there she was! Had she been shooting us from behind a column?

Before leaving on Sunday, Diane took a lovely gold Egyptian scarab ring from her finger and presented it to May's step-mother, my dear Jane. They'd always been close, and understood each other.

Two years later, Diane lost the balance that made her life bearable and her work abundantly worthwhile. Turning from the threshold of world-fame, she scrawled *"The Last Supper"* across a page of her journal, left lying open.

She prepared a warm bath, stripped her indrawn physique, stepped into the tub, reclined, and slashed her wrists.

Diane was like a lilac branch in my life. I cried bitterly over her suicide, until the night she visited me in a dream—

RESCUE MISSION

> Returning to planet Earth
> Diane conveyed instant relief.
> "How I laugh to see you sad!"
> she told me without a word.
> Her familiar chortling mirth
> swept away my stupid grief.

Now, what happened to darling Anne Dick? Following her would-be suicide, precarious recovery, and divorce from me, she moved back to Boston with May.

We corresponded some, naturally, addressing each other as friends, although not "best friends" any more.

Finally, in 1981 (ten years after Diane's suicide) Anne also killed herself.

Death does not "close the book" on Anne's radiant and brave existence here...

Jane's kid brother Sam was a charming, disarming, madly alcoholic editor, who died of his excesses.

Her elder sister Patricia dared marry the dashing German-American Konrad Kellen, who'd won a distinguished service medal for his field-intelligence coup near the climax of World War Two.

Konrad "caught a peculiar mocking glint," as he explained to me, in a captured Nazi officer's eye, and that was enough. Getting through to Headquarters, he calmly alerted General Bradley—in the nick of time—to the immanence of Germany's final Ardennes Forest push-back, now remembered as the "Battle of the Bulge."

Abetted by Pat's warmth and party-giving charm, Konrad later became the distinctly humane star of a somewhat cold-blooded intelligence outfit: the Rand Corporation.

When throat cancer finally felled Gigi, Jane's beautiful mother, Pat took her in and saw her through to the end. She also cared for

Konrad's mother. That's how it is with Pat. She always makes sure to be there for whomever needs her.

When Konrad went public with his approval of the bitterly controversial "Pentagon Papers" disclosure, and his own horrified opposition to the Vietnam war, his bosses were in a quandary. Should they fire their best analyst and resident war hero?

Instead, they re-assigned him to explore and critique California's corrupt and cruel penal system.

Konrad has since died, thoroughly vindicated. Pat and her devoted children David, Jennifer, and Elizabeth, all carry on.

My own elder sister, Torka, had a daughter Susan, who married a restaurant manager by the name of Poet, ironically enough.

She also had a son, Lincoln Jr., who became a math wizard and computer pioneer. The math lessons he'd received left him cold, so he worked out fresh versions in his head. During Linc's twenties, Harvard and MIT hired him to cosset their shared, enormous experimental computing machine.

He seemed to enjoy the task. Yet, Linc soon gave a "goodbye party" to his friends and disappeared next morning in his private plane, vanishing forever. Nobody knows how, or why.

My kid sister Patience married Will Crompton, a stalwart, highly moral Roman Catholic, who had warm feelings for African Americans. Will was among the few white men to volunteer for the Black Panther regiment in World War Two.

That combat outfit suffered decimation and hell in general. Will was badly traumatized, resulting in long hospitalization.

Finally recovered, he wooed and won Patience, ran a family Berkshire hills goat farm, cheerfully labored at a coffin factory, and fathered five children. Namely: artist and sausage-meister Joe, musician Carrie, engineer Cathy, editor Nancy, and Sam, the youngest, who has written over seventy informative books for high school and community college kids...

When I first met Albert Murray, relations between black and white authors were strained. But Al rose well above the fray. His many books beautifully convey the mostly blue but also ecstatic feel of Afro-American life. Among them stands an "as told to" autobiography of Count Basie.

Here's a twelve bar riff from Al's final effort, a poetry volume which he kindly sent me, autographed: "For Alex, on the afterbeat."

> *they used to call me schoolboy*
> *and I never did deny my name*
> *when folks called me schoolboy*
> *I never would deny my name*
> *I said you got to be a schoolboy*
> *if preparation is your aim*

Al was my favorite pal at the Century Association, a midtown Manhattan refuge for "Artists and Amateurs of the Arts." My earliest memory of the club dates from the year of my election, 1959, when I played a round in its billiard room.

The winner, a rotund old fellow whose name I forget, congratulated the runner-up with, "You're talented."

Turning to me, he added: "And YOU possess enthusiasm." Talk about politesse!

John Brooks, Matt Clark, Jack Chancellor, Charlie Collingwood, John Hammond, Jimmy Flexner, Arthur Schlesinger, and Wede Espy, also hung out at the Century, to my constant comfort and delight.

Are the people whom we love, and ourselves as well, nothing but ephemeral bundles of sensations?

The austere Scottish philosopher David Hume arrived at that conclusion via hard logic laced with acute analysis, not easily dismissed.

Ages ago, moreover, the Tibetan Buddhist patriarch Nagarjuna put precisely the same idea in paradox-packed, ecstatic Sanskrit stanzas. Nagarjuna argued that everything is arising and vanishing, and nothing is substantial. Hence, form is emptiness, emptiness form, and selfhood a peculiar human illusion.

That doctrine makes sense, yes, but it also contradicts my personal experience. Because, after all, I feel no shadow of doubt that the ghosts of Grandpa Cook, John Bennett, Diane Arbus, and finally Pop, all four, did appear to me.

What will follow the inevitable death and speedy dissolution of one's own physical aspect? Personally, I find myself persuaded by Plotinus' classic formulation—

"When a body is perishing, no longer supported by the primal, life-giving soul or by any subordinate phase of that soul, then clearly the life-principle can no longer remain present. But does this mean that the life itself perishes?

"No, it is merely no longer where it was."

Most of my friends dismiss that concept. Death is not a rite of passage, they insist, but a permanent condition of enforced serenity.

According to secular gospel, which I also took on faith for a long time, death stalks, furiously leaps upon, tears apart and gulps down, one's problem-prone identity

Wait a minute. Is human life a one-stop exhaust-shop? I mean, shall each and every one of us be sealed up and sent on a circuitous journey to the Dead letter Office—like Franz Kafka, the Czech who's in the mail?

No, not necessarily. Real time, so-called, is only one of many times, as most folks now agree.

So it's quite legitimate to question the opinion that one's being is irrecoverably removed by birth from the cosmic ocean, and utterly banished by death from our island planet.

We, the people, do keep on bumping up against *status nascens and status evanescens* (Latin for birth and death) which can only be observed from outside.

START

Within three
minutes
of breathing
for the first time
in all natural
history put together
during a rough
patch of weather
and upon being
nuzzled by his
extremely
relieved mother
this tremulous
wet slip of a
newborn zebra
staggers
abruptly upright
to discover
down-deep succor.

For Nature, the totality comes first, whereas, for each one of her creatures, continued existence matters most.

FINISH

Storm unfolding
Seagulls scolding
Fishnets dragging
Sea mist twisting
Salt foam scudding
Lightning blinking
Thunder thudding
Timbers breaking
Hail descending
Wind unending
Sailors tugging
Canvas ripping
Cries colliding
Hope capsizing
Death bending

What science describes as war to the death, "red in tooth and claw," for survival throughout nature, sustains life itself. Sex and struggle generate, while downright death regenerates.

Take for instance the green vegetation deities Osiris and Adonis, who died each year to be reborn as their Mediterranean worshippers' bread and wine.

Holding the hollow of a seashell to my ear, I seem to hear distant surf. When I was a boy, Grandpa Eliot told me that what I heard was inside, nothing but my own bloodstream.

Life itself is a circulating process, like one's thoughts, the bloodstream of the mythosphere, which people say must have a stop, although that's not necessarily so.

Ever since teaming up with Jane I've been attempting to convey the visual/artistic penumbra, verbal/poetic aura, and intrinsic music, of human consciousness.

Such matters are amorphous at best. Hence, I've been precariously sailing along upon a semantic sea.

LAST WORD

I worship this
turning, tilted world
for three delights
together twirled

Phoebus Apollo's
solar might
the Black Virgin's
starlight, and

My dear companion
who fears not because
as our forbears knew
all people expire to

CONTINUE

5. Negative Capability

Once, when we were past sixty, Jane and I found ourselves at the mile-wide juncture of the Rio Negro with the Amazon River. Since we stood alone, sweating out the noonday heat, with nobody else in sight, Jane chose to strip and have a cooling swim.

Her total fearlessness had got us into, and through, at least a dozen serious scrapes. But this time I hesitated to follow Jane's lead, until it struck me that I wouldn't wish to live minus her company.

OF TIME & THE RIVER

The Rio Negro's narrow path
pursues a thousand-mile swath
from its Columbian mountaintop
until at last this lonesome stream
ejaculates—full-out—to cream
the welcoming beige bosom
of sweltering Senora Amazon.

We came out whole, happy, and refreshed as usual. On our return to Rio de Janeiro, however, I happened to ask a doctor whether we had been at risk.

"The Amazon's man-eating piranhas are bad enough," he told me. "And her screw-worms are even worse."

"Screw-worms?"

"One never even senses the tiny buggers burrow up inside one's hide. They destroy their human hosts, by inches, as the years go by."

"I had no idea—"

"However, the Rio Negro is something else again."

"Is that good?"

"It's better than reckless voyagers have a right to expect."

"Enlighten me."

"Well, neither piranhas nor screw-worms can tolerate the Negro's rapid, relatively cold current. Hence, they steer clear of where you swam."

"In other words, we did fine. But then I foolishly forgot what my mother taught me."

"Oh, what was that?"

"To keep away from doctors!"

To tell the truth, I have nothing against doctors. They've saved my life, and the lives of my three children also. Then, too, the good ones recognize they're just as error-prone as the rest of us...

After a severe, scary, but ultimately life-saving "invasive procedure" some years ago, I convalesced at the Central Park West apartment of doctor Jim (Wilbur J.) Gould and lovely Maureen.

Jim was an ear, nose & throat specialist, endowed with secret hypnotic powers. He successfully treated a host of opera, stage, screen, and TV stars, ranging from Frank Sinatra on down. He also happened to be a wizardly diagnostician and excellent surgeon, although eventually blocked by fear of blood.

When Senator John F. Kennedy was competing against Hubert Humphrey in North Carolina's Presidential Primary, he lost his voice. So J.F.K.'s distraught entourage naturally sent for Gould.

Jim told me that Kennedy's throat "Roughly resembled the Okeefenokee Swamp. "Any reputable doctor," he went on "would have recommended at least two weeks' total rest. But I recalled something you'd said. Namely, that whoever seeks ultimate power must be insane."

"Did I say that?"

"Certainly. So I waved my magic wand, and stuffed him with sufficient antibiotics to choke a giraffe. That same night, believe it or not, he gave a rousing performance!"

The Goulds' terrace happened to overlook the "Dakota" apartment building in front of which a madman murdered one of my idols: the low-born, humorous, humanitarian Beatle John Lennon.

RECKLESS

Born a flake like William Blake
John could rock to anything.

*"Yoko, let's not touch the brake
'til some blind sot brush my wing!"*

Just across from us lay the section of Central Park called "Strawberry Fields" and dedicated to Lennon's memory. Landscaped with Japanese garden grace, this was a serene place of pilgrimage for many, and for me a scene of slow recovery. I spent three weeks of sunny mornings down there, slumped on a bench.

One fine day, Yoko Ono approached along an adjacent path. Lennon's great love was elegantly dressed, haggard, and alone.

Struggling to my feet, I bowed in her direction. She smiled, bowed back as if to say, "Thanks for your courtesy," and passed on.

Having recently been sliced open, I recalled hearing that back in London Yoko had given "Cut Piece" performances, inviting the audience to snip away her costume bit by bit with scissors that she herself supplied, thus exposing the vulnerable showgirl underneath.

Lennon turned up one night, and fell head over heels in love. Yoko soon persuaded him to exchange the worst of his drug addiction for intense sexual intimacy coupled with spiritual partnership. Thus, she initiated the final, brief but relatively happy family chapter of Lennon's existence.

QUO VADIS?

> Free Will arrives first of wonders
> mounted astride lightning, fast.
> Hand in hand with silent Wrath
> Love paces her sun-dappled path
> and the distant Future thunders
> *"Hi!"* to cherry-blossom Past.

There's a new poet and essayist on the scene whom I love, named Phil Cousineau. Witness the blazing sincerity of his verse volume titled *"The Blue Museum."*

Phil's new book has been on my bedside table for the past week. *"Fungoes and Fastballs"* consists in baseball haiku, or seventeen-syllable, triadic, 5-7-5 stanzas. Here's one of my favorites—

> *A reporter asks the owner*
> *If it's a life or death game.*
> *"No, much more important!"*

Setting physical differences aside, does any irreducible divide separate the sexes? I used to assume so, but now I don't know. Compassion could pertain more to women, for example, and passion to men, as Aristotle suggested. But one might as well argue that passion pertains more to youth, and compassion to age. That, too, is obvious in general but by no means predictable on the ground.

Among our present neighbors are no less than four female painters of local renown: Hugette Calland, Galya Pillin-Tarnu, Karen Mulkie, and especially Diane Butler, whose insightful images delight me all the time.

Diane and her Afro-American husband Abraham inhabit a waterfront van. Tourists might mistake the Butler couple for vagrants, whereas Diane's art plus Abraham's music make them the spiritual pillars of this beach-front community.

As a teen-ager, Abraham was drafted to serve in Vietnam. He adamantly declined to kill people, or "Off the Gooks," and thus increase America's highly touted everyday "body-count." At that point nobody guessed what has since become obvious to all. The more folks you slaughter, the more will sign up to do you in.

Abraham was forced to endure long, cruel, and often solitary, confinement for "desertion" at Fort Ord. The boy emerged from his torture, not the psychotic wreck you might expect, but an indomitable man.

He still gets arrested for speaking out against persistent public evils, or simply for "Disturbing the Peace" with his ecstatic songs and wonderfully throbbing hand-drums. Whose peace?

GULL ABILITY

At the beach this morning
a lone seagull, serenely floating
poised motionless upon the heaving
and crashing breakers, did nothing
whatsoever until finally, atop an
oncoming high seventh wave
she stretched out her wings
and glided directly at me
almost as if to say—

*"When you reach home, try
to remember my rapport
with relaxing ocean
and supportive sky.
Celebrate seagull
existence, better
than does my
creaking cry."*

Speaking of creaking cries, this volume has taken well over a decade to write. It's been a difficult yet generally pleasurable project, page by crumpled page, as days, nights, weeks, months and years, passed imperceptibly over, and inevitably by, this nodding head.

The book owes everything to Jane, plus our beloved offspring with their partners. Namely, May & Fred Paddock, Jefferson Eliot & Kendell Shaffer, Winslow Eliot & Tom Stier.

Minus my Magnificent Seven, I could never have got this far.

And I'm grateful to my grandchildren for all they've been to me: Jasper Eliot, Sydney Lark Eliot, Samantha Eliot Stier, and Eliot Stier, and for my more recent friends, who grew in significance after Jane's death: Peter Stowell, Jane's nephew, with whom I lunched weekly at the Rose Café. Dolores Deluce, who brought sunshine into my mornings at the Fig Tree Café. Cousin Beth Rendeiro, who was always there for me.

You and I have come quite a distance together, gentle reader. My thanks for your patient company. From your viewpoint, our connection happens at present as well as in the past, whereas, for me it's a future phenomenon.

TIME & TIDE

"No man is an island." False, or True?
John Donne, for one, thought he knew.
But what about the Isle of Man
where Manx is spoken if one can?

The "Sandwich Isles" were so named
for the filthy-rich Earl of Sandwich
unless Captain Cook referred
to the sand which he found there?

Awakening in pre-dawn dark
I half expect I'll disembark
where brown sailor sons of Ham
bred & mustered, on the lam.

Since there's no use in dwelling on old evils, let alone moaning over them or seeking needless pay-back, I've deliberately omitted the many people who did me dirt

On the negative side, I have signally failed to celebrate close to forty friends and relations whom I love and admire.

What vast omission! I apologize to all those buddies, both living and dead. They could have made good copy, so there's no excuse.

"Abstractionism" used to be the rage one year, and "objectivism" the next. But painters such as Italy's Giorgio Morandi teased out the "abstract" relationships of actual "objects".

One almost sees his pale bottles on a kitchen table think, and hears them clink.

Sergio Ladron de la Guevara follows in Morandi's footsteps via oils wherein the light seems to flow back and forth like friendship between solids.

Some years ago, Sergio showed up on our doorstep with an easel, a stretched canvas, and his trusty paint-box. "This is it!" he said. "I want you to sit for me."

Three hours later, he handed me the wet painting and said; "Keep it. See how it holds up. I'll come back in a few months to work on it further."

"Not by the Chorus of Boris Godunov," I told him. "Sign it, date it, and with all my heart I thank you for today's intensely vivid, spontaneous reflection."

"Are you sure?" Sergio asked. "Have I captured you?"

"Better than that, you've gifted me with a lovely green aura, which owes something to van Gogh. It looks shady and sunny both at once."

Sergio and his dear wife Karen still visit us now and again from Arizona. Recently, they brought along a little painting of two rectangular white boxes set upright, so close together that their corners almost touch.

Might the image be meant to represent Jane and me in sepia-drenched space?

Possibly, but its actual protagonist may be the dark line which indicates a narrow void, alive with sympathy, between the two objects.

In that case the painting offers an original thought, as Edward Hopper would say. Not layered over.

TERRA FIRMA

Rosemary bushes six feet high
with blossoms resembling
scattered fragments of sky,
flank our zen garden's gate.

Pirouetting to a passing gale's
furiously uplifted forefinger,
our flourishing bamboo pair
softly flails the darkened air.

Scarcely ruffled by the storm,
our small tea tree stands firm.
Her tiny, five-petal flowers
smile upon the dialing hours.

There's a particular legend which reflects my own experience, so I'll repeat it here. During the Fifth Century of our era, the Celtic saint known as Ninian founded a monastery called "White House" at Wigtownshire, north of Hadrian's Wall.

One winter night, a dozen Pictish raiders slithered down from their northern highlands and advanced upon White House. Those red-nosed savages shambling along in their frost-tipped wolf-skins were not bent upon bloodshed, but they did hope to steal the cattle upon which the prayerful monks depended for food.

While they were still far off, Ninian sensed the Picts' approach and guessed its purpose. Donning his long blue robe, woven of wool and starry brightness, he called for the slave boy whom he had lately been teaching to read and write. The saint had high hopes for him.

Together, they hurried out through the monastery's wicket gate. Ninian took a deep breath of the keen, cold air. "I'll need my crosier," he told the boy, who trotted back in to fetch it.

Christian bishops still carry crosiers for ritual purposes. They're "Good Shepherd" symbols, closely resembling a shepherd's crook. The saint's crosier was a seven-foot stick of polished apple wood, having a red-gold cross, inlaid with mother-of-pearl, in the down-curve at its top.

Ninian and the boy now entered the cattle-fold, and the saint employed the point of his crosier to circumscribe its dirt interior with a barely visible groove. That done, he told the boy to seek concealment amid the branches of a nearby pine tree and keep watch from there.

The saint himself withdrew and went to bed.

Soon afterward, the Picts appeared. Invading the cattle-fold, they unconsciously crossed into Ninian's magic circle. Once inside, they found themselves unable to leave it again.

Enraged by their wolf-skin apparel, the heroic old bull of the herd soon gored and trampled each hapless raider to destruction.

The slave boy in his tree was impishly delighted by all this, and much impressed. Skipping back to Ninian's quarters, he reported what had occurred.

"Don't credit me," said the saint. My magic crosier and our big brown bull, between them, have brought about a necessary but nonetheless EVIL victory."

Looking uncommonly pale and drawn, Ninian fell back upon the pillows. He closed his glittering eyes again. His withered lips parted, and he started snoring.

The saint knew what was about to happen, and he welcomed it.

"Thou shalt not kill" was a Judeo/Christian keystone of Ninian's creed.

So he desired to offer a personal sacrifice as penance for slaughtering the Picts. Sleeping, he would free the boy and relinquish his most precious treasure.

Seizing the saint's crosier from its accustomed place at the foot of the bed, the formerly filial slave sinfully runs away, heading west toward the Irish Sea.

He hopes to become "Consulting Sorcerer" to Druid Ireland's King.

QUANDARY

While telling this, I seem to sense
it happens in the present tense.
A baffled boy stands on the shore.
Have I myself been here before?

The child grips his stolen prize
in wild regret. I empathize.
He wears a many-colored coat.
The trouble is, he has no boat!

Trudging along the beach, the boy comes across the wooden skeleton of a Scots-Irish skiff or coracle, so-called, which has not yet been covered with stitched-together hides. He bravely launches it, casting himself aboard. Lo and behold, the sieve-like vessel bears him across the sea to Ireland!

The crosier conspires to make it possible, because she yearns to travel far and finally take root in the westernmost corner of the western world.

What's more, she dreams of becoming fully alive again, able to bring forth fresh gifts of wisdom, rife with pleasing ways.

While still at sea, the boy intuits what is happening. Also, that the crosier's creative power surpasses anything that he himself could ever expect to understand.

Stepping out onto dry land, he plants his crosier firmly in the sand. On his knees, he waters it with tears of happiness. A clear spring bubbles up from the place where his tears have fallen. Then, as he sleeps, the crosier quivers for joy, transformed back into a live, arboreal creature.

FULFILLMENT

I much admire Saint Ninian,
who passed his magic power on
while asleep, to an adopted son
whom he knew would run away.

Still, I would rather play the boy
who found release in loving joy
and helped his stolen sorcery
become a living apple tree.

Emerald leaves and ruby fruits
fountain from the crosier's roots.
Her foliage fills with golden sound
of bees, or ancient spells unbound.

The boy becomes a hermit thrush.
Some few fellow-songsters hush
to hear him warbling, unafraid,
sheltered in her dappled shade.

For me, Jane is the heroine of that story, resembling an apple tree in spring bloom. She's faced the music with me, all the way, and we two have literally danced for joy.

It strikes me now that three divine interventions, over a thirteen year period (1950-1963), changed my life and gave it personal significance.

The first was meeting Jane, of course. The second, encountering Apollo's deliberately ambiguous Oracle at Delphi. Third, being lovingly laughed at by the Black Virgin of Karoulia.

In a letter home from Rome, the "failed" poet John Keats (who was about to die young of tuberculosis) defined his own "Negative Capability" —

"Capable of being in uncertainties, mysteries, doubts, without any irritable reaching after fact and reason."

Keats once made a precise drawing of the Grecian urn, or "Sosibios Vase," at London's British Museum, and then conveyed its silent message via this verse which I memorized and puzzled over in youth—

> *When old age shall this generation waste*
> *Thou shalt remain, in midst of other woe,*
> *Than ours, to whom thou say'st,*
> *'Beauty is truth, truth beauty,' — that is all*
> *Ye know, and all ye need to know.*

Wonders never cease, but terrible woes as well do come to almost everyone, and I must now report on ours.

Over a period of several years, Jane suffered horribly from "Alzheimer's" and "dementia," although never to the point where I couldn't take care of her.

Jane's spirit remained empathetic as ever, and her courage never wavered.

She still gave wise and comforting counsel to old friends, without having a single clue as to each caller's personal identity!

Finally she wrote the only poem in her entire career and presented it to me more than a dozen times (each time the first, from her immediate viewpoint) in colored ink on index-cards—

What's important?
You
Ever since
I
Met
You
Today
Forever
Always

Then came the darkest hour of my life one night, when all at once—without any warning—Jane gave up the ghost in my arms.

I was there to bear witness and hug her body tight to my heart as it shuddered and shook from her feet to her throat, abandoned by the freedom-seeking spirit.

I called 911. Emergency doctors at the nearest hospital ran through their revival methods, all of which failed, and pronounced her in "critical but stable condition."

My granddaughter Samantha Stier was the only close relation around at the time, so she took charge, and alerted the others.

May could not leave Copake, N.Y., because her husband Fred was mortally ill.

Jeff and his family, who live nearby, had driven up to San Francisco to visit Benny Goodman's beloved daughter Benjie. They hurried home.

Winslow flew in from Massachusetts to care (with hospice nursing help) for Jane in our upstairs guest room.

One night I was awakened by a thump from up there. The body had rolled out of bed and gone stone cold dead upon the floor...

For weeks and months, I couldn't even weep. I was yearning for my own death to come, but instead the healing passage of time turned me sane again.

I finally realized that although death spells closure in the physical sense, it's a painful transition to welcome gladly. Like birth in that respect.

Birth and Death, between them, benefit everyone and everything. Having learned that much at last, I find myself in agreement with what my favorite philosopher, Plotinus, concluded,

"The Universe is a living body, sympathetic to itself."

That fits well with what Jesus said—

"A new commandment give I unto you, that you love one another."

Nearly every day for the past twenty-five years and more, we aging people said good morning to the Pacific Ocean.

At first, we ran along the beach.

In later years we walked, and finally we did stretching exercises or simply stood, in silent communication with seagulls, dolphins, plunging brown pelicans, an occasional seal or two, sandpipers, and "bicycle birds," as I dubbed them, who skirt the waves on their tiny legs, quicker than the eye can follow.

My own legs won't take me across the wide beach now, but I still find my way—our way—back again.

Jane and I invariably capped our homage to the Pacific with breakfast at the welcoming waterfront Fig Tree Café.

Nowadays—in fond remembrance of her—old friends on the Fig's roster, including Austin, Carlos, Ephron, George, Karen, Mael, Napo, and Ricky, in concert with owner Jose, decline to accept any payment for my customary latte and pancake!

I bow to, and enjoy, their generous hospitality.

POST MORTEM

Jane planted love, banished fear
and made very sure to pour
sheer beauty upon us here

Afterward, she passed beyond
the rock buckled burial tomb
to find a sunrise attic room

She and I shall soon explore
the fathomless mythosphere
from her further horizon door

Last night I dreamt that I could somehow sense our daughter Winslow coming around a corner toward me. I won't try to interpret that, but simply enjoy it...

Jane once posted an urgent letter to someone close to us who badly needed a boost. I was much impressed by what she wrote, and had sufficient wit to copy it out at the time. Hence I can quote her vital message verbatim—

"There are many icons still to be painted. Like a living icon of ourselves. I call this the self-appeared icon. We must 'appear', not as someone else but as we dare to try and be. So much of this icon you have already painted. Just go to, and finish up with the thrill of it.

"That stab of pain in your heart used to be joy, not pain. Identify it as joy once again. For a 'self-appeared' icon something may hurt, but that doesn't mean it's bad. A living icon is painted in blood, bone, color, and thought.

"The prayer said before painting such an icon is that it is for the Mother of God. All I know about God is that She or He, or It maybe, was creative, is creative, and will be creative."

Thanks to Jane's account of our mutual ideal, which we shared for six whole decades together, this admittedly unkempt attempt at autobiography stands finished at last, with no remorse and not a speck of regret, on Easter Sunday morning, 2015.

www.ingramcontent.com/pod-product-compliance
Lightning Source LLC
Chambersburg PA
CBHW021138160426
43194CB00007B/620